International Series i Studies

MW01274740

More information about this series at http://www.springer.com/series/15195

Giovanna Pegan • Donata Vianelli •
Patrizia de Luca

International Marketing Strategy

The Country of Origin Effect
on Decision-Making in Practice

Giovanna Pegan
Department of Economics, Business,
Mathematics and Statistics
University of Trieste
Trieste, Italy

Donata Vianelli
Department of Economics, Business,
Mathematics and Statistics
University of Trieste
Trieste, Italy

Patrizia de Luca
Department of Economics, Business,
Mathematics and Statistics
University of Trieste
Trieste, Italy

ISSN 2366-8814   ISSN 2366-8822   (electronic)
International Series in Advanced Management Studies
ISBN 978-3-030-33590-8   ISBN 978-3-030-33588-5   (eBook)
https://doi.org/10.1007/978-3-030-33588-5

This Springer imprint is published by the registered company Springer Nature Switzerland AG.
The registered company address is: Gewerbestrasse 11, 6330 Cham, Switzerland

To Stefano, who always helps me
and brings joy to our big Made in Italy family
Giovanna

To Giovanni, who makes our days magical
with the best of Made in Italy music
Donata

To Stefano, who shares our
passion for an authentic Made in Italy
atmosphere
Patrizia

Foreword

In recent decades, the influence of country image on consumer behavior has attracted significant, growing international attention from researchers and practitioners. Ernest Dichter, a noted industrial psychologist at Harvard University, published a seminal article in the *Harvard Business Review* in 1962, stating that "the little phrase 'Made in ...' can have a tremendous influence on the acceptance and success of products over and above the specific advertising techniques used by themselves" (p. 116) Since then, country image research—or country-of-origin research—has evolved into one of the most researched topics in the field of international marketing, with an estimated number of publications far exceeding 2000. The results from this body of research show that the image of a country exerts a significant influence on consumer perceptions of foreign brands, products, and tourism destinations and on perceived risk and value and likelihood of purchase.

Despite many contributions over the past 40 years, the globalization of markets has made country-of-origin research subject to increasing skepticism, and it arguably suffers from a progressively widening relevance gap, which negatively affects its value and contributions to international marketing strategy. Indeed, recent studies have pointed out the dearth of research on the managerial side of the country-of-origin phenomenon—research explaining how national companies can incorporate the country-of-origin effect into their marketing practices—rather than attempts to predict consumer attitudes toward products and brands from specific countries. This research approach has led to a fragmented view of the country-of-origin effect not conducive to a true understanding of its practical relevance.

Moreover, most country-of-origin studies are imperfect replications based on quantitative surveys with close-end questions investigating respondents' attitudes toward products and brands from different origins. According to a literature review by Lu, Heslop, Thomas, and Kwan published in *International Marketing Review* in 2016, the majority (83%) of 554 articles published in academic journals between 1978 and 2013 are quantitative in nature, and only 6% are qualitative. The prevalence of quantitative studies has led to significant growth in publications over the past 60 years, but the lack of qualitative research has undoubtedly constrained theoretical advancements in the field.

This book addresses these gaps and makes three major novel contributions to country-of-origin research and practice.

First, this book is the first to adopt a managerial perspective on the country-of-origin phenomenon and to provide a comprehensive view on how national manufacturers, importers, and retailers can exploit the competitive advantages of a favorable country image to create value for foreign buyers. Today, most consumers are exposed to a wide diversity of products from different countries. Modern advances in manufacturing, digital technologies, and transportation enable products to be made virtually anywhere, so some authors have recently argued that country-of-origin information is no longer a source of differential advantage. To the contrary, however, this book clearly shows that, especially in the case of highly typical products, connections to countries with strong, favorable images (such as Italy) facilitate the internationalization process. Moreover, the authors provide managers with practical insights into the immediate usefulness of formulating country-of-origin-related strategies and policies.

Second, the book not only covers the basics of country-of-origin research, with a thorough literature review that sets a necessary foundation for the subsequent discussion. Far more importantly, the book supplies new empirical evidence through a mixed scientific approach combining secondary data and qualitative and quantitative research. In this way, the authors build a solid theoretical frame that connects the country-of-origin effect to strategic entry modes and relationship management in international marketing channels. Although this book is not the first academic contribution to investigate the role of country of origin in the context of international retailing, it offers a significant example of how a more solid, integrative research approach can improve the understanding of country-of-origin effect and its theoretical foundations. The book, therefore, presents interesting reading for academic and applied researchers with interest in this topic and related areas.

Third, the book illustrates the opportunity Italy presents to develop a deeper and broader understanding of what the country-of-origin effect is and why and how it influences international marketing strategies. In countries such as Italy, foreign perceptions of country image play a crucial role in explaining the competitive advantage of Made in Italy in global markets. Culture, aesthetics, manufacturing, tourism attractions, arts, and the general so-called Italian way of life create intangible associations that enhance consumers' perceptions and purchase intentions toward Italian products and brands. However, Italy and Italian products, despite their importance, have received relatively little attention in marketing studies. According to a literature review by Usunier in *European Management Studies* in 2006, Italy ranks sixth as an object of investigation in country-of-origin research. This book thus adds more Italy to country image research. Italy's unique characteristics make it relevant not only to those living and working in the country but also to all scholars and practitioners who are interested in country of origin in general and seek an ideal context in which to research and learn.

For all these reasons, this book goes considerably beyond what is known about this topic and advances the theory and practice of the country-of-origin effect.

Although amid globalization the increasing delocalization of enterprises' operations and the subsequent fragmentation of supply chains raise questions about the competitive relevance of product and brand origins, the reality is that people will always attribute functional and emotional meanings to the perceived images of places and the products associated with them.

The subject of this book and the rigorous scientific approach employed by its authors, therefore, can provide guidance and inspiration to national companies seeking ways to enhance their international competitiveness and international marketing researchers interested in unveiling how the role of country of origin will evolve in the future global scenario.

University of International Studies   Alessandro De Nisco
of Rome (UNINT), Rome, Italy

Acknowledgments

This research and writing on country of origin would not have been possible without the support, collaboration, and encouragement of many Italian colleagues to whom we are very grateful. In the past 10 years, we have conducted and actively participated in numerous national and international research projects that allowed us to receive invaluable feedback. In particular, we want to thank Gaetano Aiello, University of Firenze; Giuseppe Bertoli, University of Brescia; Elena Cedrola, University of Macerata; Alessandro De Nisco, University of Rome; Gianluigi Gallenti, University of Trieste; Vittoria Marino, University of Salento; Michela Matarazzo, University of Rome; Maria Rosaria Napolitano, University of Benevento; Riccardo Resciniti, University of Benevento; and Tiziano Vescovi, University of Venice.

We owe special thanks to James Reardon, University of Northern Colorado, USA; Ilan Alon, University of Agder, Norway; and José Antonio Ontalba Ruipérez and Carlos Gonzalo Penela, Trademetrics—Universitat Politècnica de Valencia, Spain. They shared highly useful contributions and suggestions during the research projects we carried out together.

We are also indebted to the many reviewers who provided very detailed suggestions on the contents and structure of the book.

Finally, we are grateful for the opportunity provided by Alberto Pastore, University La Sapienza, Rome, who fully endorsed the internationalization of the Italian Management Association, leading to the publication of this book.

Contents

Chapter 1
Introduction to the Country of Origin Effect in International Marketing Strategies

Abstract This chapter is aimed at providing an initial theoretical framework on the theme of the country of origin (COO) from the company's perspective. This chapter also describes the objectives of the volume and the methodology of the research. After a brief introduction on the complexity of the COO effect on consumer purchasing behavior in international markets, the chapter clarifies the particular analytical perspective of the volume and illustrates its aims. The chapter then explains the research questions that guided and inspired this theoretical and empirical investigation and summarizes the methodology used in this study.

1.1 Country of Origin Effect

Today, as digital connectivity breaks down cultural and geographical barriers, consumers can buy any product, and they often face realities, and meanings very different from their lands of origin and cultures. Consequently, the topic of the country of origin (COO) is more relevant than ever.

In the marketing literature, the COO effect is known to determine the activation of associations (positive or negative) in the consumer's mind (Aaker, 1996; Keller, 2003), which then affect the consumer's propensity to buy (or not buy) products from that specific COO (Chen, 2004; Han, 1989; Han & Terpstra, 1988; Leila & Merunka, 2006; Nagashima, 1970; Obermiller & Spangenberg, 1989; Schooler, 1965). The COO effect is exercised primarily through the country's image (Papadopoulos & Heslop, 2003). The country image (CI), as well as the brand image, identifies a set of associations with the COO, organized into groups in a significant way (Keller, 2003; Pappu, Quester, & Cooksey, 2007).

Globalization has defined a new space for comparisons of different world cultures and products. This new space for confrontation can result in very different purchasing behaviors. Indeed, there is a great variability in the ways in which products are associated with the COO, depending on the category of product considered and how the COO affects final purchasing decisions (Tseng & Balabanis, 2011). In some cases, for example, imported products (e.g., French wine) benefit from the superior image of their COO and are preferred over domestic products. In other cases,

© Springer Nature Switzerland AG 2020
G. Pegan et al., *International Marketing Strategy*, International Series in Advanced Management Studies, https://doi.org/10.1007/978-3-030-33588-5_1

however, imported goods (e.g., Chinese products) are affected by negative stereo-types that are difficult to eliminate, leading to their a priori exclusion from the set of purchasing alternatives. In addition, some products such as cars, perfumes, and food are strongly identified with their COO characteristics (e.g., French perfumes and German cars; Kotler & Gertner, 2002), while other products (e.g., detergents and tools) are not immediately linked to a COO. Although the link between the product and the COO can sometimes be irrational (Olivero & Russo, 2013), perceptions of products are influenced by their origin (De Nisco, 2006; Phau & Chao, 2008; Saran & Gupta, 2012).

Some authors have highlighted three main components whose interactions form the basis of the relationship between the COO and the consumer behavior (Obermiller & Spangenberg, 1989). First is the cognitive component, in which the consumer lacks detailed information and associates the product with its COO (its image) to evaluate its quality level. From this perspective, it is possible to regard the COO as a heuristic that can help consumers make inferences about quality and influences their beliefs about products. In fact, the availability of increasingly standardized products with intrinsic (tangible) components pushes consumers to use synthetic indicators of quality assessment such as the COO. Such indicators, like other extrinsic cues such as price and brand, can simplify consumers' decision-making process (Han, 1989; Oberecker & Diamantopoulos, 2011; Pastore, Ricotta, & Giraldi, 2011). Second is the affective component, in which the product's COO can evoke affective and symbolic value (as often happens in the case of made-in-Italy products). Finally, in the normative component, the purchase is driven by the desire to support the economy of a given country based on the level of policy shared with it.

Most studies have described the COO as a complex, multidimensional construct (De Nisco, Mainolfi, Marino, & Napolitano, 2015; Martin & Eroglu, 1993; Mattarazzo, 2012; Papadopoulos & Heslop, 2003). Highlighting its multidimensionality, Roth and Diamantopoulos (2009) defined three distinct dimensions to understand the COO effect on purchase intention: the overall CI, representing individuals' general perceptions and opinions on a country's level of economic, political, and cultural development (Nagashima, 1970; Pappu et al., 2007); country product image (CPI), reflecting the innovation, quality, and prestige of a country's manufacturing production; and the country-related product image (CRPI), referring to the reputation of a specific product from a given country that reflects the technical characteristics, reliability, and status of the product. Some scholars have highlighted how these three dimensions of the COO can interact in a nonlinear way in product purchase decisions (Bursi, Grappi, & Martinelli, 2012). The overall image of a country (CI) indirectly influences consumer purchase intentions due to two mediated effects. The first is linked to a country's manufacturing production (CPI), such as agro-food for Italy. The second is linked to the image of a specific product from a particular country (CRPI), such as Italian wine (Bursi et al., 2012).

1.2   The Evolution of the Country of Origin Construct

The new global competitive context has introduced complexities and contradictions into the theoretical analysis and interpretation of the COO. The spread of production decentralization, outsourcing, and especially the emergence of so-called hybrid products (e.g., with different countries of production and design or brand) has made it more difficult to identify the exact origins of products (Li, Murray, & Scott, 2000; Phau & Chao, 2008). The original concept of the COO reflected only the origin of production but has been extended to other aspects (Usunier, 2011) such as the countries of design, the parts, and assembly (Chao, 2001; Insch & McBride, 1998, 2004; Quester, Dzever, & Chetty, 2000). This approach, known as the deconstruction strategy, seeks to identify a set of sub-concepts that differently influence the customer's qualitative perceptions during the purchasing process based on the product origin (Chowdhury & Ahmed, 2009; Li et al., 2000). Some authors (Chen, 2004; Thakor & Lavack, 2003; Ulgado, 2002) have underlined the distinction between the country of the brand (COB) and the country of manufacture (COM), while Leila and Merunka (2006) considered the importance of the country of design and the country of production. Several studies have examined the dynamics and relationships between these variables, but it is worth noting that these different classifications make it difficult to compare the results of these studies. Hamzaoui-Essoussi, Merunka, and Bartikowski (2011) showed how knowledge of the country in which a product was designed can produce effects only if the product has symbolic value. In most cases, though, customers consider the country where a product was manufactured to be of the utmost importance (Vianelli & Pegan, 2014).

From another perspective, the association strategy considers the association's customers make among the product, its brand, and its COO (Andehn & Berg, 2011). Here, the focus of COO research shifts from production to consumption (Andehn & Berg, 2011). Numerous scholars thus have considered consumers' perceptions of products' origins based on associations made with brands (Magnusson, Westjohn, & Zdravkovic, 2011; Thakor & Lavack, 2003). Thakor and Kohli (1996) introduced a new concept: the brand of origin, defined as "the place, region or country where a brand is perceived to belong to its target consumers" (p. 26). In other words, the place to which consumers perceive that the brand belongs sometimes can overwhelm the traditional COO paradigm (Hamzaoui-Essoussi et al., 2011). The importance of the place where the product is designed or assembled diminishes, while that of customers' perceptions of the COO (the country of association) rises. In short, the previous analysis method focused on the effects of the COO considered to be a qualitative attribute of the product (i.e., linked to customers' cognitive processes), while the second approach focuses on the effects of the product's origin as identified by customers, which are taken as a starting point in the emotional and normative field of the COO effect (Dmitrovic & Vida, 2010). This second perspective, which sees the country of the brand as more important than the country of manufacture, has gained widespread use by researchers. However, it should be pointed out that in a globalized world, cognitive aspects seem to have lost relevance, but the persistence of the economic crisis has increased consumers' awareness of supporting their national economies by purchasing local products (normative component). This awareness may favor the choice to buy domestic products, thereby significantly increasing the importance of the country of production (Dmitrovic & Vida, 2010).

1.3 Theoretical Models to Understand the Country of Origin Effect in Consumer Decision-Making

The COO effect is complex, and despite the rich literature available, it remains a highly controversial issue (Bloemer, Brijs, & Kasper, 2009). Without any intention of providing a comprehensive review of the marketing literature, which is beyond the scope of this volume, three main theoretical approaches that can help clarify the effects of the COO on the consumer are briefly presented in the following section (Reardon, Vianelli, & Miller, 2017): cue utilization theory, elaboration likelihood model (ELM), and categorization theory.

According to the first theory, during the decision-making process, the consumer gets information from cues that can be intrinsic—inseparable from the product or service—or extrinsic—for example, price, brand, or COO—(Olson & Jacoby, 1972). When intrinsic cues are not readily available, the consumer relies almost exclusively on extrinsic cues (Magnusson et al., 2011). The COO, as an extrinsic signal, allows individuals to reduce their cognitive effort, accelerating the decision-making process when no other information is available. According to other scholars, however, the process of information processing can occur without conscious awareness (Shiffrin & Schneider, 1977; Zajonc, 1980). In this perspective, the mere presence of a COO cue activates already memorized associations and country-specific stereotypes (Herz & Diamantopoulos, 2013; Liu & Johnson, 2005). Consequently, even simple exposure to a COO indication affects product and brand evaluations. This unconscious reaction is largely affective and concerns the link between the identity of consumers and the COO or the pride of owning products originating from that country (Batra, Ramaswamy, Alden, & Steenkamp, 2000; Oberecker & Diamantopoulos, 2011).

Another contribution to the understanding of the COO effect comes from the revision by Bloemer et al. (2009) of the ELM model (Petty, Cacioppo, & Schumann, 1983). As is well known, the ELM describes two different paths an individual can follow to process information. A first central way foresees a process of accurate, intentional elaboration of various information cues. This way assumes that the subject has the motivation and cognitive ability to process the information stimuli. A second peripheral way instead provides a superficial, automatic mechanism of information processing based on emotional responses, stereotypes, and habits. In this case, the individual is less involved and, therefore, less interested in making the cognitive effort to process the information. The moderating effect of involvement in ELM is discussed by Petty et al. (1983), who demonstrate that high involvement leads to central processing and that low involvement is associated with the peripheral pathway. To better understand the effects of COO on consumer decision-making, Bloemer et al. (2009) revised this approach by suggesting that a halo mechanism results from weak COO effects caused by insufficient information. These authors described a cognitive outcome that results in a central processing called a summary construct. Previous experience with a country and its products involves the use of a summary construct to determine the cue selection (Bloemer et al., 2009).

A particular contribution to the understanding of the mechanisms underlying the functioning of the COO effect on the consumer decision-making process is provided by categorization theory (Alba & Hutchinson, 1987; Cohen & Basu, 1987). Categorization is a process that involves determining which elements belong together (Barsalou, 1983). According to this theory, categorization is the cognitive process that "expresses the characteristic way in which individuals organize and structure perceptual inputs derived from the external environment" (Block, Buss, Block, & Gjerde, 1981, p. 770; see also Smith, 1995). The categories then influence the processing of consumer information by acting as heuristics to make decision-making more efficient (Hadjimarcou & Hu, 1999). In fact, the consumer likes to structure the knowledge of specific product alternatives into categories (Gutman, 1982; Punj & Moon, 2002) and then use category structures to organize and differentiate products and brands. According to this theory, to deepen the COO's influence on consumers' behavior, it is essential to focus on the concept of brand and product typicality (Loken & Ward, 1990; Tseng & Balabanis, 2011). The typicality, or strength of the association with the origin of the product and brand, refers to the extent to which an object represents a category (Barsalou, 1983; Rosch, 1978). The most typical members of a category tend to be named first in free recall and become the standard for the product category when comparing products (Tseng & Balabanis, 2011). In the COO literature, categorization theory has determined the concept of national typicality, which occurs when a product seems to be highly typical of a given country. Adapting to the stereotypes of its COO is expected to produce more favorable evaluations of the product and increase its probability of purchase (Tseng & Balabanis, 2011). For example, products made in advanced economies are rated more favorably than those made in less developed countries, especially for more complex manufactured goods (Pappu et al., 2007). Moreover, brands typical of their origin activate stereotyped country beliefs and increase the COO effect (Aboulnasr, 2006; Hamzaoui-Essoussi et al., 2011; Reardon et al., 2017).

1.4 Country of Origin as a Driver to Create Value

The progressive, qualitative homogenization of products, the competitive pressure exerted by low-cost countries, and the diffusion of hybrid products have contributed to revitalizing research on the COO, enriching it with analyses from different perspectives (Hamzaoui-Essoussi et al., 2011; Insch, Prentice, & Knight, 2011). In addition to numerous studies in the consumer field, there are also contributions, albeit small, aimed at understanding whether and how particular COOs represent drivers for value creation in companies' international marketing strategies (Bertoli & Resciniti, 2012; Mattarazzo, 2012; Vianelli, de Luca, & Pegan, 2012). The importance of the COO effect on the global level places it at the center of a lively, still open debate (Diamantopoulos, Schlegelmilch, & Palihawadana, 2011; Samiee, 2011; Usunier, 2011).

In today's increasingly fluid, changing, connectivity-driven business world, operating abroad is a necessity not only for growth but also for firms' very survival. Creating value in international markets introduces new challenges that require companies to constantly search for possible sources of value, even in the most traditional sectors (Vianelli, de Luca, & Bortoluzzi, 2012). According to several scholars, companies that base their offerings on products characterized by strong links to a territory (place specific) historically perceived as associated with these specific products (time specific) can find in the COO a strategic resource for value creation in different markets (De Nisco, 2017; Golinelli, 2012; Marino & Mainolfi, 2013; Sims, 2009). Some researchers, however, have suggested that companies achieve the best performance abroad when they exploit the value of the attributes underlying particular COOs to enrich the distinctive positioning of their brands (Busacca, Bertoli, & Molteni, 2006; Pastore et al., 2011). It has been repeatedly emphasized that if the link between the product and the territory of origin represents an important driver of firm internationalization, then firm growth abroad requires investment in the brand even amid ideal conditions to exploit the COO effect (Hamzaoui & Merunka, 2006; Roth & Romeo, 1992). The process of creating value through the COO seems to depend on companies' ability to merge brand enhancement activities with the qualitative excellence and product expertise inherent to particular territories of origin (Bertoli & Resciniti, 2012; Pegan, Vianelli, & de Luca, 2014; Vianelli & Pegan, 2014). Here emerges the importance of the concept of the brand of origin, which, as mentioned, emphasizes perceptions of the product's brand origins (Thakor & Kohli, 1996).

Researchers have found that customers' perceptions may vary depending on the products' place of manufacture (linked to specific brands) and the location of manufacturing companies (Balabanis & Diamantopoulos, 2008; Samiee, 2010; Samiee, Shimp, & Sharma, 2005). Consumers can be misled by several factors such as ignorance and a lack of information and interest in products' origins. The confusion is related to the lack of consumer awareness and therefore calls into question the decisions of marketing managers on how much to invest in marketing communication. The communication investment should allow managers to convey to consumers the positive associations between product quality and brand image, thus, reducing the impact of the country of production. Several strategies can be adopted to ensure this linkage, including but not limited to the use of a brand suggesting the company's location (Thakor & Lavack, 2003; Usunier & Cestre, 2007), symbolic images related to a particular country (e.g., the stylized colors and shapes of a flag; Insch and Florek, 2009), and language that recalls a particular country or geographical area through specific brand name and logo (Harun, Wahid, Mohammad, & Ignatius, 2011). Sometimes, without any commercial effort, consumers might spontaneously evoke some effects of the product origin due to strong associations with countries, such as pasta with Italy and sushi with Japan (Pastore et al., 2011; Usunier & Cestre, 2007).

Other studies have further developed the concept of the brand origin and presented a more elaborated paradigm for assessing the COO effect. Called the brand origin culture, it focuses on the cultural–linguistic (phonetic, morphological, and semantic) aspects added to the brand to stimulate positive perceptions among customers (Harun et al., 2011; Lim & O'Cass, 2001; Usunier, 2006, 2011) and to indicate the origin of the product to consumers (Li & Shooshtari, 2003; Thakor & Lavack, 2003). Diamantopoulos et al. (2011) assessed the influence of the CI and brand image on purchasing intention, taking into account differences in brand familiarity, and sought to capture consumer assessments of the COO at both the overall country level (CI) and the specific product category level (PCI). The results of these authors show that the COO has important indirect effects; in particular, the CI and the product category image (PCI) strongly influence purchase intention through their impacts on brand image. In addition, consumers associate the image of a country not only with the capabilities of a specific sector or product category but also with the ability to produce good brands. According to Diamantopoulos et al. (2011), to understand the role of the COO from a managerial perspective, it is necessary to consider explicitly the image of both the product and the brand. Figure 1.1 illustrates four cases that consider the COO effect on these two aspects.

The first case analyzed is the ideal one because the COO has a positive influence on both the product and the brand. For example, Germany has a good reputation in car manufacturing in general and produces strong brands such as BMW and Mercedes. In the second case, we see a strong product image but a weak brand image. For example, Turkey has a very positive image related to carpets but lacks the capability to transform these product-related skills into strong, well-known brands. In the third case, a country such as Austria develops very strong, well-known brands such as Red Bull and Swarovski but has weak product images. In the fourth and most

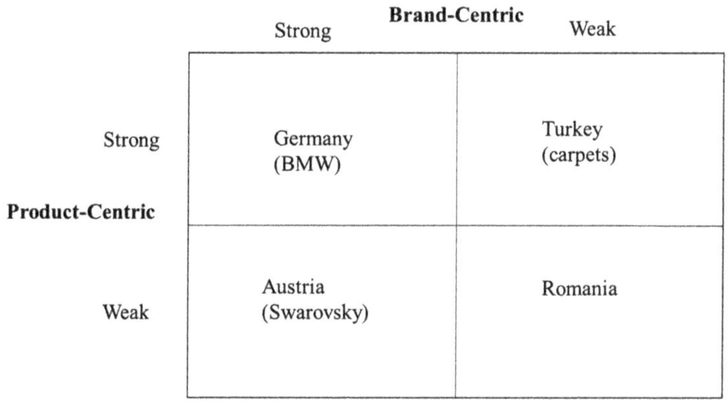

| | **Brand-Centric** | |
	Strong	Weak
Product-Centric Strong	Germany (BMW)	Turkey (carpets)
Product-Centric Weak	Austria (Swarovsky)	Romania

Fig. 1.1 Country-of-origin effect and brand image (Source: Adapted from Diamantopoulos et al. (2011))

unpleasant case, countries such as Romania have neither an especially strong product image nor solid, well-known brands. This case is the most challenging situation because it requires knowledge of how to create a strong image for the product or brand.

1.5   The Perspective of This Book

As mentioned, companies offering products with a high national typicality should be able to translate the high intrinsic potential value of the COO into effective value perceived by the foreign market. However, it is not so obvious that the company can create real value for the market through the COO and thus be able to effectively differentiate its product offering from the competitive ones. The value creation process to which the positive country and product stereotypes of the COO can contribute by creating superior perceived value for foreign customers is not sufficient to determine competitive advantages in foreign markets. In fact, the company must accompany value creation with a value appropriation process, drawing on the ability to transform the value of the product into long-term sales and profits (Mizik & Jacobson, 2003). Both competition and consumers can hinder value appropriation. In the first case, the company creates value but fails to impose itself on the competition. In the second case, the consumer might want to acquire a valuable product but is not willing to pay a premium price reflecting the real product value. In both cases, the company fails to appropriate the value it has created and is hindered from acquiring profits. In this context, the marketing channels used to convey the product value to the final consumer assume key roles.

More than ever, it has become a strategic imperative to concretely support decisions aimed at long-term business development and consolidation by identifying possible sources of new value creation for the market through the COO and the ways in which the company can appropriate this value in foreign markets, even mature ones. Problems encountered in the management of marketing channels often cause the loss of competitiveness of many companies linked to place- and time-specific production (i.e., linked to highly typical national productions) in more traditional foreign markets and their difficulties growing in emerging markets (Bortoluzzi, Chiarvesio, & Tabacco, 2012; Vianelli, de Luca, & Bortoluzzi, 2012). An analysis of some good practices (Pegan, Vianelli, & de Luca, 2013; Pegan et al., 2014) has highlighted how the COO value creation for the market and companies' appropriation of that value depends on their ability to strategically manage marketing channels in various markets (Alon, Jaffe, & Vianelli, 2013).

In international marketing strategies, the choice of channels is fundamental to the success of the company. Indeed, the basis of any international marketing strategy is not only the creation of value for the customer, but also the delivery of value through channels to the end market (Ancarani & Scarpi, 2016). The channels consist of the online and offline intermediaries used by customers to interact with the product and brand. Channels generally can be of two types: communication channels and distribution channels. Communication channels encompass all the media that allow the transmission of information and content such as television, radio, press, social media, and contact centers. Distribution channels include all the channels that facilitate transactions such as points of sale, sales networks, and e-commerce sites. Distribution and communication channels are often very closely linked without a clear division of roles, as in the case of a company's e-commerce website and flagship store (Kotler, Hermawan, & Iwan, 2017).

In this perspective, communication plays a very important role in the value appropriation process. Clearly communicating the origin of the product involves using the COO as an extrinsic cue that acts cognitively, emotionally, and normatively on the consumer to give brief indications of intrinsic cues such as product quality and positive national associations (Herz & Diamantopoulos, 2013; Liu & Johnson, 2005; Magnusson et al., 2011). Effective communication allows companies to enhance their ability to create and appropriate the value of the COO effect (Batra et al., 2000; Hirschman & Holbrook, 1982). The possibility of successfully communicating the COO is strongly influenced by the type of channel adopted and the relationships established among the various actors in the supply chain. In fact, in the communication process, the channel partners, above all, constitute the link to the final customer and can convey a COO valorized upstream by the manufacturing company. The channel actors can also reduce the COO value so that it does not appear to have strong distinctiveness to the final foreign customer. If not properly managed, intra-channel relationships can hinder the value creation and appropriation processes through the COO, influencing the firm's potential future growth and even its very survival (Insch et al., 2011).

Companies' distribution choices are closely related to the specific entry modes selected to penetrate foreign markets. Globalization and the changing roles of emerging market countries inevitably affect companies' entry modes and perceptions of the origin effect (Fong, Chun-Ling, & Yunzhou, 2014). Manufacturers, therefore, need to understand how the COO effect is influenced by the ways in which they enter foreign markets to correctly manage the value creation process for the market and value appropriation through the COO.

Figure 1.2 presents a visual summary of framework of the book's perspective. As highlighted in Chap. 2, the technical and organizational modalities that can be implemented can be divided into three main groups: export modes, intermediate modes, and hierarchical modes (Alon, Jaffe, Prange, & Vianelli, 2016). These modalities reflect different degrees of investment risk and channel control by manufacturing companies. Exports are an entry mode often used by small companies and have low risk but often afford little control over the sales process, which has important implications for the ability to effectively communicate proposals' distinctive COO value to the final customers (Fig. 1.2).

To exercise greater control over the market and to be able to enhance the COO and the entire distribution channel, many companies instead opt for intermediate entry modes. They choose contractual forms (e.g., international licensing and franchising) that require sharing ownership and control with local partners. In this way, the partners share the risk and contribute equally to product promotion in foreign markets.

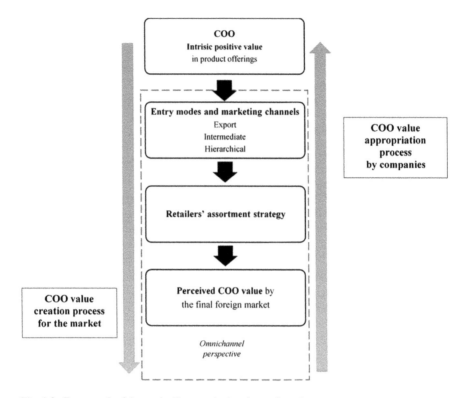

Fig. 1.2 Framework of the study (Source: Authors' own figure)

Other companies decide to make direct investments in production and commercial subsidiaries. This strategy increases the business risk but also allows greater control of the supply chain and adaptation of the product offerings to the needs of overseas consumers, which facilitates company development in foreign markets. In this perspective, it is clear that, by directly overseeing the market, the company gains a greater capacity to create and appropriate value through the COO.

These different entry modes result in specific distribution choices. In the case of indirect marketing channels, both short and long, the importer and the retailer also define the assortment policies. These figures can be especially critical in determining the manufacturer's value creation process for the market and value appropriation through the COO (Pegan & Vianelli, 2013; Reardon et al., 2017). The long-term relationships created between the company and the distribution partners, such as the importer (as further developed in Chap. 3), are a key factor in control of the foreign market and the image built through the partners' marketing choices (Pegan, Vianelli, & Reardon, 2017).

In intermediate entry modes, the distribution channel is configured as an integrated vertical marketing system in which the company and the partners that adhere to the agreement share the risk, with relevant implications for management of the COO. For example, as discussed in Chap. 4, contractual agreements can introduce important challenges to strategic management of the relationship between the COO and the country of brand, with implications for brand perceptions, product value, and thus the final consumer's purchase propensity. However, as analyzed in Chap. 5, further aspects of the COO and its contradictory relationship with the concept of brand origin concern the experience gained by companies that invest directly through greenfield types in foreign markets. Indeed, these companies find that they need to understand the complex relationships between the country of manufacture and the country of the brand. Often debated from theoretical perspectives (Chen, 2004; Thakor & Lavack, 2003; Ulgado, 2002), this relationship becomes more crucial than ever from a managerial perspective, especially for small and medium companies that are linked to time- and place-specific products (historically and traditionally linked to a specific place of origin) and aim to grow in very geographically and culturally distant foreign markets. In this perspective, the company that decides to integrate vertically with the Directly Operated Store (DOS) has a very effective communication tool for the COO and the brand abroad. The point of sale becomes the platform for the privileged relationship with the foreign market because it is able to more directly communicate to the final consumer the distinctive values of the brand and the COO, facilitating the creation of an effective customer experience (de Luca & Pegan, 2014; Kotler et al., 2017). Monitoring this physical touchpoint in the foreign market helps the company get the best out of the COO and brand dynamics in its activities.

In this volume, particular attention is paid to analysis of the influence the COO construct may have on the determination of retailers' assortment, as discussed in Chap. 6. How the COO affects retail buyers' purchase decisions has largely been overlooked but has recently been identified as an important area of study (Chen, Mathur, & Maheswaran, 2014; Koschate-Fischer, Diamantopoulos, & Oldenkotte, 2012). As noted, this lack of research is especially evident when compared to the impressive volume of literature on the consumer's COO. However, understanding whether and to what extent the made-in variable weighs in decisions to purchase new products in retailers' assortment has high importance given the gatekeeper role distribution plays in end customers' choices (Insch et al., 2011). In fact, from among the many new products presented each year to retail buyers, only a small percentage actually go on the shelves and are then further evaluated by the final consumer (Fig. 1.2). The spread of hybrid products, as mentioned, increases the importance of studying the dynamics that play a role in international retailers' assortment strategies (Reardon et al., 2017).

In the digital age, particular relevance is seen in studying the dynamics of the COO in online channels that function as privileged places for building and overseeing relationships with potential and current customers to create value. Given the growing importance of e-commerce, it is necessary to understand, as investigated in Chap. 7, how companies manage and enhance the COO effect in fluid environments where both geographical and cultural boundaries are weak. The theme of search engines takes on high importance in scenarios characterized by connectivity. Indeed, the new customer journey (Kotler et al., 2017) is guided and influenced by the 5 As (aware, appeal, ask, action, and advocacy) and, above all, by what is collected through online search engines such as Google (Jerath, Ma, & Park, 2014), which are generally the main traffic sources for websites (Netmarketshare, 2016). From a managerial perspective, company success depends heavily on online searches using specific keywords and on search results, which can reflect the effectiveness of companies' website (Chen, Liu, & Whinston, 2009).

Furthermore, the types and amounts of data growing rapidly, spurred by new and emerging new services such as social networks and the Internet of Things. In this new era of big data, companies have to gain the skills necessary to effectively manage and analyze large amounts of data. If born-digital companies are already masters of big data, traditional companies have to learn how to gain advantages from big data (de Luca, Pegan, & Gonzalo Penela, 2019; McAfee & Brynjolfsson, 2012). The collection of big data should allow companies to optimize marketing activities in different channels, particularly the various online and offline intermediaries used by customers to interact with the product or brand. Only by studying their customers' journey can companies implement an omnichannel marketing strategy based on the integration of the channels used (Fig. 1.2). As mentioned, channels can be both distribution and communication channels, which frequently are closely linked without a distinct separation of functions, as in the case of a company's e-commerce site. The company, therefore, must use big data to map and monitor the various touchpoints in which the product or brand and its COO interact to communicate and sell to customers (Kotler et al., 2017).

1.6   Aim and Methodology

This book is the result of a long, rich research process of the authors, on the internationalization of enterprises from the perspective of the COO, aimed at making both theoretical and managerial contributions. From a theoretical perspective, the main research objective is to contribute to integrating the economic and managerial literature on the COO by analyzing its manifestations and valorization throughout international marketing channels. Only a few studies from companies' perspective have deeply explored the value creation process through the COO, with its possible definitions, and companies' mechanisms to appropriate this value, particularly in different international marketing channels (Insch et al., 2011; Knight, Holdsworth, & Mather, 2007; Reardon et al., 2017). From a managerial perspective, this book, which gives space to the voices of companies and distribution partners, is aimed at providing useful operational suggestions. Through the stories of the numerous companies interviewed and through a constant dialogue between theory and practice, the authors have attempted to answer questions important to business development in foreign markets. The main research questions that inspired and guided the theoretical and empirical investigation were:

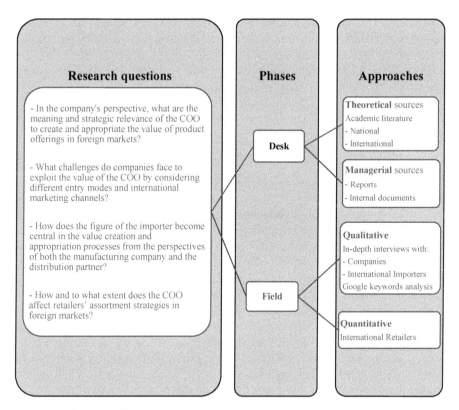

Fig. 1.3 Study process (Source: Authors' own figure)

- In the company's perspective, what are the meaning and strategic relevance of the COO to create and appropriate the value of product offerings in foreign markets?
- What challenges do companies face to exploit the value of the COO by considering different entry modes and international marketing channels?
- How does the figure of the importer become central in the value creation and appropriation processes from the perspectives of both the manufacturing company and the distribution partner?
- How and to what extent does the COO affect retailers' assortment strategies in foreign markets?

These research questions were the subject of a theoretical and empirical study conducted in two distinct but complementary main phases. Figure 1.3 summarizes the complete study process. In the first phase, desk research was carried out to collect and interpret data from multiple national and international sources, both theoretical–scientific and operational–managerial. This phase served two purposes. First, analysis of the international management literature enabled outlining the theoretical framework of reference that provided the basis for the rest of the research. Second, to enrich the knowledge from an operational–managerial perspective, the analysis was extended to many secondary data sources, including sector and company reports, specialized websites, and other internal documents provided by the companies involved in the research.

In the second phase, field research was carried out in several steps using both qualitative and quantitative methodologies, as detailed in Fig. 1.3.

1.6.1 Qualitative Study: Different Methods and Tools

To deeply understand the multiple facets of the COO and its different roles in international marketing channels, the use of qualitative methodologies (Yin, 2011) was especially appropriate. It permitted grasping the complexity of the value creation process through the COO and companies' mechanisms to appropriate this value. This process allowed fully understanding the nuances of this nonlinear phenomenon in international marketing channels (Denzin & Lincoln, 1998). The qualitative phase was conducted with different data collection and analysis methods (Fig. 1.3).

The focus was on manufacturing companies selected through purposive sampling to obtain a group of cases with heterogeneous businesses, internationalization levels, entry methods, and marketing channels. The choice of the companies studied[1] was motivated by the fact that despite their diversity, they were small- and medium-sized firms characterized by time- and place-specific product offerings. As mentioned, in these business contexts, the processes of creating value through the COO for the market and appropriating this value for the producer in international distribution channels become highly strategic to obtain competitive advantages and grow abroad (Bertoli & Resciniti, 2012).

These companies' multiple stories allowed gathering an especially significant patrimony of experience because in those specific product and market contexts, the dynamics of the processes analyzed were truly representative of both opportunities and threats. Primary data were collected through in-depth interviews personally conducted by members of the research group both face to face and at a distance (via Skype or telephone). For each company, several interviews were held with different figures, mostly owners and export managers. The interviews, which lasted on average 45–60 min, were taped, transcribed verbatim, and appropriately translated by the authors. The collected data were analyzed using different tools (Fig. 1.3).

The parts of these interviews focused on exporting companies, as described in Chap. 3, were then subjected to qualitative content analysis using the Atlas.ti program. To provide a structure and to attribute meaning to the collected data, a coding scheme was developed to identify the central themes of the interviews (Strauss & Corbin, 1990). The text of the interview transcripts consisted of

---

[1]For the purpose of greater clarity, the details of the different companies considered in the study are presented in later chapters.

180 pages and 89,282 words. The coding scheme consisted of a multistage, iterative process guided by both the data (inductive method) and the authors' theoretical sensitivity to the issues studied (Zarantonello & Luomala, 2011). First, after carefully re-examining the material many times, both authors separately elaborated a coding scheme. Second, the authors shared their coding schemes to reach intercoder agreement. Third, two researchers not involved in the study independently analyzed the transcribed documents to check the validity of the themes and codes identified by the authors. Although intercoder agreement was not quantified, the final scheme was elaborated only after making further modifications suggested by the two consultants and obtaining concurrence between the different codes of the interview manuscripts (Miller, Besser, & Weber, 2010). Chapter 3 presents the results of the content analysis, examining the different codes and families of codes identified during the coding process.

Other parts of the interviews with manufacturers were used to build short cases, particularly on the significant experiences of some companies that decided to use intermediate and hierarchical entry modes (see Chaps. 4 and 5). These experiences were captured in a constant dialogue between theory and practice and, together with the collection of secondary data, enabled deeply understanding the main criticalities for the value creation and appropriation processes through the COO, including in relation to brand. As mentioned, it was relevant to investigate what, from companies' perspective, the role of the concept of "manufactured in" was in the associations drawn between the country and the brand. Specifically, when considering companies' marketing strategies at an international level—particularly in cases with good relationships between the country's image country and the product category—it was interesting to understand whether the importance of the country of manufacture increased or decreased as the importance of the country of brand increased.

To explore the role of intermediaries in the value creation and appropriation processes, in-depth interviews with international importers were also conducted (Fig. 1.3). From an initial list of 50 international importers suggested by the manufacturers and contacted by email, 12 expressed interest in collaborating in the research. Of these, seven were available for interviews. To ensure anonymity, each respondent was assigned a descriptive code (see Table 3.7).

The analysis was carried out through interviews via Skype and email. The chosen respondents were company representatives in active roles in the specific fields investigated. Before the interviews, general data on the companies were collected from their official websites to get an overview of their relative size and conditions. The Skype interviews were recorded and immediately transcribed. Similarly, once the email interviews were completed, the responses were transcribed verbatim. In this case, the focus on the specific context of foreign products and markets symbolic of various peculiarities, as analyzed in Chap. 3, allowed developing an interpretive framework useful to stimulate theoretical and managerial reflections valid in other foreign markets. As can be seen, the various importers came from heterogeneous areas and were of different sizes, ranging from family businesses to large groups of importers (Fig. 1.3).

The study then investigated the current and potential roles of the online channel in the valorization of the COO from the omnichannel perspective, taking into account specific experiences in international markets. The aim of this research phase, as presented in Chap. 7, was to examine user-generated online data to create new knowledge and support companies' marketing decisions on content and digital strategies. Understanding online research behavior has become a critical challenge (Gebauer & Ginsburg, 2010), especially for traditional actors historically linked to particular products such as wine production. In this phase, therefore, descriptive research was performed to understand the configurations of online wine information searches in specific foreign markets. The research followed the digital method approach, which views the Internet as a source of methods rather than an object of study. Data were obtained from various search engine optimization (SEO) tools, primarily Google Trends, Google AdWords, and Sistrix. Google Trends tracks trends in keyword searches from January 2004 to the present day. This tool is usually used to display keywords and their long-, medium-, and short-term evolution. Google AdWords provides national and international search statistics for keywords on general and specific topics over the past 12 months. Sistrix offers website visibility reports based on organic keywords. This tool weekly queries and saves more than 15 million keywords in different Google indices. The reports list the website rankings for these keywords and trace their evolution. As explained in Chap. 7, the study took into account users' Google search requests in 2016, highlighting and analyzing the popularity of keywords.

A research process with three phases was developed (Gonzalo-Penela, de Luca, & Pegan 2017). First, the search keywords of foreign users related to products and their corresponding frequencies were extracted from the Google AdWords Keyword Planner tool. Second, qualitative analysis of the keywords was carried out to better understand the users' searches and classify the keywords into three categories according to users' intentions (navigation, information, and transactional). Third, the keywords referring to the particular COOs of the main players in the competitive arena of the specific product analyzed were identified.

1.6.2   Quantitative Research: A Focus on International Retailers

Within this rich framework, quantitative research with a sample of retailers was then carried out to fill the main theoretical gap, namely, the lack of studies on the COO's role in influencing retailers' assortment choices (Fig. 1.3). The quantitative research was based on the development and administration of a structured questionnaire sent to retail buyers (see Chap. 6). A population list obtained from LexisNexis® Academic had 14,579 potential respondents, of whom 7478 included the word "buyer" in their titles. Three emails with a link to the Qualtrics® survey were sent at two-week intervals. Participation in the survey was voluntary, and the participants were promised individual confidentiality. To increase the number of responses, the potential respondents were promised (and later received) the study results as an incentive for participation. In all, 221 responses were received, and 205 were sufficiently complete for the analysis (see Table 6.1). Nine retail buyers with otherwise complete information chose not to compile information on their companies' characteristics (Reardon et al., 2017).

References

Aaker, D. A. (1996). *Building strong brands*. New York: The Free Press.
Aboulnasr, K. (2006). Country of origin effects: The role of information diagnosticity, information typicality and involvement. *Marketing Management Journal, 16*(1), 1–18.
Alba, J., & Hutchinson, W. (1987). Dimensions of consumer expertise. *Journal of Consumer Research, 13*(4), 411–454.
Alon, I., Jaffe, E., Prange, C., & Vianelli, D. (2016). *Global marketing. Contemporary theory, practice, and cases*. New York, NY: McGraw-Hill.
Alon, I., Jaffe, E., & Vianelli, D. (2013). *Global marketing. Contemporary theory, practice, and cases*. New York, NY: McGraw-Hill.
Ancarani, F., & Scarpi, D. (2016). *Marketing internazionale. Nuovi mercati per le eccellenze globali*. Milan, Italy: Pearson.
Andehn, M., & Berg, P. O. (2011). *Place-of-origin effects: A conceptual framework based on a literature review*. Stockholm, Sweden: Stockholm University School of Business.
Balabanis, G., & Diamantopoulos, A. (2008). Brand origin identification by consumers: A classification perspective. *Journal of International Marketing, 16*(1), 39–71.
Barsalou, L. W. (1983). Ad hoc categories. *Memory and Cognition, 11*(3), 211–227.
Batra, R., Ramaswamy, V., Alden, D. L., & Steenkamp, J.-B. E. M. (2000). Effects of brand local/foreign origin on consumer attitudes in developing countries. *Journal of Consumer Psychology, 9*(2), 83–95.
Bertoli, G., & Resciniti, R. (Eds.). (2012). *International marketing and the country of origin effect*. Cheltenham, UK: Edward Elgar.
Block, J., Buss, D. M., Block, J. H., & Gjerde, P. F. (1981). The cognitive style of breadth of categorization: Longitudinal consistency of personality correlates. *Journal of Personality and Social Psychology, 40*, 770–779.
Bloemer, J., Brijs, K., & Kasper, H. (2009). The CoO-ELM model: A theoretical framework for the cognitive processes underlying country of origin effects. *European Journal of Marketing, 43*(1/2), 62–89.
Bortoluzzi, G., Chiarvesio, M., & Tabacco, R. (2012). La meccanica innova nei servizi per competere nei mercati emergenti. *Economia e società regionale, 3*, 55–63.
Bursi, T., Grappi, S., & Martinelli, E. (2012). *Effetto country of origin un'analisi comparata a livello internazionale sul comportamento d'acquisto della clientela*. Bologna, Italy: Il Mulino.
Busacca, B., Bertoli, G., & Molteni, L. (2006). Consumatore, marca ed effetto made in: evidenze dall'Italia e dagli Stati Uniti, finanza marketing e produzione. *Finanza Marketing e Produzione, 2*, 5–32.
Chao, P. (2001). The moderating effects of country of assembly, country of parts and country of design on hybrid product evaluations. *Journal of Advertising, 30*(4), 67–81.
Chen, H. L. (2004). Testing the role of country of origin in consumer adoptions new products. *International Advances in Economic Research, 10*(3), 245–256.
Chen, J., Liu, D., & Whinston, A. (2009). Auctioning keywords in online search. *Journal of Marketing, 73*(4), 125–141.

Chen, C. Y., Mathur, P., & Maheswaran, D. (2014). The effects of country-related affect on product evaluations. *Journal of Consumer Research, 41*(4), 1033–1046.

Chowdhury, H. K., & Ahmed, J. U. (2009). An examination of effects of partitioned country of origin on consumer product quality perceptions. *International Journal of Consumer Studies, 33* (4), 496–502.

Cohen, J., & Basu, K. (1987). Alternative models of categorization: Toward a contingent processing framework. *Journal of Consumer Research, 13*(4), 455–472.

de Luca, P., & Pegan, G. (2014). The coffee shop and customer experience: A study of the U.S. market. In F. Musso & E. Druica (Eds.), *Handbook of research on retailer–consumer relationship development* (pp. 173–196). IGI Global: Hershey, PA.

de Luca, P., Pegan, G., & Gonzalo Penela, C. (2019). Insights from a Google keywords analysis. What can the internet tell us about Italian wine in the US market? *Micro & Macro Marketing, 1*, 93–116.

De Nisco, A. (2006). Country of origin e buyer behavior: Una meta-analisi dalla letteratura internazionale. *Mercati e Competitività, 4*, 81–101.

De Nisco, A. (2017). *Immagine Paese. Il vantaggio competitivo di essere italiani*. Napoli: Editoriale Scientifica.

De Nisco, A., Mainolfi, G., Marino, V., & Napolitano, M. R. (2015). Tourism satisfaction effect on general country image, destination image, and post-visit intentions. *Journal of Vacation Marketing, 21*(4), 87–110.

Denzin, N. K., & Lincoln, W. S. (1998). *Handbook of qualitative research*. Thousand Oaks, CA: Sage.

Diamantopoulos, A., Schlegelmilch, B., & Palihawadana, D. (2011). The relationship between country-of-origin image and brand image as drivers of purchase intentions. *International Marketing Review, 28*(5), 508–524. https://doi.org/10.1108/02651331111167624.

Dmitrovic, T., & Vida, I. (2010). Consumer behaviour induced by product nationality: The evolution of the field and its theoretical antecedents. *Transformation in Business & Economics, 9*(1), 145–165.

Fong, C.-M., Chun-Ling, L., & Yunzhou, D. (2014). Consumer animosity, country of origin, and foreign entry-mode choice: A cross-country investigation. *Journal of International Marketing, 22*(1), 62–76.

Gebauer, J., & Ginsburg, M. (2010). The US wine industry and the internet: An analysis of success factors for online business models. *Electronic Markets, 13*(1), 59–66.

Golinelli, G. (Ed.). (2012). *Patrimonio culturale e creazione di valore. Verso nuovi percorsi*. Padua, Italy: Cedam.

Gutman, J. (1982). A means-end chain model based on consumer categorization processes. *Journal of Marketing, 46*(2), 60–72.

Hadjimarcou, J., & Hu, M. (1999). Global product stereotypes and heuristic processing: The impact of ambient task complexity. *Psychology and Marketing, 37*(3), 96–108.

Hamzaoui, L., & Merunka, D. (2006). The impact of country of design and country of manufacture on consumer perceptions of bi-national products' quality: An empirical model based on the concept of fit. *Journal of Consumer Marketing, 23*(3), 145–155.

Hamzaoui-Essoussi, L., Merunka, D., & Bartikowski, B. (2011). Brand origin and country of manufacture influences on brand equity and the moderating role of brand typicality. *Journal of Business Research, 64*(9), 973–978.

Han, C. M. (1989). Country image: Halo or summary construct? *Journal of Marketing Research, 26* (May), 222–229.

Han, C. M., & Terpstra, V. (1988). Country of origin effects for uni-national and binational products. *Journal of International Business Studies, 16*(4), 235–256.

Harun, A., Wahid, A. N., Mohammad, O., & Ignatius, J. (2011). The concept of Culture of Brand Origin (COBO). A new paradigm in the evaluation of origin effect. *International Journal of Academic Research in Business and Social Sciences, 1*(3), 282–290.

Herz, M. F., & Diamantopoulos, A. (2013). Country-specific associations made by consumers: A dual- coding theory perspective. *Journal of International Marketing, 21*(3), 95–121.

Hirschman, E. C., & Holbrook, M. B. (1982). Hedonic consumption: Emerging concepts, methods and propositions. *The Journal of Marketing, 46*, 92–101. https://doi.org/10.2307/1251707.

Insch, A., & Florek, M. (2009). Prevalence of country of origin association on the supermarket shelf. *International Journal of Retail & Distribution Management, 37*(5), 453–471.

Insch, G. S., & McBride, J. B. (1998). Decomposing the country-of-origin construct: An empirical test of country of design, country of parts and country of assembly. *Journal of International Consumer Marketing, 10*(4), 69.

Insch, G. S., & McBride, J. B. (2004). The impact of country-of-origin cues on consumer perceptions of produce quality: A bi-national test of decomposed country-of-origin contrast. *Journal of Business Research, 57*(3), 256–265.

Insch, A., Prentice, R. S., & Knight, J. G. (2011). Retail buyers' decision-making and buy national campaigns. *Australasian Marketing Journal, 19*, 257–266.

Jerath, K., Ma, L., & Park, Y. (2014). Consumer click behavior at a search engine: The role of keyword popularity. *Journal of Marketing Research, II*, 480–486.

Keller, K. L. (2003). *Building, measuring and managing brand equity*. Upper Saddle River, NJ: Prentice-Hall.

Knight, J. G., Holdsworth, D. K., & Mather, D. W. (2007). Country-of-origin and choice of food imports: An in-depth study of European distribution channel gatekeepers. *Journal of International Business Studies, 38*(1), 107–125.

Koschate-Fischer, N., Diamantopoulos, A., & Oldenkotte, K. (2012). Are consumers really willing to pay more for a favorable country image? A study of country-of-origin effects on willingness to pay. *Journal of International Marketing, 20*(1), 19–41.

Kotler, P., & Gertner, D. (2002). Country as brand, product, and beyond: A place marketing and brand management perspective. *The Journal of Brand Management, 9*(April), 249–261.

Kotler, P., Hermawan, K., & Iwan, S. (2017). *Marketing 4.0. Dal tradizionale al digitale*. Milano: Hoepli.

Leila, H., & Merunka, D. (2006). The impact of country of design and country of manufacture on consumer perceptions of bi national products quality: An empirical model based on the concept of fit. *Journal of Consumer Marketing, 23*(3), 145–155.

Li, Z. G., Murray, W. L., & Scott, D. M. (2000). Global sourcing, multiple country-of-origin facets, and consumer reactions. *Journal of Business Research, 47*(2), 121–133. https://doi.org/10.1016/S0148-2963(98)00061-7.

Li, F., & Shooshtari, N. H. (2003). Brand naming in China: Sociolinguistics implications. *Multinational Business Review, 11*(3), 3–22.

Lim, K., & O'Cass, A. (2001). Consumer brand classifications: An assessment of culture-of-origin versus country-of-origin. *Journal of Product and Brand Management, 10*(2), 120–136.

Liu, S. S., & Johnson, K. F. (2005). The automatic country-of-origin effects on brand judgements. *Journal of Advertising, 34*(1), 87–97.

Loken, B., & Ward, J. C. (1990). Alternative approaches to understanding the determinants of typicality. *Journal of Consumer Research, 17*(2), 111–126.

Magnusson, P., Westjohn, S. A., & Zdravkovic, S. (2011). Further clarification on how perceived brand origin affects brand attitude: A reply to Samiee and Usunier. *International Marketing Review, 28*(5), 497–507.

Marino, V., & Mainolfi, G. (2013). *Country brand management*. Milan, Italy: Egea.

Martin, I. M., & Eroglu, S. (1993). Measuring a multi-dimensional construct: Country image. *Journal of Business Reviews, 28*(3), 191–210.

Mattarazzo, M. (2012). Country of origin effect: Research evolution, basic constructs and firm implications. In G. Bertoli & R. Resciniti (Eds.), *International marketing and the country of origin effect* (pp. 23–42). Cheltenham, UK; Northampton, MA: Edward Elgar.

McAfee, A., & Brynjolfsson, E. (2012). Big data: The management revolution. *Harvard Business Review*, October 3rd–9th.

Miller, N. J., Besser, T. L., & Weber, S. S. (2010). Networking as marketing strategy: A case study of small community businesses. *Qualitative Market Research: An International Journal, 13*(3), 253–270.

Mizik, N., & Jacobson, R. (2003). Trading off between value creation and value appropriation: The financial implications of shifts in strategic emphasis. *Journal of Marketing, 67*(1), 63–76.

Nagashima, A. (1970). A comparison of Japanese and U.S. attitudes toward foreign products. *Journal of Marketing, 34*(1), 68–74.

Netmarketshare. (2016). *Market share statistics for internet technologies.* Retrieved April 20, 2018, from https://www.netmarketshare.com

Oberecker, E. M., & Diamantopoulos, A. (2011). Consumers' emotional bonds with foreign countries: Does consumer affinity affect behavioral intentions? *Journal of Marketing, 19*(2), 45–72.

Obermiller, C., & Spangenberg, E. (1989). Exploring the effects of country of origin labels: An information processing framework. *Advances in Consumer Research, 16,* 454–459.

Olivero, N., & Russo, V. (2013). *Psicologia dei consumi.* Milano: McGraw Hill.

Olson, J., & Jacoby, J. (1972). Cue utilization in the quality perception process. *Proceedings of the third annual conference of the Association for Consumer Research,* 167–179.

Papadopoulos, N., & Heslop, L. A. (2003). Country equity and product country images: State of art in research and implications. In S. C. Jain (Ed.), *Handbook of research in international marketing* (pp. 402–433). Cheltenham, UK; Northampton, MA: Edward Elgar.

Pappu, R., Quester, P. G., & Cooksey, R. W. (2007). Country image and consumer-based brand equity: Relationships and implications for international marketing. *Journal of International Business Studies, 38,* 726–745.

Pastore, A., Ricotta, F., & Giraldi, A. (2011). Innovare l'offerta attraverso le caratteristiche estrinseche del prodotto. Il ruolo creativo del country of origin. In L. Pilotti (Ed.), *Creatività innovazione e territorio. Ecosistemi del valore per la competizione globale* (pp. 629–650). Bologna, Italy: Il Mulino.

Pegan, G., & Vianelli, D. (2013). Il ruolo degli importatori nella valorizzazione del country of origin: Un'indagine qualitativa sul vino Italiano nel mercato statunitense. In *Atti del X Convegno Annuale della SIM—Società Italiana di Marketing.* Milan, Italy.

Pegan, G., Vianelli, D., & de Luca, P. (2013). Il ruolo della distribuzione nella valorizzazione dei marchi made in Italy ad alto valore simbolico in USA: Casi, esperienze e criticità. In G. Aiello (Ed.), *Davanti agli occhi del cliente. Branding e retailing del Made in Italy nel mondo* (pp. 174–197). Rome, Italy: Aracne.

Pegan, G., Vianelli, D., & de Luca, P. (2014). Competere e creare valore nei mercati maturi: Alcune evidenze empiriche del made in Italy negli Stati Uniti. *Economia e Società Regionale, XXXII, 2,* 55–67.

Pegan, G., Vianelli, D., & Reardon, J. (2017). *Wine importers and their country of origin proclivities.* In Conference proceedings XXIX Sinergie-SIMA: Value co-creation in foreign markets: Le sfide di management per le imprese e per la società (1–5).

Penela, C. G., de Luca, P., & Pegan, G. (2017). Insights from Google search user-generated data: a study on European Wine in the US Market. In *Contributo in Conference proceedings XIV SIM conference: "Il marketing di successo, imprese enti persone".* ISBN: 978-88-907662-9-9, pp. 1–7.

Petty, R. E., Cacioppo, J. T., & Schumann, D. (1983). Central and peripheral routes to advertising effectiveness: The moderating role of involvement. *Journal of Consumer Research, 10*(2), 135–146.

Phau, I., & Chao, P. (2008). Country-of-origin: State of the art review for international marketing strategy and practice. *International Marketing Review, 25*(4), 349–353.

Punj, G., & Moon, J. (2002). Positioning options for achieving brand association. A psychological categorization framework. *Journal of Business Research, 55*(4), 275–283.

Quester, P. G., Dzever, S., & Chetty, S. (2000). Country of origin effects on purchasing agents product perceptions: An international perspective. *The Journal of Business and Industrial Marketing, 15*(7), 479–489.

Reardon, J., Vianelli, D., & Miller, C. (2017). The effect of COO on retail buyers' propensity to trial new product. *International Marketing Review, 34*(2), 311–329. https://doi.org/10.1108/IMR-03-2015-0080.

Rosch, E. (1978). Principles of categorization. In E. Rosch & B. B. Lloyd (Eds.), *Cognition and categorization* (pp. 27–48). Hillsdale, NJ: Lawrence Erlbaum.

Roth, K. P., & Diamantopoulos, A. (2009). Advancing the country image construct. *Journal of Business Research, 62*, 726–740.

Roth, M. S., & Romeo, J. B. (1992). Matching product category and country image perception: A framework for managing country-of-origin effects. *Journal of International Business Studies, 23*(3), 477–497.

Samiee, S. (2010). Advancing the country image construct—A commentary essay. *Journal of Business Research, 63*, 442–445.

Samiee, S. (2011). Resolving the impasse regarding research on the origins of products and brands. *International Marketing Review, 28*(5), 473–485.

Samiee, S., Shimp, T. A., & Sharma, S. (2005). Brand origin recognition accuracy: Its antecedents and consumers' cognitive limitations July 2005. *Journal of International Business Studies, 36* (4), 379–397.

Saran, R., & Gupta, N. (2012). Country of origin vs. consumer perception: A literature review. *The IUP Journal of Marketing Management, XI*(4), 66–75.

Schooler, R. (1965). Product bias in the central American common market. *Journal of Marketing Research, 2*(2), 394–397.

Shiffrin, R. M., & Schneider, W. (1977). Controlled and automatic human information processing: II. Perceptual learning, automatic attending and a general theory. *Psychological Review, 84*(2), 127–190.

Sims, R. (2009). Food, place and authenticity: Local food and the sustainable tourism experience. *Journal of Sustainable Tourism, 17*(3), 321–336.

Smith, E. E. (1995). Concepts and categorization. In E. E. Smith & D. N. Osherson (Eds.), *An invitation to cognitive science. Thinking: An invitation to cognitive science* (2nd ed., pp. 3–33). Cambridge, MA: The MIT Press.

Strauss, A., & Corbin, J. M. (1990). *Basics of qualitative research: Grounded theory procedures and techniques*. Thousand Oaks, CA: Sage.

Thakor, M. V., & Kohli, C. S. (1996). Brand origin: Conceptualization and review. *Journal of Consumer Marketing, 13*(3), 27–42.

Thakor, M. V., & Lavack, A. M. (2003). Effect of perceived brand origin associations on consumer perception of quality. *Journal of Product and Brand Management, 12*(6), 394–407.

Tseng, T., & Balabanis, G. (2011). Explaining the product-specificity of country-of-origin effects. *International Marketing Review, 28*(6), 581–600.

Ulgado, F. (2002). Country of origin effects on E-commerce. *Journal of American Academy of Business, 2*(1), 250–253.

Usunier, J. C. (2006). Relevance in business research: The case of country-of-origin research in marketing. *European Management Review, 3*, 60–73.

Usunier, J. C. (2011). The shift from manufacturing to brand origin: Suggestions for improving COO relevance. *International Marketing Review, 28*(5), 486–496.

Usunier, J. C., & Cestre, G. (2007). Product ethnicity: Revisiting the match between products and countries. *Journal of International Marketing, 15*(3), 32–72.

Vianelli, D., de Luca, P., & Bortoluzzi, G. (2012). Distribution channel governance and value of made in Italy products in the Chinese market. In G. Bertoli & R. Resciniti (Eds.), *International marketing and the country of origin effect* (pp. 133–150). Cheltenham, UK: Edward Elgar.

Vianelli, D., de Luca, P., & Pegan, G. (2012). *Modalità d'entrata e scelte distributive del made in Italy in Cina*. Milan, Italy: Franco Angeli.

Vianelli, D., & Pegan, G. (2014). Made in Italy brands in the US and China: Does country of origin matter? *Journal of Euromarketing, 23*(1&2, January–June), 57–73.

Yin, R. K. (2011). *Qualitative research from start to finish*. New York, NY: Guilford Press.

Zajonc, R. (1980). Feeling and thinking: Preferences need no inferences. *American Psychologist, 35*(2), 151–175.

Zarantonello, L. & Luomala, H.T.. (2011). Dear Mr Chocolate constructing a typology of contextualized chocolate consumption experiences through qualitative diary research. *Qualitative Market Research: An International Journal, 14*(1), 55–82.

Chapter 2
Strategic Entry Modes and Country of Origin Effect

Abstract The role the COO can play in the international entry strategy depends heavily on how the distribution channel is structured, especially in relation to the choice of entry mode. The entry method must be chosen with great care as a long channel can lead to the paradox of selling a product abroad at a much higher price than in the domestic market while encountering many difficulties in enhancing the product's brand and the COO to justify the premium price. In fact, indirect and long marketing channels with many intermediaries between the company and the final customer often make it difficult to enhance the typicality of the product, its brand and its origins. However, if the company is directly present and works closely with foreign customers, the valorization of its origins as an element of differentiation is more effective. Moreover, the length of the channel has impacts on price escalation, due to the presence of intermediaries, transport costs, taxes, insurance costs, and other factors. This chapter describes the different entry modes, i.e., export modes, intermediate entry modes (contractual and equity based), and hierarchical modes, with the aim to identify in which cases management of the COO is especially critical and relevant.

2.1 Introduction

The role the COO can play in the international entry strategy depends heavily on how the distribution channel is structured, especially in relation to the choice of entry mode. As shown in Fig. 2.1, companies can go abroad through export modes, intermediate entry modes (contractual and equity based), and hierarchical modes. Some of these methods are related to production activities in foreign markets, while others involve the company's commercial choices and affect the enhancement of the product, its brand and its origin (Cateora, Gilly, Graham & Money, 2019).

The export strategy is often necessary for SMEs that approach foreign markets in ways that present low or moderate investment risks. However, this choice allows for very limited control as in the management of foreign markets, the company relies entirely on intermediaries who hold in their hands the company's business strategy in the target market. Intermediate entry procedures involve the collaboration of the

23

G. Pegan et al., *International Marketing Strategy*, International Series in Advanced Management Studies, https://doi.org/10.1007/978-3-030-33588-5_2

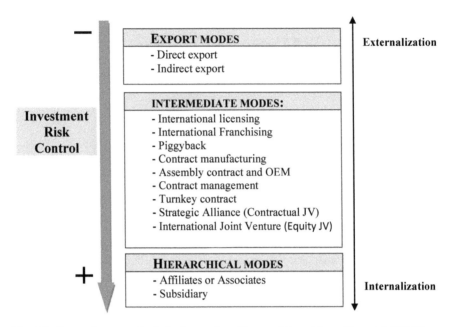

Fig. 2.1 Types of entry modes in foreign markets (Source: Adapted from Alon et al. (2016))

company with a foreign partner in production and commercial activities. In this case, the company has greater commitment to investing resources, resulting in higher degree of risk. However, the company gains increased control over activities developed abroad through its direct presence in the foreign market alongside the foreign partner. Finally, the choice to make direct investments abroad through the hierarchical entry mode maximizes the company's commitment of resources and thus its business risk but also allows it complete control of its business, sales, and production activities (Lowe, Kenyon & Doole, 2019).

Indirect and long marketing channels with many intermediaries between the company and the final customer often make it difficult to enhance the typicality of the product, its brand and its origins. However, if the company is directly present and works closely with foreign customers, the valorization of its origins as an element of differentiation is more effective. Consequently, much depends on the strategic choices made upstream by the company, which may vary over time to improve the company's visibility and distinctiveness in foreign markets.

Moreover, the length of the channel has impacts on price escalation due to the presence of intermediaries, transport costs, taxes, insurance costs, and other factors. The entry method, therefore, must be chosen with great care as a long channel can lead to the paradox of selling a product abroad at a much higher price than in the domestic market, while encountering many difficulties in enhancing the product's brand and the COO to justify the premium price.

This chapter describes the different entry modes, with the aim to identify in which case management of the COO is especially critical and relevant. This discussion is the subject of further analysis in the following chapters.

2.2   Export Modes

Companies that choose exports as an entry mode often are in the early stages of their internationalization strategy or choose this less demanding investment as they prefer caution when entering abroad. The reasons can be as diverse, from the choice of potentially attractive but culturally distant countries to the scarce information available on the market and especially difficult competitive environments. However, investing marginally and consequently taking little risk also results in limited control over the distribution channel, which makes it difficult to implement marketing strategies aimed at creating the distinctiveness of the COO. The company outsources management of the foreign market to intermediaries operating in the domestic market in the case of indirect exports or the foreign market in the case of direct exports. The high flexibility provided by outsourcing offers a quick exit if the market turns out to be unprofitable but does not allow for control over intermediaries' activities. As seen in Chap. 3, this lack of control can weaken the brand and COO value in the distribution channel.

2.2.1   Indirect Export Modes

Specifically, in the case of indirect exports, the company relies on an intermediary in the domestic market, which can be an export company, buying office, trading company, or broker. In these cases, the distance from the foreign market risks preventing a strategic definition of the origin of the product and brand. The product is managed by the local intermediary, which exports it to several countries and often uses additional intermediaries that significantly lengthen the distribution channel and increase the distance from the final consumer. Put short, in indirect exports, the manufacturer can do little to enhance the COO, for instance, by communicating it differently in various countries of export. To the contrary, the manufacturer often delegates the choice of countries to the national intermediary on which it relies and views exports as a way of assessing opportunities abroad and/or placing products not absorbed by the domestic market.

A type of indirect export mode that can be considered more favorable for enhancing the COO of the product is offered by export consortia, voluntary aggregations created to develop common activities, such as foreign export and global communication. Especially in the case of mono-sectorial aggregations, such as the Prosciutto di Parma and Parmigiano–Reggiano Cheese Consortia, the product's origin and typicality can be efficiently promoted, and the COO can give a competitive advantage against products of other nationalities.

2.2.2 Direct Export Modes

In direct exports, the company has direct contact with a foreign intermediary (Fig. 2.1). If in this case the relationship with the final clients is mediated by an intermediary, then the direct contact with the foreign market allows the company to get more information and awareness about the actions taken to create value from the product's origins.

Direct exports can be implemented in two different ways:

1. First, the company can create direct contact with foreign clients and can offer and receive information useful for adapting its product portfolio based on perceptions of its *made in* in the foreign market. This direct relation is important to implement brand strategies in the best way to create value around the product's origin. It can be developed not only in business-to-business relationships directly managed by the company's own sales force but also through the use of online channels. Although the Internet cannot replace a physical market presence and only marginally reduces the use of intermediaries, its diffusion represents an important factor that, especially in recent years, has favored exports, increasing export performance (Sinkovics, Sinkovics, & Jean, 2013). As seen in Chap. 7, the Internet can represent a significant opportunity for the company to promote the COO as the online direct relationship with the final consumers can enable conveying the value of the product and brand's COO.
2. Second, the company can rely on distributors, importers, and dealers operating in the foreign market. Identifying them is very important in short-term penetration of the foreign market. Moreover, they play a central role in enhancing the image of the foreign manufacturer they represent in their assortment. This brand awareness is not always easy to achieve in the case of exports, as seen in Chap. 3. It is the intermediary, such as the importer, who has to implement the company policies to create differentiation from the competition and enhance intrinsic characteristics, such as the product's COO. For SMEs in certain sectors, such as the Italian wine and olive oil industries, this differentiation based on COO is especially important, and the product's COO must be effectively conveyed.

In the case of direct export, even if there is a direct relation with the foreign partner, the control of the COO can still be weak, as can be seen in Fig. 2.2. The brand of the chocolate cream Nutella, positioned in the shelf of a Chinese retailer, in the communication to target consumers has lost the Italian origin of the brand, switching to made in Germany that is one of the country of production.

Fig. 2.2 A made-in-Italy brand with a German COO in a Chinese store (Source: Authors' own figure)

2.2.3 Choice of Distribution Partner from the Perspective of the Country of Origin

Particularly in the field of exports, the choice of the distribution partner is important because the company's success in a specific market depends almost entirely upon the partner it has trusted. Financial strength, commitment to the company's product and distribution, marketing, and sales skills are all important characteristics that affect export performance (Dong, Tse, & Hung, 2010). Companies that have products in foreign markets where it is necessary to enhance the COO should consider some characteristics of distributors.

First, it is important to verify the compatibility between the producer and the distributors in image, quality, and positioning. This is often done by examining the brands and complementary products represented by the foreign intermediary. For example, premium positioning of the brand strengthened by a premium COO has to be coherent with the image and the positioning of the distributor.

Second, marketing and sales factors are especially relevant when the distributor has to manage not only the product but also the brand image abroad. The distributor's marketing and sales skills can be evaluated by checking its business contacts and capacity to develop promotional activities and after-sales services in the local market. In particular, when the distributor has to deal with clients and enhance the characteristics of products and their origins, strong knowledge of the production of a country or of a specific region of origin is highly significant.

Third, among the characteristics of foreign distributors, commitment is extremely relevant to developing long-lasting relationships. Especially when the brand's success is based on the heritage of a product and its origins, a long-lasting relationship is important to convey these values and support the distributor in transferring them to the foreign clients. In general, commitment can be evaluated by examining factors such as the volatility of the distributor's product portfolio over the past 10 years, the (central or marginal) role the distributor assigns to a specific brand and the distributor's willingness to drop competing products with the same or different COOs (Alon, Jaffe, Prange, & Vianelli, 2016).

In partnerships with distributors, capability building programmes, and motivational programmes can be important to enhance the relationship and support the promotion of the brand and its origins. For example, the manufacturer can provide marketing and sales support, such as promotional material describing the value of the product's COO. Furthermore, the manufacturer can give the partners' sales personnel early training and visit clients together to show the sales force how to present the product to the final clients. Finally, the partners' motivation can be increased not only through monetary benefits but also the provision of updated information on production, new products, and company developments and visits by the partner to the company's headquarters to share common values and motivate the partner to achieve channel goals in foreign markets (Kashyap & Sivadas, 2012).

2.3 Intermediate Entry Modes

Internationalization through exports, as we have seen, can limit the company's effectiveness at enhancing its brand and its typicality of origin. The independent intermediary that acts as a filter for the company's end customers, risks curbing opportunities for growth and, above all, failing to consolidate the image of the company's brand through enhancing its COO.

Intermediate modes are entry strategies that can be considered to lie halfway between exports and, as seen later, hierarchical modes. Intermediate modes include contractual modes that assume that ownership and control can be shared by the company and the local partner. The risk thus is shared between the partners, and they can contribute equally to product promotion in foreign markets. This approach can open possibilities to support the product's origin and manage the brand image throughout the distribution channel.

Partners can choose from among a number of intermediate entry modes to benefit from their respective strengths and exercise stronger control of the brand image and COO. Contract-based entry modes are non-equity agreements with no investment in risky capital. The various alternatives include:

- International licensing
- International franchising
- Piggyback
- Contract manufacturing, assembly contract, and Original Equipment Manufacturing (OEM)
- Contract management
- Turnkey contract
- Strategic alliances

Equity-based entry modes are organized entities with social capital shared between the partners. These modes are a form of foreign direct investment (FDI) set up in the form of minority joint ventures, 50/50 joint ventures and majority joint ventures. The choice of different agreements, as analyzed in Chap. 4, can affect the company's possibilities to create value around the product's origins.

2.3.1   International Licensing

In international licensing, the firm transfers the rights to its products to a foreign company for the purpose of production and sales. For a set royalty fee, the licensee may use the licensor's technology, trademarks, patents, characters, and other intellectual properties to expand its presence in the target foreign markets. Like exporting, licensing is an attractive entry mode for many companies as the expenditures and risks are limited, and the licensee takes the entrepreneurial risk. From the COO perspective, though, there are some advantages and disadvantages. If production is carried out in the foreign market, the value of the domestic market as the country of manufacture is lost, which risks weakening the concept of origin linked to the typicality of the product associated with a given country.

Nevertheless, entrusting production to a foreign partner can not only reduce costs and limit price escalation but also helps adapt the product to local demand. The licensee should have a better knowledge of the market and be able to maintain the typicality of the product while meeting local needs. Through the partnership relationship, the company can strengthen its brand presence abroad while maintaining strong influence on the product's distribution channel and associated values linked to the country of origin. More specifically, there is the opportunity to support the country of brand and the country of design as the licensor can guide the licensee in enhancing the country's image associated with the product and at the same time ensure widespread dissemination at the international level. Obviously, all this is possible only if there is strong, favorable collaboration. Otherwise, even if the entry method is contractual and has the aforementioned benefit of greater control, there remains the risk of not developing the full potential of the brand and its COO in both profitability and customer value.

2.3.2   International Franchising

In international franchising, a foreign independent company (franchisee) receives from another company (franchisor) the right to operate its business. With the goal to penetrate foreign markets, the franchisor offers to multiple franchisees its trademarks, products, services and production, and operation processes. The relationship between the franchisor and the franchisee is closer than in licensing, especially in terms of control. Consequently, companies that invest in brand image prefer franchising as they can control the activity, provide promotional materials, conduct training, and offer support to the franchisee. With a view to enhancing the COO, franchising is also especially suitable to enhance the brand's origin, explain its values, and define a coordinated image in the various countries where the company's brand is present.

This arrangement constitutes a win–win agreement between the franchisor and the franchisee. On one hand, the franchisor has the opportunity to expand abroad while minimizing its financial risk and maintaining control of its brand image, which can enhance the origin through communication at the point of sale. SMEs find it especially important that franchising offers the possibility to enhance the COO through product communication and the creation of a store experience that can enhance the origin of the product. The franchisee, for its part, can benefit from a consolidated brand and effectively manage its business with the support of the franchisor's experience and consulting and training activities.

Many characteristics of franchising can contribute to the enhancement of the COO. First, franchising makes it possible to create a network of points of sale in a relatively short time, especially compared to the development of a network of owned shops. The store network is especially important when the company wants to create a strong brand image in a foreign country, particularly in sectors such as clothing in which strengthening the brand through the store experience is fundamental. Opening the company's own stores risks taking too much time, undermining the company's efforts to reinforce the product's COO to differentiate the brand from other foreign brands in the market. Compared to direct investment by the company in more than one owned store, time can be shorter as the company relies on foreign partners who can open franchised stores simultaneously. However, it is important to emphasize that the upstream identification of the most suitable and reliable partners, especially in particular countries, often takes a long time.

The second advantage of this mode of entry is the low financial risk, which makes it also feasible for SMEs. Often the latter need to differentiate themselves abroad through enhancement of the COO. Think of sectors such as fashion and furniture in which companies that cannot enter abroad with a famous brand can leverage the COO to positive effect. These companies do not have many opportunities to invest and frequently select export methods that, by their nature, tend to reduce brand value in the transition among intermediaries along the distribution channel, increasing the gap between value creation and value appropriation by the final consumers. For SME, therefore, franchising can be an opportunity. With limited investment, they can exercise good control over the brand image, enhance the product's COO, and minimize the risks associated with the length of the distribution channel.

Finally, COO management also often requires adaptation to the foreign market, for example, in the way it is communicated. The most appreciated symbols of a specific country of origin can be different in many cultures. Consider how the senses of smell, touch, sight, and hearing can be used in the store experience to convey the image of a country. Depending on the culture, a country can be recalled by a musical style, a particular song, perfumes, images (e.g., family and landscapes) and materials (e.g., the color of wood). Collaboration with franchisees close to a particular market, therefore, can offer an opportunity to implement effective adaptation policies, especially in store management.

2.3.3 Piggyback

In piggyback agreements, the company (rider) becomes international by including some of its products in the assortment of another company (carrier) that enters foreign markets with a more diversified product portfolio. The rider has the advantage of exploiting the foreign distribution network of a company that offers complementary products. The carrier gains more bargaining power vis-à-vis the distributor as it presents itself with a wider, more complete assortment range.

Piggybacking is an interesting entry mode for SMEs working with niche products often linked to craft traditions in which the COO plays a central role. For these companies, choosing piggybacking instead of exports allows them to avoid making investments while maintaining control over brand identity, which risks disappearing over a long distribution channel with many intermediaries. However, the choice of a partner is very important. Its COO must be consistent with that of the rider company. For example, in the food sector where some products can be especially enhanced by a positive made in, the choice of a partner company with a brand with consistent made in and product quality can be a winning strategy to enter foreign markets.

2.3.4 Contract Manufacturing, Assembly Contract, and Original Equipment Manufacturing

The use of contract manufacturing (outsourcing) is very common among companies operating internationally. In this arrangement, these companies decide to outsource production to a third party through an assembly contract or OEM. In the first case, the company sends the components to the foreign partner, who transforms or assembles them and then re-exports the finished product to the company of origin. In OEM, the company buys the original product from a foreign partner and then refines it to resell it as its own product. The company thus appears to be the official producer of the product.

While offering numerous advantages, particularly cost reduction, outsourcing production also changes the country of manufacturing. The same applies, albeit in a different way, to assembly contract and OEM. In some sectors, it is difficult to be competitive without reducing production and assembly costs. These entry modes can accomplish this goal without high investments that SMEs otherwise could not muster. The main advantage enjoyed when a company outsources production, buys original products or requires assembly abroad is reduced costs while maintaining control over marketing activities and marketing channels. The persistent risk is decreasing the final quality of the product. The decomposability of the COO in the country of manufacturing and the country of brand (to mention only the main components) can open an opportunity for the country of manufacturing to cease investing heavily in enhancement of the country of brand. This approach can be conducted along with other entry modes the company chooses from a distribution perspective, such as franchising and direct investment in directly operated stores (DOS).

2.3.5 Contract Management

Contract management is typically used in sectors such as tourism, which includes hotels and airports. To a property owned by a foreign partner, the company can offer its experience, technology, specialized services, and human resources for a certain period of time in exchange for a fee or a percentage of the sales. The difference between franchising and licensing is that in addition to proposing a business and sales model to follow, the company that enters the foreign market also has responsibility for management. Especially in countries where managerial skills tend to be lacking, the company can then manage and control the image of the services offered. Management of the positioning strategy, therefore, is always entrusted to the management company, while the financial, political, strategic, and ownership aspects are left to the foreign partner, who can maximize the revenues and profits of its investment.

The company that enters a foreign market through contract management has several advantages. First, it can be present in the target market without the financial, legal, and political risks of direct investment. Second, the company can focus on and retain complete control of brand management. In particular, a COO connotation can be achieved if the COO offers some element of differentiation for the service brand. For example, the Accor group, with the Sofitel Legend brand, offers foreign partners the possibility of entering contract management to own a hotel "where heritage is infused with French luxury and grace."[1] However, contract management offers the risk that when the contract expires, the foreign company will want to regain control of management activities related to the business. Through contract management, that same foreign company will have had the opportunity to assess the profitability of the business and the opportunity to proceed to direct investment.

---

[1]https://group.accor.com/en/hotel-development/brands/sofitel-legend

2.3.6 Turnkey Contract

A turnkey project is an entry mode that involves the creation of a turnkey facility for the foreign client, often a government body. Such a project involves the design, construction, and equipment of a large, complex facility (e.g., an airport, hotel, or power plant) and often also staff selection and initial training. A turnkey project can be self-engineered versus construction to specification, depending on whether the realization is defined by the exporting company based on the client company's parameters or directly by the client company that requires the exporting company undertake a project already outlined in all its characteristics. Given the project type, turnkey projects do not involve the dimension of the COO, which is difficult to associate with the sectors in which these large projects tend to be implemented.

2.3.7 Strategic Alliances and International Joint Ventures

Strategic alliances, also called contractual joint ventures, are a mode of entry based on a contractual relationship between two or more companies that agree to share resources and expertise to achieve a common goal. Joint ventures are strategic alliances that base the relationships between partner companies not on a contract but on equity. In contrast to the contractual method, joint ventures involve the creation of a new company, with capital contributions from the companies involved in the agreement. It is, therefore, possible to create a minority joint venture (less than 50% of the shares), a 50/50 joint venture, or a majority joint venture (more than 50% of the shares) (Peng & Meyer, 2019).

The advantage of strategic alliances and joint ventures is that they exploit the partners' mutual complementarity in resources, such as technology, brands, and qualified personnel. An essential prerequisite is the definition of a common strategic goal, without which both strategic alliances and joint ventures have no reason to exist. Through these agreements, companies can become more competitive, overcome entry barriers to new markets, expand their product portfolios, and acquire and manage resources more effectively and efficiently.

However, joint management is not always easy. Values, management styles, and corporate cultures can be different, and it is essential for the success of the agreement to choose an appropriate, reliable, and highly committed partner. In addition, there may be significant difficulties in managing leadership and problems related to poor planning and capitalization. From the COO perspective, the possibility of effectively managing the image linked to the made in very much depends on the form in which the strategic alliance or joint venture was set up.

If two or more companies from the same country agree to enter a foreign market, the COO's image is strengthened, and the commitment of several partners allows maximizing control of the COO in the distribution channel. If the company enters a foreign market by forming a joint venture or a strategic alliance with a local partner, the COO can be maintained if the exporting company retains control of the brand (country of brand). The product probably would lose the connotation of COO in terms of the country of production, so while localizing production in a foreign market, it becomes important to exercise high control of the quality of production associated with the country of brand. In this form of agreement, the local partner assumes an important role in management of the distribution channel, exploiting its greater knowledge of the domestic market.

Finally, management of the COO as a competitive advantage becomes difficult if two or more companies from different countries decide to create a joint venture in a third market. Unless one partner has significantly greater weight, it becomes difficult to defend both a country of brand and a country of manufacturing position.

2.4 Hierarchical Modes

Hierarchical entry modes are a form of FDI in which the company takes ownership of facilities in the foreign market. This entry mode is recommended for companies that want to ensure control of their activities abroad and to invest to achieve significant penetration of sales in the target market (Peng & Meyer, 2019). Obviously, this is the riskiest way of entry. In fact, even if the company acquires greater knowledge of the market and the competitive environment and exercises a high degree of control over the activities developed in the foreign market, the business risk associated with the investment remains high. Much obviously depends on the type of direct investment.

The company can go directly abroad by creating a representative office or a branch. The representative office represents the company in the foreign market, supporting marketing, and service activities. This approach is taken in countries where it is not considered advantageous to establish a sales subsidiary, such as countries with high political risk or low sales potential but high future growth prospects. In the COO perspective, a representative office can oversee the foreign market by controlling implementation of the company's branding strategy, suggesting possible adaptations and maintaining closer relationships with importers, distributors, and retailers.

A more demanding choice is opening a branch that does not have legal autonomy from the parent company but, unlike the representative office, can sign contracts and sell products and services. The branch's actions, therefore, can certainly more decisively enhance the brand and its COO in the client companies.

A sales subsidiary involves more direct investment than a branch. This company has its own legal personality, operates independently of the parent company and is subject to the laws and tax system of the country where it is located. It becomes a sales and production subsidiary if, in addition to sales, it also performs production activities. Like the joint venture, this type of direct investment can be classified as a wholly owned subsidiary if ownership of the foreign subsidiary is 100% or a subsidiary if the parent company's share is higher than 50% (majority stake). If the parent company's share is lower than 50% (minority stake), the company in the foreign market is called an associate or an affiliate. With respect to the COO, as discussed in Chap. 5, if the subsidiary is only responsible for the sales of the product imported from the domestic market, the country of manufacturing and the country of brand are maintained, with the possibility of controlling the implementation of the country of brand throughout the distribution channel. If production is moved to a foreign country, the country of manufacturing is lost, but the country of brand remains, and the COO can be adapted to the foreign country where the company decides to invest. For instance, making adaptations, even to product and packaging, can enhance perceptions of the COO in the target market. For example, in the USA, Barilla has succeeded in enhancing Italian-made products, enriching them with specific adaptations necessary to meet the needs of US consumers.

Direct investments can be developed in the form of new establishments (greenfield investments) or mergers and acquisitions (brownfield investment).

2.4.1   Greenfield Investments

In greenfield investment, the company has the advantage of creating a completely new, ad hoc entity for the foreign market based on its strategies and objectives and the characteristics of its target customers. A new company has the advantage of bringing innovation and creating new jobs in the foreign country. However, the investment takes a long time and is often not quantifiable, and the introduction of a new company can increase competitive pressures in a country, risking negative consumer perceptions and boycotts. However, it is important to underline that greenfield investments can also be used to strengthen the company's presence in retail, with investment in Directly Operated Stores (DOS). This choice is made mostly by companies operating in sectors where the brand value and the COO can be significantly enhanced by the shopping experience, as is the case for luxury brands. Greenfield investment is perceived as a real investment by the company in a foreign market and therefore also carries the perceptions of the company's COO.

2.4.2   Brownfield Investments

In brownfield investment, the company decides to acquire a company in the foreign market. Acquisition shortens entry times as the company can operate almost immediately, but there are other factors to consider. First, before the acquisition, identifying the company to be acquired can be very long as it is not easy to find a company with the right characteristics for investment. Second, operating time can be faster or slower depending on the characteristics of the new company. Often, the process of integrating technology, production, information technology, and organizational cultures requires much time. From a competitive perspective, a brownfield investment is less aggressive as it does not alter the competitive structures. The disadvantage for the local economy is that unlike greenfield investment, brownfield investment does not create new jobs.

From the COO perspective, brownfield investment tends to limit the value of the made in as it acquires a foreign company already operating in the local market and therefore is perceived with the COO of the country of entry. However, this perception may change over the long term as the integration of the acquired company within the group becomes complete. Obviously, if the local brands of the acquired company are maintained in brownfield investment, the COO does not offer value. This choice, however, is in line with the logic of diversifying the product portfolio of many foreign companies, which use acquisitions to combine the brand of the foreign company positioned in a premium range and some local brands with different positioning and target.

2.5 Conclusion

Considering the analysis of the entry strategies, it clearly emerges that COO can play a different role depending on how the distribution channel is structured, especially in relation to the choice of entry mode. Thus, if a company wants to enhance the product's brand and the COO, especially if it is necessary to justify a premium price in foreign markets, the entry method must be chosen with great care.

In the case of export modes, investing marginally and exercising a limited control over the distribution channel, makes it difficult to implement marketing strategies aimed at creating the distinctiveness of the COO. Especially in the case of indirect exports, where the company relies on an intermediary in the domestic market, the manufacturer can do little to enhance the COO. Only in the case of export consortia, where the product's origin and typicality have to be efficiently promoted, much importance is given to the COO that can create a competitive advantage against products of other nationalities. In the case of direct exports, the direct contact with the foreign market allows the company to get more information and awareness about the actions taken to create value from the product's origins, but also in this case the control can be weak, as pointed out in the example of the Nutella brand. In general, in the case of export modes, companies that export products in countries where it is necessary to enhance the COO should pay much attention to the characteristics of distributors.

Intermediate modes are entry strategies that can be considered to lie halfway between exports and hierarchical modes, hence the company can exercise stronger control of the brand image and COO if compared to export modes. However, there are some differences depending on the choice of the mode of entry.

In the case of licencing, if production is carried out in the foreign market, the value of the domestic market as the country of manufacture is lost, which risks weakening the concept of origin linked to the typicality of the product associated with a given country. Nevertheless, through the partnership relationship and a favorable collaboration, the company can strengthen its brand presence abroad while maintaining strong influence on the product's distribution channel and can associate values linked to the country of origin.

International franchising is a mode of entry especially suitable to enhance the brand's origin: through a win–win agreement between the franchisor and the franchisee, the company can explain its values and define a coordinated image in the various countries where the company's brand is present. In particular, with international franchising, a company can enhance the origin of the product through communication at the point of sale, accordingly to the importance of the store experience to convey the COO of the product, as will be pointed out in Chap. 6.

Also, piggyback agreements can be interesting in the COO perspective, especially for niche products linked to craft traditions, provided that COO must be consistent with that of the rider company.

The decomposability of the COO in the country of manufacturing and the country of a brand can open an opportunity also for entry modes such as management contract or contract management, giving the possibility to invest heavily in enhancement of the country of brand instead of the country of manufacturing.

If the company enters a foreign market by forming a joint venture or a strategic alliance with a local partner, the COO can be maintained if the exporting company retains control of the brand. Vice versa, management of the COO as a competitive advantage becomes difficult if two or more companies from different countries decide to create a joint venture in a third market. Unless one partner has significantly greater weight, it becomes difficult to defend both a country of brand and a country of manufacturing position.

Hierarchical modes can certainly more decisively enhance the brand and its COO in the foreign markets. A representative office or a branch can oversee the foreign market by controlling implementation of the company's branding strategy. This control can be exerted in a stronger way with a subsidiary, that is responsible for the sales of the product imported from the domestic market, thus giving the possibility to maintain the country of manufacturing and the country of brand. Furthermore, with a subsidiary, the company has the possibility of controlling the implementation of the country of brand throughout the distribution channel. If production is moved to a foreign country, the country of manufacturing is lost, but the country of brand remains, and the COO can be adapted to the foreign country where the company decides to invest.

References

Alon, I., Jaffe, E., Prange, C., & Vianelli, D. (2016). *Global marketing. Contemporary theory, practice, and cases*. New York: McGraw-Hill.

Cateora, P., Gilly, M., Graham, J., & Money, R. B. (2019). *International marketing* (17th ed.). New York: McGraw-Hil-Irwin.

Dong, M., Tse, D., & Hung, K. (2010). Effective distributor governance in emerging markets: The salience of distributor role, relationship stages, and market uncertainty. *Journal of International Marketing, 18*(3), 1–17.

Kashyap, V., & Sivadas, E. (2012). An exploratory examination of shared values in channel relationships. *Journal of Business Research, 65*(5), 586–593.

Lowe, R., Kenyon, A., & Doole, I. (2019). *International marketing strategy: Analysis, development & implementation* (8th ed.). Andover, Hampshire: Cengage Learning EMEA.

Peng, M., & Meyer, K. (2019). *International business* (3rd ed.). Andover, Hampshire: Cengage Learning EMEA.

Sinkovics, N., Sinkovics, R. R., & Jean, R.-J. (2013). The internet as an alternative path to internationalization? *International Marketing Review, 30*(2), 130–155.

Chapter 3
Country of Origin Valorization in Exporting: Insights from Companies and Foreign Importers

Abstract Studies on the COO management of channel relationships in exports are especially scarce. In this context, companies, typically small and medium enterprises (SMEs), must enhance the value and symbolic content of the product offerings linked to the COO, using distribution channels involving one or more independent commercial intermediaries such as importers. The aim of this chapter is to contribute to the COO literature by identifying the variables in the relationships between companies and importers that favor and limit appropriation of the value generated by the COO. Giving voice to some companies and importers operating in a representative context (the United States wine market), this chapter serves the purpose of enriching the theoretical background of the COO in three ways: first, by investigating the COO value creation from the company's perspective; second, by understanding whether and to what extent importers assume a key or marginal role in the management and communication of the COO that favors or hinders the value appropriation process; and third, by identifying key factors in value appropriation and destruction through the COO in relationships between SMEs and importers.

3.1 Introduction

As mentioned, the topic of the COO assumes undoubted importance in small and medium enterprises' (SMEs) internationalization processes (Fong, Chun-Ling, & Yunzhou, 2014; Mattarazzo, 2012; Vianelli, de Luca, & Bortoluzzi, 2012). For these firms, the COO's value and symbolic attributes are important factors in value creation for the market. Often, small businesses try to base the creation of competitive advantages in various markets on the geographical origins of their offerings (Marino, Gallucci, & Mainolfi, 2009; Marino & Mainolfi, 2013; Pastore, Ricotta, & Giraldi, 2011; Roth & Diamantopoulos, 2009; Roth & Romeo, 1992). In some cases, the COO may constitute the only strong element of symbolic distinctiveness and guarantee of product quality, especially if consumers perceive a high degree of consistency in the synthetic evaluation of the distinctive attributes of the country and those of the product category of the product (Hamzaoui & Merunka, 2006; Roth & Romeo, 1992; Sims, 2009). As pointed out, the value creation process to which the COO can contribute by creating superior value for foreign customers is not sufficient to determine competitive advantages in the foreign market. In fact, the company must accompany value creation with a process of value appropriation, which consists of transforming the product value into long-term sales and profits for the company (Mizik & Jacobson, 2003). However, the company's ability to appropriate the value of COO seems to derive mainly from the level of control exercised at the level of the distribution channel. Recent studies on some business cases have highlighted that resolving many small businesses' loss of competitiveness related to place- and time-specific production in more traditional foreign markets and their difficulties growing in emerging markets, such as China, demands knowledge of how to enhance the COO in international distribution channel relationships (Bertoli & Resciniti, 2012; Pegan & Vianelli, 2016; Vianelli, de Luca, & Bortoluzzi, 2012). It, therefore, is essential to understand whether and to what extent intermediaries assume a key or marginal role in the management and communication of the COO that favors or hinders the value appropriation process. Indeed, researches on COO management in marketing channel appear to be very limited (Hansen & Skytte, 1998; Insch, Prentice, & Knight, 2011; Reardon, Vianelli, & Miller, 2017). Studies are especially scarce in export contexts where companies, typically SMEs, must enhance the value and symbolic content of the product offerings linked to the COO, using distribution channels involving one or more independent commercial intermediaries, such as importers (Pegan & Vianelli, 2013).

3.2   Importers and Country of Origin Effect

Exports, as pointed out in Chap. 2, are the most widely used approach to foreign markets because they involve lower financial, marketing, human resources, and time investments. Due to these low commitment requirements, exports are the preferred entry mode for most SMEs. Exported products may be sold abroad by intermediaries who distribute them directly through retailers and importers in the target country (Alon, Jaffe, Prange, & Vianelli, 2016). Importers provide the same services as distributors but may be either wholesalers or retailers and generally do not have exclusive territorial rights. The manufacturer has limited control over importers because they may sell the products of many suppliers, sometimes even competing product lines. Similar to distributors, importers negotiate their margins with the supplier, with different pricing policies across countries depending on the levels of service required and local competition (Alon et al., 2016; Pegan, Vianelli, & Reardon, 2017).

The importer is the first actor in the international marketing channel to select the new products offered by companies. Importers must constantly review and choose which products to include in their assortments. The price of the products and the bargaining power of the producers are only some factors considered during this selection (Alpert, Wilson, & Elliot, 1993). Indeed, many factors are involved in importers' purchasing decisions. First, as Newall (1977) pointed out, it is important to note that, in the purchasing process, the perceived risk is more articulated and higher in the business market than the consumer market because in the business area, this risk concerns perceptions of negative consequences not only for the buyer (personal risk) but also for the company (business risk). In this perspective, the decision-making process of importers can be conceived of as a general process aimed at minimizing perceived risk (Hakansson & Wootz, 1975; Sheth, 1973). In addition, given the vastness of the foreign and domestic purchasing options from which importers may choose, their decision-making processes are complex and have various implications for businesses. These processes are aimed at ensuring good margins and turnover to maximize gross margin return on investment (GMROI). Turnover results are mainly determined by the final consumers through the price and volume of sales (Hamzaoui-Essoussi, Merunka, & Bartikowski, 2011; Koschate-Fischer, Diamantopoulos, & Oldenkotte, 2012), while margins also depend on the efficiency of the purchasing system at reducing the costs of the goods sold and transactions. Effective, efficient supply chain management clearly also has indirect impacts on turnover. For the purposes of GMROI, therefore, the importer must be able to combine satisfaction of the demands expressed by the final consumer with those of efficient supply chain management (Da Silva, Davies, & Naudé, 2001).

Importers who are retail buyers can be considered to be the custodians of customer choice (Sternquist, 1994). Investigating whether and how the COO can influence their purchasing decisions is a crucial issue because such decisions determine the architecture of choices (Thaler & Sustein, 2009) to which customers are exposed in the next stages of the supply chain. In general, intermediary members of the international marketing channel are considered to be more rational and less emotional in their purchasing behavior than consumers due to the lesser information asymmetry that characterizes their decision-making process (Alpert et al., 1993). However, some studies (Bahng & Kincade, 2014; Hansen & Skytte, 1998; Kline & Wagner, 1994) have pointed out that intermediaries, even if they follow "more formalized purchasing procedures," can be considered to be "no more rational than consumers in making purchasing decisions" (Insch, 2003, p. 1) and can be influenced by COO perceptions. Consumers and retail shoppers seem to share various aspects of preferences, product choice decisions, and COO (Sheth, 1973). One of the few studies exploring the issue of the COO effect in importers' decision-making highlights the importance of investigating the role of COO in industry-specific terms (Knight, Holdsworth, & Mather (2007). In addition, the authors suggested conceiving of the importer's COO perceptions as based more on summary constructions that include product-specific attributes and manufacturers than on the country's image as a halo (Knight et al., 2007). In other words, importers, as members of the international marketing channel, can be considered to be "expert consumers" with high product capabilities (Sternquist, 1994, p. 171). The influence of the country's image, therefore, is exercised at the level of associations between the specific product domain and the country where it was produced rather than a generic image of the country.

As already mentioned, for GMROI purposes, the importer must combine customer satisfaction with efficient supply chain management (Da Silva et al., 2001).

Selecting from among a multitude of products from several countries and buying for a diverse customer audience, importers must purchase what they think their target segments will appreciate (Levy & Weitz, 2007). In this case, therefore, it is important to know how consumers perceive the COO in relation to products from different countries involved in the importer's commercial activity.

Considering supply chain management, the COO, as in the case of consumers, can be utilized by importers as a heuristic to simplify the treatment of information in supply chain decisions. For example, small importers may perceive large producers in developed countries as being too strong and powerful and, therefore, tend to exclude them as suppliers. However, an importer may also consider that remote producers have significant transaction costs due to logistics or alternatively those that are geographically closer and have relatively lower transaction costs. In general, importers may avoid or be attracted to producers in certain regions because the development of a relationship of trust is easier due greater (lesser) mental distance (Johnston, Khalil, Jain, & Cheng, 2012) or the different levels of corruption present (Reardon et al., 2017).

3.3 Country of Origin, Value Creation, and Value Appropriation: The Role of Importers

As mentioned, the value appropriation process defines the amount of the advantage connected to value creation from which companies can make profits in the market. When SMEs rely on importers to penetrate foreign markets, the conversion of value creation into value appropriation depends on the characteristics of the relationship between the supplier (the SME) and the buyer (the importer). The product value does not depend only on the product itself but also on a joint dialogue between the seller and the customer, especially in foreign markets where customers' experience and knowledge can be significantly different, making the preferences and the buying process different than in the home market. The choice of the intermediary entrusted with sales in the export market is crucial not only to achieve short-term profitability but also to set the foundation for continuous growth based on the development and strengthening of the producer company's image (Alon et al., 2016; Pegan, Vianelli, & de Luca, 2013). In a prime position to communicate, influence, and manage the final individual customers, importers act as mediators in enterprises' value appropriation process, helping them appropriate the value they have created and defend it in the long term. The long-term relationship created between the company and the importer becomes a key factor in control of the market and the image transferred to the final customer.

The relationship with the importer can become especially crucial in highly dynamic, complex product, and market contexts where it is important to be able to invest in the distinctiveness of offerings and to strategically manage symbolic attributes such as the COO. The importer managing the relationship with the foreign market can contribute to the appropriation of value originating from the COO (Pegan et al., 2017).

To fill the gap on this topic in the literature, the objective of this chapter is to present an investigation of whether and to what extent companies operating in sectors that traditionally exploit the positive halo linked to the COO effect can take advantage of a distinctive positioning in which value creation and value appropriation are two processes in agreement. Put differently, this study examines whether a tense relationship is created between value creation and value appropriation when the value created by the COO is partly lost in the relationship between the enterprise and the importer. The latter operates in foreign markets that often have some characteristics that hinder value appropriation and, therefore, must be managed (Pegan & Vianelli, 2013, 2016). In particular, the study aim is to identify the variables in the relationship between companies and importers that favor and limit appropriation of the value generated by the COO. This chapter presents, especially representative testimony gathered from the stories of the experiences of particular companies (wineries) that have decided to export wine to the world's largest wine market (the USA), along with importers operating in that market. Before giving voice to these companies and importers, the reasons that led to focusing the study on this particular product and market context are explained in detail.

3.4 Wine and Terroir in a Traditional Foreign Market: A Challenge for Exporters

3.4.1 Why Italian Wine in the US Market

Traditional wine-producing countries face more difficulties penetrating foreign markets due to changes in the international competitive arena caused by the gradual rise of new producing countries (e.g., Australia and Chile). The latter are spreading a culture of wine decontextualized from the territory of origin and promoting so-called international grape varieties (e.g., merlot and sauvignon). These countries also make strong investments in their brands to bridge the competitive gap resulting from their lack of recognized winemaking traditions (Bardají & Mili, 2009; Campbell & Guibert, 2006; Rea & D'Antone, 2010). Conversely, traditional producers such as France, Italy, and Spain are highly fragmented and base their differentiation strategy on *terroir*, emphasizing the designations of origin (DO). The DO represent a critical success factor but restrict growth in size, requiring production in certain geographic areas and the use of traditional systems that limit production capacity (Anderson, Norman, & Wittwer, 2001). These challenges are even more critical for small wineries such as Italian wineries that decide to export and aim to grow in foreign markets but face highly complex macro- and micro-environments, especially in the

USA, the largest wine marketplace in the world.[1] Laws (a three-tier system[2]), market segmentation, and intense competition demand the use of independent importers, wholesalers, and retailers, which are generally less suited to facilitating growth and controlling the foreign market (Alon et al., 2016). They, in fact, are distributors who do not always have exclusive sales rights in a given geographical area, making it difficult to control products' final destination. Moreover, these entities may represent different companies in the same sector, sometimes partial competitors, with obvious consequences for penetration of foreign markets.

These importers operate in markets where a link to a specific country or region constitutes a distinctive attribute of wine production (Bruwer & Johnson, 2010). Indeed, the ability to create strong, intense links between the company's product and the territory can generate maximum value in the wine sector, while success abroad is strongly correlated to the company's ability to enhance and effectively communicate the *terroir* (D'Amico, 2002; Rea & D'Antone, 2010). According to the literature, the multidimensional concept of *terroir* understands territory in its broadest sense as including not only the physical environment but also the human, historical, and cultural factors that directly affect the peculiarities of the wines produced in a given territory (Callon, Meadel, & Rabehariosoa, 2002; Mattiacci & Maralli, 2007). Emphasizing the unique conditions of a specific physical territory and thus enhancing its cultural identity, the idea of *terroir* recalls the concept of the quality economy typical of niche productions (Callon et al., 2002). Quality that comes from being rooted in particular areas and certified by relevant institutions is widely recognized by the market and permeates consumers' experiences and perceptions. The

---

[1]The USA continues to be one of the most attractive wine markets in the world. The USA is in fact considered a growing market, together with Canada, South Korea, and the newcomer Brazil, where wine is a mainstream product that is going through a dynamic development (Source: https://www.vinitaly.com/it/news/wine-news/gli-usa-sono-ancora-il-mercato-piu-attraente/, accessed August 8, 2019). Although volume consumption in the American market is slowing down, spending on wine is not slowing down. In 2018, the data show a growth of 0.8% and 4.3%, respectively, very similar to the pace of the last 5 years (an annual increase of 1.6% in volume and 5.0% in value). The largest market in the world is drinking better and better: with these data we can easily calculate an average price per liter of 18.6 dollars, which means 14 dollars per bottle, 12.3 euros at the current exchange rate (Source: http://www.inumeridelvino.it/2019/07/usa-vendite-al-dettaglio-di-vino-aggiornamento-2018.html, accessed 20 July, 2019). In 2018, the exports of Italian wine to the USA recorded the largest increase in the last 5 years. In terms of value, there was an increase in 2017 of 6.8% to 1.984 billion dollars, after the +3.4% recorded the previous year. In terms of quantity, the annual increase was 1.2%. The market share also improved, rising in 12 months to 32% from 31.4%, as did average prices, which rose by 5.4% to 5.9 dollars per liter (Source: http://america24.com/news/vino-italiano-export-in-usa-al-top-di-cinque-anni-nel-2018, accessed June 16, 2019).

[2]The three-tier alcohol distribution system for distributing alcoholic beverages was established in the USA after the abolition of the Prohibition. The three levels are importers or manufacturers, distributors, and retailers. In the basic structure, manufacturers may only sell their products to wholesale distributors, who then sell them to retailers, and only retailers may sell to consumers. Producers include brewers, wine producers, distillers, and importers. More details about this system could be found here (Source: https://beveragetradenetwork.com/en/btn-academy/articles/three-tier-system-and-pricing-overview-for-usa-market-305.htm, accessed February 15, 2019).

management literature recognizes precisely this close product–territory link as a distinctive identifying factor in wine production (Bruwer & Johnson, 2010). In this context, a dynamic, interactive relationship is created between the product and the territory. The territory enriches the wine with meaning and value, transmitting to the wine its own historical, cultural, and environmental values. The wine, thus enriched, contributes to developing the territory's identity and reputation, increasing its attractiveness and value (Mattiacci & Maralli, 2007; Pegan & Vianelli, 2013; Pegan & Vianelli, 2016).

As mentioned, a qualitative study on Italian wineries was conducted. The methodology is discussed in Chap. 1. Here, we recall that we collected data through in-depth interviews with 18 Italian winery SMEs in the main Italian wine exporting regions (five in Tuscany, six in Veneto, one in Piedmont, and six in Friuli Venezia Giulia) present in the US market through importers (Table 3.1).

3.4.2   The Meaning and the Strategic Role of the Country of Origin from Italian Wineries' Perspective

The stories of the wine entrepreneurs interviewed and the content analysis[3] indicate the importance and multidimensionality of the COO, particularly made in Italy (Table 3.2), as a driver of value creation in their experiences of exporting to the USA. The respondents emphasize that it is precisely the strong perceived link between the product and its territory (*terroir*) that offers a strategic source for starting the internationalization process to create value in the foreign wine market.

The Italian product typicality attracting the interest of potential foreign importers often provides the basis for the activation of exports:

> There was an importer looking for a small business with a niche wine. My company produces 5,000 bottles of high-quality Brunello di Montalcino. (P2)

> He was looking for us because he was interested in our small niche production and especially because we were already known then to produce very traditional wines with very little technique, technology, and chemistry. (P7)

The COO of made in Italy creates value due to its strong cultural and symbolic identity. The concept of intangible cultural heritage[4] (Napolitano & Marino, 2016;

---

[3]The methodology is discussed in Chap. 1. As mentioned, content analysis of the interviews identified 33 codes. These codes were then classified into four main families of codes, each distinguished by a different number of citations and frequency in the data (Pegan & Vianelli, 2013; Zarantonello & Luomala, 2011). Each company was assigned a primary document, named with the acronym P and numbered in ascending order. Each quotation in the text is associated with the specific company whose representative was interviewed (e.g., P2 and P3, as shown in Table 3.1).

[4]Cultural heritage is a set of resources inherited from the past that, independent of ownership, people see as a reflection and expression of their constantly evolving values, beliefs, knowledge, and traditions. Cultural heritage includes all aspects of the environment resulting from the interactions between people and places over time.

Table 3.1 Main characteristics of exporters

Cases	Sector	Italian region	Entry strategies	Specific foreign markets	Predominant data
Case 1 (P1)	Food/wine	Tuscany	Exports	USA	Primary
Case 2 (P2)	Food/wine	Tuscany	Exports	USA	Primary
Case 3 (P3)	Food/wine	Friuli Venezia Giulia	Exports	USA	Primary
Case 4 (P4)	Food/wine	Friulia Venezia Giulia	Exports	USA	Primary
Case 5 (P5)	Food/wine	Friuli Venezia Giulia	Exports	USA	Primary
Case 6 (P6)	Food/wine	Veneto	Exports	USA	Primary
Case 7 (P7)	Food/wine	Friuli Venezia Giulia	Exports	USA	Primary
Case 8 (P8)	Food/wine	Tuscany	Exports	USA	Primary
Case 9 (P9)	Food/wine	Tuscany	Exports	USA	Primary
Case 10 (P10)	Food/wine	Veneto	Exports	USA	Primary
Case 11 (P11)	Food/wine	Veneto	Exports	USA	Primary
Case 12 (P12)	Food/wine	Piedmont	Exports	USA	Primary
Case 13 (P13)	Food/wine	Veneto	Exports	USA	Primary
Case 14 (P14)	Food/wine	Friuli Venezia Giulia	Exports	USA	Primary
Case 15 (P15)	Food/wine	Veneto	Exports	USA	Primary
Case 16 (P16)	Food/wine	Friuli Venezia Giulia	Exports	USA	Primary
Case 17 (P17)	Food/wine	Tuscany	Exports	USA	Primary
Case 18 (18)	Food/wine	Veneto	Exports	USA	Primary

Source: Compiled by authors

Pegan & Vianelli, 2016), strongly connected to the concept of *terroir*, helps understanding of the intrinsic, strongly distinctive value of Italian products as an expression of a specific community and culture. The strong cultural value of the wine emerges and marks it as an expression of the Italian intangible cultural heritage represented by food and all the related rituals and events. The symbolic value of made-in-Italy wine is even more evident for particular wines such as Prosecco that represent a new style of drinking, synonymous with the Italian lifestyle. Prosecco's simplicity, essentiality, and informality have made it different and have determined its success. The symbolic and emotional value of prosecco wine and its ability to communicate the tangible and intangible values of Italy's cultural heritage are strongly emphasized by an interviewee:

> For them, it is more a concept linked to the simplicity of life, to know how to take problems with the right weight, to eat well, to drink well, to not be overwhelmed by the problems of work. [. . .] The made in Italy, they also consider it from the point of view of elegance. As opposed to the French one that is sophisticated elegance, Italian elegance is more original,

Table 3.2   Family 1—Context of the country of origin

Codes of family 1	Number of quotations	Frequency in the data
Terroir	28	
Symbolic value of made in Italy	28	
Value of Italian wine image	25	
Value of Italian food image	24	
Value of the Italian image	21	
Place of origin effect	28	
Total	154	24.6%

Source: Compiled by Authors
The percentage was calculated by dividing the total of 627 selected quotations in the transcribed empirical material by the number of quotations per family

> less sumptuous, more authentic and balanced, more natural, and more a way of being. [...] And the Prosecco most characterizes us [...] because it is simple, fragrant, floral and everyday [...] It is a product that is elegant and that makes you look good when you go out to drink with friends [...]. (P12)

Similarly, an interviewee with a company that had operated in the USA for many year states that:

> An Italian wine is bought for the simple fact of being Italian. There is a different image linked to the territory compared to other products from other countries. There is consumer awareness that Italy is an inexhaustible source of flavors, recipes, and fragrances, (P13)

The COO effect, as highlighted by many studies in the consumer field (Bursi, Grappi, & Martinelli, 2012; Papadopoulos & Heslop, 2003; Roth & Diamantopoulos, 2009; Roth & Romeo, 1992; Samiee, 2010, 2011; Usunier, 2006, 2011), is present in its complexity and multidimensionality. The respondents identify as a relevant source of value the image of a specific manufacturing production (the value of the Italian food image), which is a country product image (Italian cuisine). The COO in the made-in-Italy designation creates value in wine primarily due to the strong symbolic and emotional connotations of both the country image and the country product image (e.g., Italian agro-food), rich with cultural values and strong perceptions in the US market. The Prosecco Valdobbiadene wine can transmit to the final consumer an experience that recalls the pleasant, envied Italian lifestyle. In the mind of the US customer, this wine is associated with the freshness, joy, and conviviality typically present in Italian cuisine:

> It must not be separated from Italian cuisine, appreciated for its variety and quality. The wine was successful because it was presented as something you could have with Italian cuisine. As the taste for Italian cuisine evolves, so also the taste for Italian wine evolves. (P13)

Similarly, it is stressed that made in Italy is fundamentally important, especially due to the positive connotations associated with the country's overall cultural image in the minds of foreign consumers:

> I believe that made in Italy is very important. There's art; there's fashion; there's Ferrari; there's the Italian lifestyle. (P3)

The driving effect of the appeal of the strong, prestigious cultural image associated with Italian cuisine (country product image) found abroad in the distinctive value of the image of the specific product is clearly underlined by an interviewee:

> In other markets, the penetration of our wines always goes hand in hand with catering. This is also the case in the most remote corner of the world. [. . .] In New York in the 80s began the decline of French cuisine and the boom of Italian cuisine that presented fresh elements, local products, then also local wines and bubbles that were not yet known. Prosecco has begun to have its own small demand from these Italian restaurateurs. (P13)

However, it emerges that in this specific area, the COO effect can be reread as the place-of-origin effect (Andehn & Berg, 2011) in which not only the country but also a specific region of origin is perceived as historically linked to a particular production and, therefore, endowed with strong, distinctive know-how (Barber, Taylor, & Deale, 2010). The region then can enrich the product with strong symbolic connotations for foreign consumers:

> The American market loves us and has always loved us. Everything that comes from Italy makes them dream. I see many guests who come here in the summer in our farm and some Americans who book for the eighth, ninth time. They really need to come here because Italy has nothing in common with their imagination and Tuscany above all. In fact, what calls them most for all our wines is Tuscany, so the fact of being in this territory: Florence . . . the Renaissance . . . and everything else. (P1)

> More than made in Italy, Pinot Grigio is known as an Italian product but has a great appeal for the area. That is, traditionally, Pinot Grigio comes from Friuli, from northern Italy, and in the U.S. is known to be a product that comes from here. And when one speaks of Italian white wine in the USA, many identify with Pinot Grigio and Friuli. (P14)

In this regard, the experience of another company emphasizes with great force that what has allowed it to gain a competitive advantage is the strategic importance of the place-of-origin effect in its specific designation of the made in Venice:

> When Americans asked me where I came from, I said that I was coming from Venice. Unconsciously, I had created a pass for myself in the American market because, I realized, the world goes crazy for Venice. [. . .] Venice is seen as the dream. Perhaps it is more famous than Italy itself. In Venice, there is no great food or wine produced due to geographical problems. Venice is an island in a lagoon, so it is almost impossible to cultivate vineyards. I believe that these two characteristics should be exploited even more because they are huge potential. (P17)

According to the company, the appeal of the strong territorial identity of Italian wine manifested in the appeal of made in Venice, rich in symbolic connotations especially loved by foreign consumers, paradoxically presents a strategic resource more relevant to gaining competitive advantages in foreign markets than in Italy:

> We export about 70% of our production abroad. Italy is suffering from an economic crisis. The company reinvests in the Italian market all the profits obtained from the foreign market to keep its products in the local market. (P18)

The creation of value through the exploitation of the strong place-of-origin effect should be implemented not only through increasing valorization and communication of the product–territory link of the origin in the market but also through changes in location in some stages of the production process. For example, white peaches should be cultivated in the province of Venice rather than bought in Emilia Romagna:

> We do not limit ourselves to an association of name and image, but through a long journey (which is underway), we want to bring the entire production of wine and Bellini in the mainland around Venice. [...] Our mission is to make the consumer recognize Bellini as a product made in Venice: prosecco wine from our hills, peaches grown near the lagoon, prepared and bottled in San Donà di Piave. (P17)

Another company highlights how important it is to remember and constantly communicate to the often inexperienced final market the special bond of Italian wine with its particular territory of origin, culture, and community. The wine nearly crosses the border of the Italian nature to become synonymous, as in the case of Prosecco, with the category of sparkling wines at international level:

> We must always draw attention to the fact that we are in Venice, that there are the Dolomites. The fact that it comes from Veneto, for example, is something unknown. The fact that it is Italian is known by 50%. [...] The brand is Prosecco. The fact that we call it Valdobbiadene, that it has DOCG (that is controlled and guaranteed designation of origin), that it is heroic viticulture and all the rest, America doesn't care. [...] That it has another denomination can interest some sommeliers, some tasters, but if we reach 2%–3% of consumers, we are lucky. (P16)

3.4.3   Characteristics of the Importer and the Importer's Role in Valorization Process of the Country of Origin

The content analysis highlighted some dimensions that, from the perspective of the companies interviewed, characterize the figure of the importer, influencing both the evaluation and the management of channel relationships (see Table 3.3).

In the process of enhancing the territorial identity of Italian wine, the distribution network plays a critical role. It is essential that the network include partners willing to transfer the values of excellence and the cultural value of made-in-Italy products downstream. Only in this way can companies escape the speculative logic of price wars inevitable in a global market:

> A great, strong, essential product–territory bond is a competitive advantage if supported by a distribution network that knows how to enhance this feature, always aiming at excellence and avoiding speculation that leads nowhere. (P12)

An especially important criterion is represented by the degree of centrality the importer attributes to the company's product and, therefore, the importer's propensity to enhance it in the subsequent channel levels, namely, the level of commitment. The relationship between importers and SMEs is immediately conditioned by the

Table 3.3 Family 2—Context of importers

Codes of family 2	Number of quotations	Frequency in the data
Level of commitment of the importer	29	
Importer—High product knowledge	25	
Market coverage	20	
Importer—High market knowledge	15	
Importer—Sales oriented	4	
Total	93	14.8%

Source: Compiled by authors

perception that the firm and the importer have the same ability and desire to increase the wine in the assortment, improve the perceived product quality among the target customers, and effectively communicate the product's typicality and uniqueness throughout the channel:

> The importer was born with our portfolio. [. . .] Our products weigh 40%. When we entered, we preferred to choose a small importer that has represented us well, obtaining a great focus on our products. (P18)

It is essential to have the right importer because it facilitates the sales process. The importer decides the marketing of the product and must understand the peculiarities, strengths, and characteristics to communicate to convince distributors to push one product rather than another. The value given to the brand depends on the quality of the partnerships the company has managed to cultivate:

> The importer in the United States takes the place of the manufacturer, and he creates and decides the marketing of the product. In our case, there is a partnership. We decide together but usually the importer. Distribution, therefore, is very important, especially in a market where distribution commands as in the United States. [. . .] It is important that your distribution works for you and not for others. (P13)

The choice of which importer to rely is also guided by evaluation of his contribution to knowledge of the product and thus the wines most suitable for marketing (importer—high product knowledge) and the specific needs of the foreign market context (importer—high market knowledge). This knowledge is crucial and closely related to ensuring appropriate enhancement of Italian wines within the distribution channel up to the final consumer:

> The importer/distributor is quite familiar with the wine, the names, the classifications, and how it is produced because he often takes part in trade fairs. He is interested, studies, goes to companies in Italy, and comes to directly know the production in the area. (P6)

> Your importer must be very skilled at creating a marketing policy. It must be all around: it must understand what the characteristics of the wine are, what is to be communicated, what the strengths of your brand are. That's why it's better to be wary of importers born from the evening to the morning. (P10)

> The importer knows the market well, tells us how to enhance the product, knows the marketing, understands what can be useful to enhance the product. (P13)

> My importer always keeps me informed about trends and what is happening in the American market. (P9)

It is emphasized that a distinctive aspect of the US wine market is precisely the gap in knowledge and expertise between the importers and the final consumers, which, as we will see, is an obstacle to the growth of Italian products:

> There is a big gap between the business customer and the final consumer market. This is also one of the big differences with the Italian market. Here in Italy, for better or for worse, everyone understands something about wine. In America, consumers find it hard to understand the difference between good wine and bad wine. As far as the business is concerned, American distributors, on the other hand, are prepared. [...] They do tastings. They are the consumers' consultants. (P13)

> I meet importers with a strong knowledge of Italian wine. There is a strong love for wine and for Italian culture. Most of the operators come periodically to Italy. They know what happens. [...] They are also careful not to take into account a made in Italy that is sometimes a bit forced, made in series. Importer gives us input to improve [...]. Sometimes our importer gives us advice on the label [...] or helps us to improve the product from a visual point of view and, in some cases, even to modify, albeit only slightly, the taste of the wine, perhaps softening it a little to better adapt it to the local consumer. (P12)

However, even if the importer is prepared and interested in praising the distinctive characteristics of the Italian product, it does not guarantee that there will be many receptive actors downstream. In addition to often unskilled consumers, retailers sometimes might be uncooperative:

> Few consumers are able to really distinguish things and, therefore, also the prices that logically change. There are many products at very low prices, competitive, and not distinguishing between one thing and another. Consumers cannot understand the real reason for this price difference. Many times, we have come up against even a lack of willingness to understand, to be educated. We deal mainly with the importers, but they also tell us about the attitudes of the end customer and the distributor. The importers may have a clear idea of what the company is like but cannot pass it on to their employees. (P4)

This experience is rather rare. However, in a couple of cases, it emerges that the establishment of a relationship with an overly commercial importer (importer—sales oriented) likely results in failure due to, for example, overly aggressive sales policies based on discounted prices rather than the qualitative distinctiveness of the product.

> They also sell wine at cost. This often creates discomfort. They are nothing more than harmful disturbances that in fact determine the sale of the product. (P5)

> Opportunities in the U.S. are the possibility of selling large quantities, while the greatest threat is the risk of seeing the price squeezed by demand always downward by the importer. (P16)

The product's knowledge is strongly linked to the market coverage guaranteed by a specific importer, which is a fundamental strategic factor in penetrating and growing in such a vast, complex market:

> We have not sought a domestic importer able to cover all the American states. Instead, we have preferred to take individual importers for the various states. At the moment, we have focused on seven, eight states. (P3)

Table 3.4 Family 3—Context of foreign consumers, market, and competition characteristics

Codes of family 3	Number of quotations	Frequency in the data
Not-expert consumer	39	
Complexity of Italian DO	29	
Price escalation	22	
Dimensions of the US wine market	18	
Weak institutions	6	
Threats in the macro-environment	12	
Inability to enhance the value of made in Italy	11	
Italian sounding	11	
Made-in-France value	7	
Competition from new producers	18	
Private label	5	
Total	178	28.4%

Source: Compiled by authors

3.4.4 Critical Issues: The Role of the Foreign Context

As mentioned, companies must associate value creation with a value appropriation process, which demands the ability to transform the product value into long-term sales and profits for companies (Mizik & Jacobson, 2003). In the companies' perceptions, the most critical factors in value appropriation through the COO are the specific characteristics of foreign consumers, the market, and the competitive scenario (Table 3.4).

Among the most relevant factors, two distinct but closely related aspects emerge. First, the intrinsic complexity of the DO system on which the differentiation of Italian products is based makes it difficult to communicate the intrinsic value of Italian wine to the final market. Second, the inexperienced foreign consumer has to deal with an articulated product offering whose quality is difficult to evaluate compared to other simpler, perhaps cheaper alternatives. Lacking competence, the final consumer is often attracted more by the symbolic connotations of the COO than perceptions of the real higher quality of the Italian product. This situation is a problem that Italian producers often encounter abroad, even in traditional export markets. As found in previous studies (Pegan, Vianelli, & de Luca, 2014; Vianelli, de Luca, & Pegan, 2012), even in markets such as the USA where there is a spontaneous association between a positive country image and its manufacturing excellence (as in the case of made-in-Italy wine), this association is not enough to induce purchases. In this case, too, a knowledge gap and the need to fill it are confirmed (de Luca & Pegan, 2014; Pegan et al., 2014). Compared to importers, the final consumers are generally considered to be less competent (not-expert consumer), especially in certain geographic areas of the country.

> Unfortunately, the American consumer of the coasts, in cities like New York and San Francisco is an attentive consumer, updated, a traveler who knows Italy not only on the map and maybe has already been there. If, on the other hand, we move to the American

provinces, which are where 90% of wines are sold, the central provinces of the Midwest, the consumer is not so careful. He takes what is proposed to him as "made in Italy." (P12)

The customers—in a market context characterized by the presence of new exporting countries such as Australia with competitive prices and the availability of catalogue sales based on market demand and not linked to particular vineyards—pay little attention to the product origin unless they are adequately guided by commercial intermediaries in the choice of wine products. Consequently, it is difficult to communicate to the market the superior, certified quality of the Italian offer (the complexity of Italian DO). In the experiences of one company:

> The American doesn't care about origin. [...] Prosecco for him can also be made in China. He doesn't care. This is because there is very little wine culture. For example, many people don't even know where Venice is. The made in Italy is a mix of fashion, cuisine, ideas. The American does not care that they are actually produced in Italy. [...] Italian wines are made in Italy, but for the consumer, it is not important. The American doesn't even care about names. The American doesn't care where the products were born. (P13)

Some other factors related to particular market contexts also seem to hinder value appropriation by the SMEs interviewed. The difficulty in appropriately enhancing the qualitative superiority of the DO product is associated with the challenges justifying to the consumer premium prices not only due to the product quality but also to the structure of the distribution system and the length of the US three-level market channel (price escalation).

> The threats come from the structure of the American distribution system. It's very expensive. It doesn't allow properly planning commercial and marketing plans. The biggest threat [...] is the consolidation of the big distribution groups, which [...] concentrate their strength and manage the wine flows. And unfortunately, we have to go through them as we can't go over them. (P17)

> The noble wine is sold to the importer for €8.50, but then I find it in restaurants' wine lists at up to $80. There are the costs of transportation and a whole series of intermediate steps. ... It depends on the American states and the different types of licenses. In some markets, my importer makes me have direct contact with the distributor, and you can be more competitive. In others, you can't. (P1)

The threats for Italian wine are even more significant in light of the spread of a new business model for wine due to the entry of new producer countries such as Australia. With considerable marketing resources, these countries are much more open and flexible (competition from new producers) and, therefore, more competitive than traditional producer countries such as Italy strongly bound to their own territories:

> Australians sell you with their wine samples. They make it for you the way you want it. Vice versa, a small company, for example, in the Tuscan territory must be dignified and must be able to distinguish itself for its quality and not for its wine samples. [...] You can adjust the label, but you can't start making chianti or pinot noir just because they want it. Pinot noir will never be produced here. Identity is above all the territory where you are located. (P9)

Increasing global competitive pressures are linked to precisely the numerous opportunities offered by the constantly growing and evolving demand for wine, even in taste (dimensions of the US market):

It's a market that's definitely evolving and expanding. It's a very large and very varied market. (P6)

It's a market with great potential where everyone wants to be, but it's certainly a market that, from many points of view, is difficult. It's not so easy either to enter or to promote the product. (P10)

In some interviewees' views, weakening the image of the made-in-Italy product in the US market would reduce possibilities to appropriate the value of the COO. This scenario would contribute to some contingent events linked to political–economic changes in the macro-environment. These events could undermine the country's overall image and concretely damage the value of Italian wine in the USA, particularly the possibility to charge premium prices (threats of the macro-environment):

The floating currency, Italian politics: negative news arrives and influences general perceptions. (P6)

Precisely for this reason, several companies realize that made in Italy, despite its potentially high intrinsic and symbolic value, is not sufficient by itself to effectively distinguish the product and, above all, drive growth in the US market:

In America, the largest share of imported wines belongs to Italy. Italian wine is a brand in itself. Even Tuscany, to which we belong, is still a very strong brand, but it is not enough to ensure growth in the market. (P17)

The lack of Italian product's distinctiveness in the US market is also partly attributed to an extremely fragmented sector system in which companies find themselves very inexperienced and incapable of promoting the made-in (inability to enhance the value of made in Italy). The COO intrinsic value thus remains a mere potential:

I bring with me the quality of the Italian product, but Italian entrepreneurs, especially in the wine sector, have never been able, as the French have been doing for years, to really enhance the made in Italy. You never look at the long term. You always want to do what the Americans call a "one-shot deal;" that is, you get the quick shot but do not build. (P12)

Unfortunately, we as a country are disconnected. We are disjointed, and therefore, we are not able to exploit the driving force of certain sectors. And we are essentially sectarian: everyone goes their own way, and this potential is never fully exploited. (P14)

This not fully exploited value opens room for competition from non-original (Italian-sounding) products that, especially in categories of wine well known in international markets such as prosecco, threaten the competitiveness of Italian SMEs:

Italian sounding for the industry is a problem, a threat. There have been exchanges of requests for protection of certain trademarks through the World trade Organization in order to defend the product abroad, but reaching an agreement between the European Union and the United States is very difficult because the EU is too weak. At the points of sale of the great distributors, there are names like Rosecco, type prosecco, Quasi Secco that, however, are not reported on the label but in the exhibitors. (P11)

Several SME representatives interviewed describe difficulties differentiating themselves from other traditional producing countries. For instance, in contrast to

Italy, France can create higher value due to its ability to develop a system to much more effectively promote made-in-France products in foreign markets (made-in-France value):

> There is no coordinated proposal as there is, for example, in France, which coordinates the whole agri-food sector in terms of presence, events, image, etc. (P3).

> When the French present themselves around the world, they wear the Cartier watch, the Vuitton bag, the Dior dress, the Burgundy wine, all together. They make a French event that has a lot of appeal. Unfortunately, we are heirs of the Romans; therefore, *divide et impera* (P14).

According to some respondents, the institutional system (weak institutions) of a country weaker than others, therefore, has the responsibility to promote its country image in a coordinated manner abroad, especially in the complex, competitive US system:

> Made in Italy is the hat under which generally speaking, all Italian companies stay. [It is] a governmental approach that historically has been expressed through institutions that have done nothing but determine great expenditures of funds and [achieve] minimum effectiveness in the market. There are other countries that, with similar bodies, present themselves abroad by doing [a] system and presenting, at the same time, excellence to create a pull effect. They do it in a striking way and with an indisputable level of quality. We go in random order, and we don't care. Yet the Italian way of life is the most appreciated in the world. (P14)

A further criticism raised by some companies concerns distributors' willingness to sell under their own (private label) wine brands made in Italy, risking devaluing the product image:

> What is disturbing me and other companies so much is the presence of an incalculable and unspecified amount of private labels. These are the real scourge because under the name prosecco today, everything is sold in Italy and abroad. We have not yet managed to make it clear that prosecco is a wine that comes from here, from a certain area, that it has a tradition, certain characteristics, that the producers are these, and that it must be made in a certain way. The message has gone by that any wine with bubbles is fine with Prosecco. (P13)

3.4.5 The Role of Manufacturers in Appropriating the Value of the Country of Origin in Exports

The manufacturing company has a fundamental role in promoting and making consistent the value creation and appropriation processes through the COO. Table 3.5 summarizes the factors most under the company's control.

Although the COO can create value in the foreign market, according to different companies, the distinctiveness of the offerings and, therefore, the process of value appropriation can be activated only if made in Italy is strategically valued and managed through investments in the brand (brand value). Despite the size of SMEs, enriching the product positioning based on a strong COO through specific values linked to the company's brand, as noted in previous studies (Vianelli & Pegan, 2014), seems to be an essential aspect to appropriate the COO value:

Table 3.5 Family 4—Context of small- and medium-sized enterprises

Codes of family 4	Number of quotations	Frequency in the data
Brand value	35	
Training/support for importers	33	
Investing in *terroir* value	31	
Marketing mix adaptations	23	
SME size problem	20	
In-coming activities with importers	15	
Change in importers	14	
Company's need for an importers	12	
Commitment of SMEs	11	
Evolution of the entry mode in the US market	4	
Passive attitudes toward channel relationships	4	
Total	202	32.2%

Source: Compiled by authors

> At 100, the two parameters for us—the brand counts 70, and the origin counts 30. The strategy of the whole group is to maximize the value of the five different brands so that we have more than the origin. The origin is a consequence because then when one speaks of the company, there is a direct connection with Tuscany and Italy. (P17)

> We're doing everything we can to make a brand-building operation. Before buying prosecco, you buy Zardetto, and so you have to trust the name of the producer. For example, in my packaging, before, the word "prosecco" was written very large. Now the word "Zardetto" is written very large just for the concept of brand recognition. (P13)

It also emerges that, in line with previous studies (Pegan & Vianelli, 2016; Vianelli, de Luca, & Pegan, 2012), the process of value creation through the COO is based on the ability to merge brand enhancement activities with the qualitative excellence and the product expertise inherent to a particular territory of origin (investing in *terroir* value):

> We are betting on the territory. [...] It would be easier to make a very soft wine for the American market, full of merlot, a Coca-Cola wine I call it, so a wine similar to one another. [But] we have to carry because it's our strength; it's our territory. (P5)

The opinion of the director of the Consortium for the Protection of Conegliano Valdobbiadene in this regard is interesting:

> While the difference in the denominations of origin is well perceived by importers and often also by distributors, the difference should be noted that the consumer [is], on average, not very experienced, also because of the lack of tradition and culture regarding the wine sector in that country. (P17)

The challenge, according to the respondent, is to be able to communicate and disseminate to the final customer the value of the *terroir* and the true meaning of the DO (e.g., the difference between Italian DOC and DOCG) overseeing the entire supply chain and the market itself:

> We as DOCG are obliged to create a product culture. We must ensure that those who buy it know what they are buying. Every time we offer our product, we must be able to explain why it is so good, why it is the authentic expression of an Italian invention. Our wine is an

invention, something that did not exist before, was born here [in] a set of environmental factors. On the contrary, without the channel control, intermediaries can decide to market any of the other myriad of labels they have in their price list. This process of "training" the consumer can only take place thanks to constant and persevering work on the part of the producer, who must be able to communicate effectively the value of the *terroir* and its cultural value. (P17)

The importer plays a key role in this respect. In particular, investing in the marketing channel partnership relationship provides important support for the importer in product distribution. In this synergic relationship, the company shares its complementary skills of product knowledge, and the importer shares its knowledge of the demand and the market context (importer training/support):

Our importer works a lot on the development of the brand compatible with the difficulties of the American market. The American market is huge, and we do not have critical mass to do things that are particularly adaptable throughout the market. But for all the policies that we put in place and that are focused on creating brand value, we give very specific directives to the importer, and he gives us suggestions to do our job the best. (P18)

The partnership is very important. [...] The importer is fundamental for the promotion and sale of our product and to create branding with us. You have to visit him, beat the territory, and visit the customers with him. (P10)

The importer also plays a key role in facilitating adaptation strategies for the company's product offerings, guaranteeing effective enhancement to effectively match US market needs (marketing mix adaptations):

They give us inputs to improve, such as packaging. (P12)

The importer takes care of the valorization, must contextualize it in the market, work in an orderly way in the market, and then get to the final consumer. My importer believed in prosecco, invested a considerable amount of resources to make it known in the market. This is a true entrepreneurial spirit. For me, it was, therefore, a positive experience. My importer valued me. There was a partnership. It is important to have a long-term relationship. (P13)

The role of the importer to effectively meet market needs becomes even more evident given the limited size (SME size problem) of the companies surveyed:

The market is very difficult, and in order to approach it, you need to have a knowledge far superior to that which a small producer normally has. So only companies of a certain size can afford it because you have to be willing to invest for several years, stay there, know the various problems before you can make something real. (P13)

Similarly, another company states that its small size closes the door on market value and demands a quality-based niche strategy:

I can't think of making wine for large-scale distribution. I have to do exclusively and obligatorily of medium–high quality, and you understand that in short, having a small company, I can't do otherwise. (P9)

A synergic relationship with the importer must be based on shared values linked to the territory where the company's incoming actions (incoming activities with the importer) play a fundamental role in strengthening the importer's commitment and knowledge:

> The reason why the distributor prefers your wine to others [...] is because he knows you directly; he believes in what you do; he came here to visit you. [...] He saw how you work. He fell in love with the place and can describe the territory, transmitting our passion to the final consumer. (P1)

> He often comes to Italy and makes small experiences, even harvesting and visiting the territory. He is passionate about this area; he is passionate about the language. However, he tries to explain and bring the Italian language to its sellers to understand even more concepts. This is important for the made in Italy, so in our case, we can speak of a partnership. (P6)

Several companies point out that the type of market strengthens the need for a distribution partner (company's need for an importer):

> The idea was to find an ideal partner who could give us an appropriate and important future. (P10)

In some cases, however, the relationship does not last in the long term due to the evolution of the company's strategy (change in partner). The type of importer (local or national) may act as a constraint if the company wishes to extend its market coverage at a national level:

> We were working with smaller companies and importers, but we saw that they were not able to give us development and increases. Today, we have found the right partner. In this way, we can see the business from the perspective of long-term growth. (P10)

> The change was linked to the need to increase the market coverage [...]. As the company grew, we felt the need to change the model. Now, we have an importer who focuses on the whole portfolio. He covers all the U.S. states, and he does all the commercial and marketing policies. (P17)

In particular, it is important that the company recognizes the importance of the market (SMEs' commitment), approaching it with a long-term perspective. The company should be aware that for effective positioning, it is no longer sufficient to create distinctiveness through the COO. It instead is necessary to invest in the relationship with the importer, which becomes a central figure in the enhancement of the COO and all its components: the image of the country and territory and the typicality of the product.

> We adopt strategies that do not go from here to a year but five to 10 years. We invest a lot because it is a market that requires considerable investment in marketing. (P10)

> Investing a lot in people, which means taking a plane, going from one side of the ocean to the other, and at the same time hosting to immerse the importer in the reality of the company, make him live Italian experiences and make him understand how the product is lived, distributed, and consumed in Italy. (P6)

A direct, on-site producer's presence offers the opportunity to provide information to assist distributors in selling the product and justifying its price superiority:

> I think it depends a lot on the relationship between the distributor, importer, producer. [...] From what I have been able to see, the results are achieved through support and presence in the country. (P17)

In some cases, awareness of the strategic importance of direct control of the foreign market leads SMEs to modify their US presence and to resolve possible channel conflicts upstream due to importers' inability to effectively enhance their products (evolution of the entry mode in the US market).

> You are in the hands of only one, and he does what he wants in all the USA. It can happen that importers do not care anything about your wine and does not sell it [for] you because he already has three others in his portfolio in the same territory. [. . .] I don't want to know more about it than a national importer, so today, a distributor is our sales subsidiary. (P5)

The centrality of the importer as a figure in the valorization of the COO and the brand requires a change in mentality. In some cases, this shift is not noticeable because the entrepreneur still seems to take a passive attitude toward the relationship, seeing it as a constraint imposed by law rather than as an opportunity (passive attitude toward channel relationships).

3.4.6 Key Factors in Value Appropriation and Destruction Through the Country of Origin

Content analysis of the experiences that emerged from the voices of the interviewees, although not generalizable, enabled outlining an interesting framework (Table 3.6) of the key factors that determine value appropriation and value destruction through the COO in the relationship between manufacturers and importers. To identify these factors, we first considered up to three main important codes of Family 2, 3, and 4 (see all the codes of each Family in Tables 3.3, 3.4, and 3.5), while we did not include family 1. Indeed, one of the aims of this phase of the study, as mentioned, was to identify the key factors that may favor the appropriation rather than the destruction of the value created by the COO (family 1) by the producers within the marketing channel relationship.

The importer's fundamental role in the value appropriation process emerges in this analysis. Channel intermediaries are considered to be able to grasp the distinctiveness of the offers proposed by Italian companies, especially when the product knowledge is associated with a high degree of commitment (level of commitment). The value of the COO heavily depends on the knowledge and skills of the importers, who are generally considered to be very well prepared and, therefore, able to interpret products, territories, and countries (high knowledge of product and market). In many cases, a synergistic relationship between knowledge about *product offering* of the company and importer's commitment is created. The desire to make the product central in the assortment leads the importer to acquire increasing skills that enable enhancing the product of a particular territory for its target audience. This increased knowledge, in turn, makes the importer more involved and thus more inclined to invest in the product made in Italy. This positive approach, however, tends to be lacking when the importer is sales oriented, which negatively affects not only the degree of commitment but also the quality of the relationship more generally.

Table 3.6 Key factors in value appropriation and destruction through the country of origin between wineries and importers

Families of codes included in the analysis	Value appropriation (main codes)	Value destruction (main codes)
Family 2: Context of importers	Importers' level of commitment Importer—High product knowledge Market coverage	Importer—Sales oriented
Family 3: Context of foreign consumers, market, and competition characteristics	Dimensions of the US market	Not-expert consumer Complexity of the Italian DO Price escalation
Family 4: Context of SMEs	Brand value Training/support for importers Investment in *terroir* value	Problem of SMEs' size Passive attitude toward channel relationships

Source: Compiled by authors

The ordinary consumer's rather superficial knowledge often tends to reduce the recognized value of the Italian product. Indeed, according to the respondents, the main obstacles to value appropriation by wineries are the complexity of the DO, not-expert consumer and price escalation. The first two aspects are linked to the knowledge and competence of the end customers who cannot clearly understand the benefits of high-quality products. The strong place- and time-specific value of Italian wine, which forms the foundation of the value creation process for the Italian winery analyzed, does not guarantee value appropriation by these SMEs. Communication—above all, communication through certifications of origin (e.g., DO), which serve as a tool to differentiate and protect the superior quality of products—become complex, especially for consumers who are potentially attracted by such goods but have not developed an adequate level of general competence about these products.

The third main obstacle is related to price escalation, which is a crucial issue given the attention to fair pricing that characterizes the US consumer. Indeed, as Nowak and Washburn (2002) stressed, the price of wine must be perceived as offering value. However, the intrinsic value of Italian wine is recognized by the intermediate client but rarely the final customer, so the value thus remains mere potential. In a modern market characterized by the growing massification of production by new countries such as Australia and the increasing power of large retailers, this situation risks missing the symbolic and distinctive value of the territory that constitutes the essence of the distinctiveness of Italian wine. However, recognizing the strategic role of the importers requires investing in the relationship with them to increase their commitment and knowledge of the territory and the product (high partner knowledge). The importers thus are considered to be an essential resource for the valorization of the COO and the transfer of knowledge even to the still inexperienced end consumer (nonexpert consumer). At the same time, a synergic relationship between the SME and its importer can only be based on the sharing of values linked to the territory in which the SME's incoming actions play a fundamental role in enhancing commitment and knowledge (high partner knowledge).

3.5   Challenge of Country of Origin Valorization from Importers' Point of View

The already very colorful, well-illustrated story of the wine-producing enterprises is enriched by the nuances of the voices, perspectives, and analyses of some importers. As mentioned in Chap. 1, seven in-depth interviews with international importers were also conducted to explore deeply the role of the intermediary in the value creation and appropriation processes in exports. Table 3.7 summarizes the main characteristics of the importers interviewed, with each respondent assigned a descriptive code from the letter A–G to ensure anonymity. The US importers interviewed give a multifaceted overview of how this particular definition of the COO, that is, made in Italy, affects the process of creating and appropriating value by importers and manufacturers.

3.5.1   Relevance of made in Italy Wine in the US Market

Regarding the importance and the role assumed by the COO in the US wine market in importers' perceptions, the common opinion among the importers is that made in Italy, as a particular definition of the COO, is a strategic factor because it can create added value for both commercial purposes and the company's image. A strong reputation for reliability, uniqueness, and product quality is the key factor in the strength of made in Italy, as cited by importer (D):

> The country of origin is very important to us, both for the value wines category and for the premium wines. Italy has a reputation that is unique in variety and price. From north to south, there are thousands of wineries producing wines of all types covering every price range. The American consumer has always been fascinated by the made in Italy, and even if he often feels scared by the complexity of our wine in general (the names of grapes or areas that do not have the right knowledge)—in the end, when they taste it, they recognize the value/quality ratio that, in my opinion, is the highest of all the other wines from the rest of the world. (D)

It is clear that Italy, along with other wine-producing countries such as France, Spain, Australia, and Chile has a large following. This factor affects the decisions of the final consumer, who feels comfortable choosing among these countries tradi-tionally linked to wine production. The strategic importance of the time- and place-specific concepts underlying Italian production is highlighted by Case C:

Table 3.7 Main characteristics of the international importers interviewed

Cases	Market coverage	Location	Main countries of origin of imported products
Case A	Medium-sized business Distributes and markets at the local level (Minnesota and the US Midwest)	Minnesota	Italy, France, Spain, and Argentina
Case B	Group Distributes and markets at the national level	Virginia	Around the world
Case C	Family business Distributes and markets at the local level	Washington state	Different countries, with special attention to Italian products
Case D	Medium-sized business National importer and distributor	California	Focus on traditional producer countries
Case E	Group National importer and distributor	New York	Special products and brands from new and old producer countries
Case F	Medium-sized business National importer and distributor	North Carolina	Special Italian wine
Case G	Medium-sized business National importer and distributor	Virginia	France, Spain, Australia, Italy, and New Zealand

Source: Compiled by authors

> As an importer and distributor, I work with wines that come from Italy for the great tradition it has in this sector. These wines are part of our corporate identity, but they are also important from a strategic point of view because they attract customers who are looking for a unique and interesting product. (C)

Betting on wines from Italy and enhancing the bond between the product and the territory allow the importer to differentiate and create value. The resulting benefits are not only economic; the company's overall image also improves. As highlighted by Case A, the intrinsic value of made in Italy is unquestionable, but it clearly emerges that appropriating this value demands adequate marketing actions and, above all, investment in the distribution partnership relationship:

> From the point of view of importers, it is essential to focus on the COO effect for differentiation in the U.S. market. But for this to be a real added value, it is necessary that there is financial support in marketing from the manufacturing company combined with common efforts in distribution. These are vital practices for the success of European brands in the United States (A).

Case B adds that Italian wine stands as an increasingly expanding business in the US market, whose durability confirms the importer's upstream assortment choices:

> Imported wines represent one third of total wine consumption in the USA. Italian wine, in turn, represents one third of imports, usually like French wines that are just as important. Italian wine, therefore, is important in the preferences of U.S. consumers, and consequently, those who import it know they can count on a segment of consumers who choose Italian wine. (B)

Case E clearly stresses the relevance of the COO in made in Italy:

I think it's huge. In the U.S., it is a significant added value, and I always see it. [...] Italian food is very popular in the United States, and many Italians want to make purchases through Italian restaurants. Wine shops are increasingly widespread and inclined to devote more space to the category of imported wines where Italy plays the lion's share. I think that the country Italy is a brand . . . . great marketing always . . . in the United States, ... for sure, for all food and wine. (E)

What emerges is a common line of thought among all the companies underlining the importance gained by the COO. In particular, Case C argues that selling and distributing Italian wine generates better profits by appropriating the value:

It is important for us because we have close ties with Italy. We started by importing exclusively Italian wine, and we have maintained this tradition. From a budget point of view, Italian wine is important because we can make better profit margins on the wine we import. Moreover, at a commercial level, it is important to have Italian wine as it is generally recognized as one of the, if not the most important, wine-producing countries in the world. And people want Italian wine! (C)

Case B also highlights the role played by the COO in its experience:

Personally, the country of origin is fundamental for me because I only import Italian wines. Moreover, especially with regard to trade customers (restaurants, wine bars), the country of origin is closely linked to perceptions of the value, style, quality, organoleptic characteristics, and varieties of grapes grown. [...] Italian wine, apart from prosecco, pinot grigio, and chianti generico, has a high-quality connotation linked to the perceptions that consumers have of Italian products in general due to the spread of Italian gastronomy and catering in the USA. (B)

Similarly, the respondent in Case F states:

The COO is fundamental for me. ... When you say Italy beyond wine, you evoke the beautiful country, culture, food. ... Surely, selling a product from Italy is an added value that has no price. (F)

The interviewee in Case A, which imports only premium wines from Italy and France, gives an interesting example about the strategic value of the COO:

I would, therefore, say that the COO is very important in the consumers' conception. For example, if a U.S. consumer has the opportunity to buy a $10 Pinot grigio from California and a $10 Pinot grigio from Friuli, the consumer will go and buy the Friulian pinot grigio. He will go and buy an Italian Pinot grigio because he has confidence in the product. Now, at the same time, if the consumer has the opportunity to buy a $10 pinot noir from California and a $10 Pinot noir from Italy, he will buy the one from California. That's because he trusts the latter more. (A)

The degree of consumer awareness emerges as a very important factor in marketing wine in the US market:

In the context of value wines, the COO effect is less important because consumers are buying a fresh point or varietal, but for premium wines, the consumer is looking for the sense of place, especially in my small business because we work with wine shops or families. Our consumers, our shops, and restaurants are looking for sense of place, so the COO for some particular categories of wine is very important. (G)

This company trading only premium wines tends to enhance the product–territory bond. Finally, with the term "sense of place," the importer highlights the peculiar characteristics of a particular geographical place the consumer wants to find in wine.

3.5.2   Importers' Perceptions of Their Role in the Process of Valuing Country of Origin

In a market such as the USA, the importer is especially important because it has to transmit the product value to the final consumer. The importer must be able not only to create value but also to appropriate that value through effective communication actions. Case B operates throughout the USA and shares very clear thoughts on the figure of the importer:

> In a market like the USA characterized by "long" distribution chains and with many intermediate players, the importer is, in his own territory and with his own customers, the interpreter and communicator of the strategies, values, style, characteristics, and needs of the companies he represents. Importers' contribution to the creation of value for the company lies in accurately communicating to its customers the characteristics of the company it represents, in creating a distribution network capable not only of selling the company's products but also of communicating the company's message. (B)

Case D is a direct importer of Italian wines, and its business is mainly concentrated in California. It distributes and markets wine differently than traditional importers and buys wine directly from producers:

> The importer is a very important central figure in the creation of value, especially importers at the national level (covering the whole of the American territory) who have a lot of power in creating the distribution and reputation of the product sold. This type of importer has contacts with various media or has people who work directly with the salesforces of various distributors and also directly with customers either on premise (restaurants and bars) or off premise (shops)—all these elements that create your reputation and value. (D)

In the value creation and appropriation processes, direct contact with the customer seems to be a key factor because it allows effectively communicating the qualities of the product sold. According to Case A, a fundamental element in importers' ability to differentiate in the market is becoming recognized through sales of quality products. Sales strategies based on price reductions communicate low originality and may not be enough to enable the importer to work profitably in the market:

> My company only imports Italian wines, so we work as importers and distributors, or we work with a company called Enotec. They have a reputation as an importer to the United States for their excellent quality. I, therefore, would say that the importer must become known for his quality and value. If an importer such as a wine shop or even smaller becomes known as a valuable resource in a region or country, it is very attractive for retailers or distributors from other states to work with those brands. I think that lowering the price and reducing the quality does not work. You have to work on specialization and originality. (A)

3.5.3   Importers' Perceptions of the Role of Wineries in the Process of Valuing the Country of Origin

Some interviewees reveal the concrete actions producing companies can take to establish good relationships with importers. Personal relationships based on trust have strategic importance, functioning as an essential vehicle for information transmission. Supporting this view, Case D proposes concrete actions to improve the synergies between importers and distributors:

> The manufacturer must be present with a production philosophy that is clearly in tune with its importer. Logically, quality both in the vineyards and in the cellar is very important, but having a physical presence in the American market [with a winery representative] that travels and works with the importer in various states can be very effective and certainly adds value to the brand. (D)

Case D also argues that in today's increasingly globalized and digital contexts, a clear, attractive web portal should inform visitors about the product origin and quality:

> Websites have become very important for the consumer, so even a good site is of strategic importance. (D)

Similarly, Case B argues that it is essential for the manufacturing company to know the characteristics of the market in which it wants to create a business:

> The manufacturing company is required first of all to understand the characteristics of the U.S. market and to have a clear vision of its needs, to know how to translate these into objectives actually achievable in the market. From a financial point of view, it is required that the company support the activities and investments that contribute to the development of its brand. (B)

Likewise, Case F emphasizes that the creation of value and, above all, the possibility of appropriating that value depends on the investment the producer intends to make in the market and the relationship with the distribution partner:

> Much depends on how much time the producers spend to come and talk about their own companies, about how the wines are produced; this is certainly fundamental. Every time you have a visiting producer, those wines are pushed a lot, and people have more interest, surely, in buying that kind of wine. This type of partnership is fundamental; i.e., the manufacturer comes personally to tell us about his products because no one else can do it better. I am an importer, so I have several wines. I certainly know them, but [it is] one thing is that I talk about them. [It is another] thing is that their "father" talks about them. (F)

In summary, as highlighted by Cases D, B, and F, what is most required of the manufacturer is to be present in the US market in proximity to the importer, thereby establishing a relationship based on increasing confidence. It is essential that the winery decides to invest time and resources in direct on-site supervision. This approach enables effectively communicating the distinctive values of the product. However, as expressed by the interviewee in Case G, it is difficult to appropriate the intrinsic value of Italian wine—which risks remaining only a mere

potential value—without support and promotion coordinated by international organizations such as the European Community:

> There are some who do not dedicate this time. Alas, bad for them. I have seen it in some
> products I have had from producers who have never come. They would have had much
> better results. It is also a shame because at the European level, there are funds [...] that
> Europe offers in subsidies to wine producers to cover travel or similar expenses. (G)

3.6 Opportunities and Threats for Valuing the Country of Origin in a Traditional Foreign Market

Analysis of the interviews reveals the main opportunities and threats for Italian wine
in the US market. Although the interviewees commonly think that made in Italy has
enormous potential, different opinions on the advantages and obstacles to the sale of
Italian wine come to light.

Case G argues that the root of the main threats is a lack of knowledge and
competence with the product among the final consumers, who may sometimes feel
almost lost amid the extreme variety of Italian wine:

> In my opinion, the opportunities and threats are the same. There is a lot of variety! On one
> hand, the great variety is exciting because there is always something new to discover. There
> is always a new and unique Italian wine to fall in love with, a new variety of grappa to
> discover. There is always a small DOC/DOCG that we have never heard [of] to try. As a
> wine lover, these are the most exciting and intriguing aspects of Italy. At the same time, this
> great variety is intimidating and overwhelming for many occasional wine drinkers. So many
> great Italian wines go unnoticed because there is too much variety for people to learn. The
> majority (85%) of the U.S. wine market wants simplicity: individual varieties, known
> varieties, and known producers. This is a pity because there is a lot of extraordinary wine
> that does not fall into the category. But for those who try to get out of that category, there is
> an almost infinite world of Italian wine to discover. (G)

The degree of knowledge in the final market greatly varies geographically and,
therefore, must be taken into account. In this regard, the respondent in Case F states
that:

> There are fifty states, and they are all completely different, even in tastes. Surely, in
> New York, I think there are wine connoisseurs who have more culture than maybe areas a
> bit more remote than the United States, as in the case of North Carolina. I've even met people
> who didn't know where chianti came from [...]. [It] even once happened to me, but maybe
> they just wanted to make fun. Otherwise, it would be just worr[isome]—to meet someone
> who thought it was French. (F)

US customers, therefore, still have little awareness of the great wealth Italy offers.
Customers thus lose all the peculiarities to differentiate Italian wines from those of
other countries.

Supporting this thesis, Case B indicates a lack of training among consumers; there
are no common synergies in marketing and communication activities. Despite this,

as reported in Case C, Italy can take advantage of the great variety and quality of wines it offers to diversify and create a competitive advantage:

> The main opportunity is represented by the native Italian vines, which represent a strong element of differentiation from other producing countries and an element of uniqueness and value creation. In addition, another opportunity is linked to the perceptions of quality brought by the many regions and designations of excellence present. The main threats are instead the perceptions of low-quality products such as prosecco and pinot grigio; the lack of a common direction in the formulation of marketing strategies for the Italian wine sector in general, with initiatives often useless and not oriented to the training and education of trade customers; and excessive fragmentation of promotional activities. (C)

The US wine market is the largest in the world and offers manifold possibilities for creating profitable businesses, but a major problem faced by manufacturing companies is strict rules governing alcohol consumption and sales. In fact, according to Case D, if Italian wine prices were to rise due to import taxes, this would increase demand for local wine:

> The opportunities are immense because the consumption of American wine per capita is still very low compared to Europe, so there is still plenty of room to grow. Unfortunately, there are so many threats, and in my opinion, the most important at the moment are political threats, where a tax on imports is enough to cause wine prices to rise and accelerate the growth of the local wine market. The other great threat is the growth of large distributors in the United States that continue to buy small wines, so they are creating a homogeneity that certainly does not favor small producers but only larger companies. This is very problematic for Italian wine precisely because it has an enormous diversity that could gradually have less space in the U.S. market. (D)

It should also be emphasized that Italy treats its variety and peculiarities of wine as fundamental characteristics that create value. An obstacle encountered in this process is large distributors' sole aim to generate turnover, not enhance the uniqueness of their wines.

Regarding opportunities for Italian wine, Case A aims to be very specific and focus mainly on the categories that, from its perspective, will constitute its main business in the future:

> I think sparkling wine represents a huge opportunity for the U.S. market, but also the red wines of southern Italy such as Campania, Basilicata, and Abruzzo, I think, have many opportunities. Not to forget the light red wines of northern Italy that are not found in California, with a retail sale of around $12–$20. To be feared by Italian wines, however, are the French red wines that are becoming very popular in our market. (A)

A clear summary of the challenges in the US market comes from the interviewee in Case E, who emphasizes the importance of investing time to accurately understand the market and its rules. Such knowledge is the key to the success of Italian wine in the US market:

> Unfortunately, they don't understand how the U.S. market works. It's a big challenge, but I don't know if the SMEs have really understood how the U.S. market really works, how important it is to have a quality product but with the right price that must be sold with great dedication. It is not enough for you to put it on the market. [...] You need to have someone in the market who represents your products and who works regularly with distributors. This is a huge country with great competition. (E)

3.7   Conclusion

This empirical analysis on the perspectives of both exporting wineries and importers has deepened knowledge of the COO's role in value creation and appropriation in partnership relationships. Particularly from the companies' perspectives, it has been possible to confirm the link with the territory typical of sectors such as wine represents a very important strategic resource. However, it has also been strongly stressed that, if not properly managed and valued in international distribution channels, the COO tends to deteriorate and lose meaning for the final consumers. The knowledge gap between the distribution partners, who are often very experienced, and the final consumers, who are not very competent, lends strategic importance and criticality to the role of the importers who oversee the foreign markets in both the off- and the on-trade sectors. In other words, as shown by other authors, the importance of the COO in the consumer purchasing process risks having a marginal or overestimated weight compared to reality (Insch et al., 2011; Usunier, 2006).

In a highly dynamic market context with the presence of new exporting countries offering increasingly competitive prices and willing to adapt their products (Bardají & Mili, 2009), the same companies interviewed consider the final consumer to be generally inattentive to the origin unless adequately guided in the choice of the wine product by the importer or the distributor. Confirming what various authors have pointed out (Bursi et al., 2012; De Nisco, Papadopoulos, & Elliot, 2017; Napolitano & Marino, 2016), the strategic link between the product and the territory in creating corporate value cannot be separated from the partnership relationship between SME and importer (Pegan et al., 2013, 2014). The latter is born and nourished due to SMEs' ability to know how to enhance the product–territory link within the distribution relationship, proactively investing through in-coming actions and continuous training. The COO is not able to impose itself on the market but provides a favorable starting point that must be consolidated with adequate *product offering* positioning.

It is also interesting to note that, even in this context, SMEs cannot ignore investments in branding. In other words, even in the presence of a strong, positive match between the country's image and the product categories—the best conditions to use the COO effect to establish the differentiated positioning of the product—several companies stress the need to invest in the brand to gain long-term competitive advantages. Even companies such as those operating in the wine sector where the product origin must be able to guide the product image, state that they must invest in the brand to grow. The necessary marketing activities, therefore, cannot be fully delegated to the foreign importer. The companies reporting the biggest increases in turnover claim to support their partners in marketing and sales but seek to exercise control over their work through control of the channel. These SMEs somehow compensate for their lack of financial resources with the relational skills they employ to reduce the physical and cultural distance with the foreign market.

Similarly, the experiences of the importers interviewed demonstrate that the product–territory bond constitutes a strategic driver of value creation that must be properly managed to be appropriated. In importers' decision-making processes, the specific COO, based on the strong product–territory link, is considered to be fundamental because it represents an element of distinction and quality that allows their businesses to feed and grow. Clearly, as channel partners, importers perceive as crucial their role in transmitting the characteristics of wine and the philosophy of the producing company to the final consumer, especially when the distribution chain is long and has many intermediate actors. Even if in a traditional foreign export market, the consumer's knowledge gap, which varies widely across geographical areas, again emerges as a possible obstacle to value creation and appropriation through the COO. The sophistication and extreme variety of the products communicated through the DO tend to confuse the final consumer who, feeling lost, may decide to buy simpler products. This threat can be countered only if the upstream company and the importer actively attempt to convey the product's potential value to the end market, investing in communication of the *terroir* (Golinelli, 2012) In other words, on one hand, wine importers believe that Italian wine has significant growth opportunities and consider it be a strategic resource for differentiating and acquiring new market segments. On the other hand, they also view as fundamental the producer's commitment to invest time in gaining knowledge of the peculiarities of the outlet market and supporting the distribution partnership relationship. It is not enough to know how to make a quality product; the manufacturer must also know how to make the market, and building that market requires knowledge from a direct, on-site presence.

Confusion, scant product knowledge, poor market perceptions of the real distinctiveness of authentic products, and thus low willingness to pay the price differential are among the main obstacles to further penetration by firms in traditional export markets. Strategic priorities for companies that want to compete successfully abroad include monitoring and understanding the needs of the multifaceted consumer, paying increased attention to value for money, being very selective in purchasing choices, and being willing to enhance local specialties rich in symbolic connotations that aid the construction and communication of the company's identity (Aiello, 2013; Bursi et al., 2012; de Luca & Pegan, 2013, 2014). This gap in end market competence toward products with high national typicality must be filled in order to exploit the positive (often affective) associations naturally evoked by this typicality in the mind of the foreign consumer. If these associations are not effectively solicited and strengthened by an international marketing strategy of the manufacturing company, the intrinsic value of the COO will remain a mere un-exploitable potential for the growth of the company abroad. Strong investments in partnerships with distributors, which are usually more sensitive and attentive to quality and authenticity of the product, and in communication activities to educate foreign consumers are the main means for companies to increase their presence in large foreign markets, including traditional ones. Importers agree with the firms that the lack of a coordinated system to communicate and promote the wine from a particular country poses a significant threat to international product penetration. The fragmentation of the sector undermines the exporting company's strength to impose its product offerings in dynamic, competitive foreign markets, even traditional exporting destinations.

Thus, there is a need to create a system to build synergies among importers, companies, and institutions that, through shared international marketing strategies and policies, can effectively convey the distinctive values of a given COO to the foreign market.

References

Aiello, G. (2013). *Davanti agli occhi del cliente. Branding e retailing del made in Italy nel mondo*. Roma: ARACNE Editrice.

Alon, I., Jaffe, E., Prange, C., & Vianelli, D. (2016). *Global marketing. Contemporary theory, practice, and cases*. New York, NY: McGraw-Hill.

Alpert, F., Wilson, B., & Elliot, M. T. (1993). Price signaling: Does it ever work? *Journal of Consumer Marketing, 10*(4), 4–14.

Andehn, M., & Berg, P. O. (2011). *Place-of-origin effects: A conceptual framework based on a literature review*. Stockholm, Sweden: Stockholm University School of Business.

Anderson, K., Norman, D., & Wittwer, G. (2001). *Globalization and the world's wine markets: Overview*. Discussion paper no 0143. Centre for International Economic Studies, Adelaide University, Australia.

Bahng, Y., & Kincade, D. (2014). Retail buyer segmentation based on the use of assortment decision factors. *Journal of Retailing and Consumer Services, 21*(4), 643–652.

Barber, N. D., Taylor, C., & Deale, C. S. (2010). Wine packaging: Marketing towards consumer lifestyle to build brand equity and increase revenue. *International Journal of Revenue Management, 4*(3/4), 215–237.

Bardají, I., & Mili, S. (2009, August 16–22). *Prospective trends in wine export markets—Expert views from Spain*. Presentation at the International Association of Agricultural Economists Conference, Beijing, China.

Bertoli, G., & Resciniti, R. (Eds.). (2012). *International marketing and the country of origin effect*. Cheltenham, UK: Edward Elgar.

Bruwer, J., & Johnson, R. (2010). Place-based marketing and regional branding strategy perspectives in the California wine industry. *Journal of Consumer Marketing, 27*(1), 5–16.

Bursi, T., Grappi, S., & Martinelli, E. (2012). *Effetto country of origin in'analisi comparata a livello internazionale sul comportamento d'acquisto della clientela*. Bologna, Italy: Il Mulino.

Callon, M., Meadel, C., & Rabehariosoa, V. (2002). The economy of qualities. *Economy and Society, 31*(2), 194–217.

Campbell, G., & Guibert, N. (2006). Old World strategies against New World competition in a globalising wine industry. *British Food Journal, 108*(4), 233–242.

D'Amico, A. (2002). *Le strategie di marketing per la valorizzazione dei prodotti tipici*. Turin, Italy: Giappichelli Editore.

Da Silva, R., Davies, G., & Naudé, P. (2001). Assessing the influence of retail buyer variables on the buying decision-making process. *European Journal of Marketing, 36*(11/12), 1327–1343. https://doi.org/10.2307/3150657.

de Luca, P., & Pegan, G. (2013). La percezione dei prodotti agro-alimentari made in Italy nel mercato USA: Orimi risultati di una ricerca netnografica. In G. Aiello (Ed.), *Davanti agli occhi del cliente. Branding e retailing del Made in Italy nel mondo* (pp. 215–234). Rome, Italy: Aracne.

de Luca, P., & Pegan, G. (2014). The coffee shop and customer experience: A study of the U.S. market. In F. Musso & E. Druica (Eds.), *Handbook of research on retailer-consumer relationship development* (pp. 173–196). Hershey, PA: IGI Global.

De Nisco, A., Papadopoulos, N., & Elliot, S. (2017). From international travelling consumer to place ambassador: Connecting place image to tourism satisfaction and post-visit intentions. *International Marketing Review, 34*(3), 425–443.

Fong, C.-M., Chun-Ling, L., & Yunzhou, D. (2014). Consumer animosity, country of origin, and foreign entry-mode choice: A cross-country investigation. *Journal of International Marketing, 22*(1), 62–76.

Golinelli, G. (Ed.). (2012). *Patrimonio culturale e creazione di valore. Verso nuovi percorsi.* Padua, Italy: Cedam.

Hakansson, H., & Wootz, B. (1975). Supplier selection in an international environment: An experimental study. *Journal of Marketing Research, 12*(1), 46.

Hamzaoui, L. M., & Merunka, D. (2006). The impact of country of design and country of manufacture on consumer perceptions of bi-national products' quality: An empirical model based on the concept of fit. *Journal of Consumer Marketing, 23*(3), 145–155.

Hamzaoui-Essoussi, L., Merunka, D., & Bartikowski, B. (2011). Brand origin and country of manufacture influences on brand equity and the moderating role of brand typicality. *Journal of Business Research, 64*(9), 973–978.

Hansen, T., & Skytte, H. (1998). Retail buying behaviour: A review. *The International Review of Retail, Distribution and Consumer Research, 8*(3), 277–301.

Insch, G. S. (2003). The impact of country-of-origin effects on industrial buyers' perceptions of product quality. *Management International Review, 43*(3), 1–11.

Insch, A., Prentice, R. S., & Knight, J. G. (2011). Retail buyers' decision-making and buy national campaigns. *Australasian Marketing Journal, 19*, 257–266.

Johnston, W. J., Khalil, S., Jain, M., & Cheng, J. M.-S. (2012). Determinants of joint action in international channels of distribution: The moderating role of psychic distance. *Journal of International Marketing, 20*(3), 34–49.

Kline, B., & Wagner, J. (1994). Information sources and retail buyer decision-making: The effect of product-specific buying experience. *Journal of Retailing, 70*(1), 75–88.

Knight, J. G., Holdsworth, D. K., & Mather, D. W. (2007). Country-of-origin and choice of food imports: An in-depth study of European distribution channel gatekeepers. *Journal of International Business Studies, 38*(1), 107–125.

Koschate-Fischer, N., Diamantopoulos, A., & Oldenkotte, K. (2012). Are consumers really willing to pay more for a favorable country image? A study of country-of-origin effects on willingness to pay. *Journal of International Marketing, 20*(1), 19–41.

Levy, M., & Weitz, B. (2007). *Retailing management* (6th ed.). New York, NY: McGraw Hill.

Marino, V., Gallucci, C., & Mainolfi, G. (2009). L'interpretazione multidimensionale della country reputation. Implicazioni strategiche per le imprese del Made in Italy. In C. Pepe & A. Zucchella (Eds.), *L'internazionalizzazione delle imprese Italiane* (pp. 93–126). Bologna, Italy: Il Mulino.

Marino, V., & Mainolfi, G. (2013). *Country brand management*. Milan, Italy: Egea.

Mattarazzo, M. (2012). Country of origin effect: Research evolution, basic constructs and firm implications. In G. Bertoli & R. Resciniti (Eds.), *International marketing and the country of origin effect* (pp. 23–42). Northampton, MA: Edward Elgar.

Mattiacci, A., & Maralli, R. (2007). Il wine marketing nell'esperienza di una media impresa leader: Banfi di montalcino. *Mercati & Competitività, 2*(2), 29–46.

Mizik, N., & Jacobson, R. (2003). Trading off between value creation and value appropriation: The financial implications of shifts in strategic emphasis. *Journal of Marketing, 67*(1), 63–76.

Napolitano, M. R., & Marino, V. (2016). *Cultural heritage e Made in Italy. Casi ed esperienze di marketing internazionale*. Naples, Italy: Editoriale Scientifica.

Newall, J. (1977). Industrial buyer behaviour a model of the implications of risk handling behaviour for communication policies in industrial marketing. *European Journal of Marketing, 11*(3), 166–211. https://doi.org/10.1108/EUM0000000005008.

Nowak, L., & Washburn, J. (2002). Building brand equity: Consumer reactions to proactive environmental policies by the winery. *International Journal of Wine Marketing, 14*(3), 5–19.

Papadopoulos, N., & Heslop, L. A. (2003). Country equity and product country images: State of art in research and implications. In S. C. Jain (Ed.), *Handbook of research in international marketing* (pp. 402–433). Northampton, MA: Edward Elgar.

Pastore, A., Ricotta, F., & Giraldi, A. (2011). Innovare l'offerta attraverso le caratteristiche estrinseche del prodotto. Il ruolo creativo del country of origin. In L. Pilotti (Ed.), *Creatività innovazione e territorio. Ecosistemi del valore per la competizione globale* (pp. 629–650). Bologna, Italy: Il Mulino.

Pegan, G., & Vianelli, D. (2013). Il ruolo degli importatori nella valorizzazione del country of origin: Un'indagine qualitativa sul vino Italiano nel mercato statunitense. In *Proceedings of X Convegno Annuale della SIM—Società Italiana di Marketing*, Rome, Italy: SIM.

Pegan, G., & Vianelli, D. (2016). L'identità territoriale come risorsa per creare valore nei mercati esteri. Una ricerca qualitativa sul ruolo della distribuzione nel comparto del prosecco in USA. In M. R. Napolitano & V. Marino (Eds.), *Cultural heritage e made in Italy. Casi ed esperienze di marketing internazionale* (pp. 297–325). Napoli, Italy: Editoriale Scientifica.

Pegan, G., Vianelli, D., & de Luca, P. (2013). Il ruolo della distribuzione nella valorizzazione dei marchi made in Italy ad alto valore simbolico in USA: Casi, esperienze e criticità. In G. Aiello (Ed.), *Davanti agli occhi del cliente. Branding e retailing del Made in Italy nel mondo* (pp. 174–197). Rome, Italy: Aracne.

Pegan, G., Vianelli, D., & de Luca, P. (2014). Competere e creare valore nei mercati maturi: Alcune evidenze empiriche del made in Italy negli Stati Uniti. *Economia e Società Regionale, XXXII*(2), 55–67.

Pegan, G., Vianelli, D., & Reardon, J. (2017). Wine importers and their country of origin proclivities. In *Conference proceedings XXIX Sinergie-SIMA: Value co-creation in foreign markets: Le sfide di management per le imprese e per la società* (pp. 1–5). Rome, Italy: Sinergie-SIMA.

Rea, A., & D'Antone, S. (2010). La sistemicità presupposto del valore della marca territoriale. Un'analisi sul mondo del vino Made in Italy. *Sinergie, 83*(10), 179–200.

Reardon, J., Vianelli, D., & Miller, C. (2017). The effect of COO on retail buyers' propensity to trial new product. *International Marketing Review, 34*(2), 311–329. https://doi.org/10.1108/IMR-03-2015-0080.

Roth, K. P., & Diamantopoulos, A. (2009). Advancing the country image construct. *Journal of Business Research, 62,* 726–740.

Roth, M. S., & Romeo, J. B. (1992). Matching product category and country image perception: A framework for managing country-of-origin effects. *Journal of International Business Studies, 23*(3), 477–497.

Samiee, S. (2010). Advancing the country image construct—A commentary essay. *Journal of Business Research, 63,* 442–445.

Samiee, S. (2011). Resolving the impasse regarding research on the origins of products and brands. *International Marketing Review, 28*(5), 473–485.

Sheth, J. N. (1973). A model of industrial buyer behavior. *Journal of Marketing, 37*(October), 50–56.

Sims, R. (2009). Food, place and authenticity: Local food and the sustainable tourism experience. *Journal of Sustainable Tourism, 17*(3), 321–336.

Sternquist, B. (1994). Gatekeepers of consumer choice, a four-country comparison of retail buyers. *International Review of Retail, Distribution and Consumer Research, 4*(2), 159–176.

Thaler, R. H., & Sustein, C. S. (2009). *Nudge: Improving decisions about health, wealth, and happiness.* London: Penguin Book.

Usunier, J. C. (2006). Relevance in business research: The case of country-of-origin research in marketing. *European Management Review, 3,* 60–73.

Usunier, J. C. (2011). The shift from manufacturing to brand origin: Suggestions for improving COO relevance. *International Marketing Review, 28*(5), 486–496.

Vianelli, D., de Luca, P., & Bortoluzzi, G. (2012). Distribution channel governance and value of made in Italy products in the Chinese market. In G. Bertoli & R. Resciniti (Eds.), *International marketing and the country of origin effect* (pp. 133–150). Cheltenham, UK: Edward Elgar.

Vianelli, D., de Luca, P., & Pegan, G. (2012). *Modalità d'entrata e scelte distributive del made in Italy in Cina*. Milan, Italy: Franco Angeli.

Vianelli, D., & Pegan, G. (2014). Made in Italy brands in the U.S. and China: Does country of origin matter? *Journal of Euromarketing, 23*(1 & 2, January–June), 57–73.

Zarantonello, L., & Luomala, H. T. (2011). Dear Mr Chocolate: Constructing a typology of contextualized chocolate consumption experiences through qualitative diary research. *Qualitative Market Research: An International Journal, 14*(1), 55–82.

Chapter 4
Country of Origin and International Contractual Marketing Channels: Evidence from Specific Product–Market Perspectives

Abstract This chapter focuses on the relationship between the COO and the international contractual distribution channel. As highlighted in Chap. 2, the main types of internationalization include intermediate modalities. To exercise greater control over the market than in export modes and to be able to strengthen the COO and the entire distribution channel, many companies opt for intermediate entry. In the intermediate entry mode, the distribution channel is configured as an integrated vertical marketing system. The companies and the partners that adhere to the agreement share ownership, risk, control, and margins through various technical forms with different implications for the valorization and management of the COO. Focusing on certain sectors (coffee and wine) and countries (China and India), this chapter presents the results of research based on secondary and primary data. These results confirm that the link between the COO and contractual agreements can be twofold. On one hand, contractual agreements are an important tool for the valorization of the COO in the foreign market, and on the other hand, the strong image of the COO can favor the possibility of concluding agreements in the target markets.

4.1 Introduction

In culturally distant, complex markets with high barriers to entry (institutional, governmental, and competitive), long-term collaboration with a local partner can be an appropriate choice to operate directly in the market without having to face the risks of direct investment (Alon, Jaffe, Prange, & Vianelli, 2016; Bursi & Galli, 2012; Vianelli, de Luca, & Pegan, 2012). The risk, in fact, is shared between the partners who adhere to the agreement and benefit from each other's strengths while compensating for each other's weaknesses.

These agreements may be equity and non-equity agreements. Equity agreements involve the establishment of an organizational unit in which the partners share the share capital, as in the case of joint ventures. Non-equity or contractual agreements do not involve investment in risk capital. In this case, there may be different alternatives depending on the purposes for which those agreements are constituted. They are a combination of different levels of externalization and internalization and

© Springer Nature Switzerland AG 2020
G. Pegan et al., *International Marketing Strategy*, International Series in Advanced Management Studies, https://doi.org/10.1007/978-3-030-33588-5_4

low and high investment in risk control. While there are many different agreement types, as pointed out in Chap. 2, this chapter focuses on the contractual agreements most closely linked to marketing and sales: licensing, franchising, and strategic alliances.

The relevance of these types of agreements has emerged, for example, in a study on the entry of Italian companies into different foreign markets (Aiello, 2013). For example, in a study on the Chinese market (Vianelli et al., 2012), 23.4% of the companies interviewed in the sample opted for collaboration agreements, and of these, 52% chose joint ventures, 25% franchising, and 23% licensing. In China, joint ventures are mainly present among companies that carry out both production and sales activities and intend to exercise greater control than guaranteed by other forms of contracts. Franchising typically has a distributive application but is the subject only of relatively recent Chinese legislation, which obviously has limited its spread (Zeidman & Xu, 2012). The application of franchising can be difficult in some sectors such as food where the consequences of the incorrect application of basic hygiene rules can be very high. At the time of the study, it was no coincidence, for example, that in China, only a limited number of McDonald's points of sale, a typical case of an international franchisor, were operated as franchises (Kwok, 2010). In fact, many companies have combined direct investment in the development of their own stores with a franchising network to more effectively increase distribution capability (Keegan & Green, 2008).

4.2   Relationships Between the Country of Origin and Contractual Agreements

Collaboration agreements in general and franchising in particular can be closely interrelated with the COO (Fig. 4.1). On one hand, the COO finds international agreements to be a strong vehicle of valorization in the foreign country. On the other hand, the same agreements can be easier to implement in the face of a strong COO effect.

At the basis of this interrelation are some elements that strengthen a brand in international markets and can assume different characteristics and levels of relevance

Fig. 4.1 Relationships between the country of origin and contractual international agreements. Source: Authors' own figure

in various reference markets. These elements include: (a) the values that define the brand; (b) the history and reputational path of the brand; and (c) the cultural references to which the brand is connected (Vescovi, 2011). Some companies, particularly Italian and other European companies, can enjoy significant advantages in building their own brand images based on specific aspects of their production traditions. To obtain these benefits, it is necessary that these companies offer a clear narrative path—precise cultural references that are linked to the origin of the brand and are easily understandable and consistent with what can be perceived by consumers—to identify the value of the alternatives of choice. The COO can influence customer assessment because people can link stereotyped perceptions of the COO to the product. For example, in China, brands from Western countries can represent status, cosmopolitanism, and modernity (Zhou & Belk, 2004).

Sometimes, however, the specific COO is not clearly distinct or perceived. In China, for example, a certain Western homogenizing factor makes it difficult for the Chinese consumer to perceive the differences between specific European countries. From a study carried out in China (Vescovi, 2011), it seems that the effect of made in Italy is not always clear. In some cases, it even seems to bring about different results than expected, surprisingly highlighting negative effects. The situation of the COO in this specific research on made in Italy, therefore, is still unclear (Vescovi, 2011). Made in Italy, which since 1990 has been used as a certification and guarantee mark for products, has more distant origins dating to the 1960s. Over time, its enhancement has been pursued with the "100% made in Italy" trademark issued by the Istituto Tutela Produttori Italiani (ITPI), that is, the Institute for the Protection of Italian Producers (ITPI, 2019) and the platform Google Arts & Culture on Made in Italy, developed by the Google Cultural Institute with the Ministry of Agricultural Policies and Unioncamere (Google Arts & Culture, 2019) to improve the knowledge and visibility of Italian manufacturing excellence.

The lack of knowledge on products' and brands' history and manufacturing tradition reduces the value of the COO. The entry modes through contractual forms can also contribute to cultural mediation between the COO and the country of destination. In this perspective, those entry modes, therefore, contribute to enhancing the value of the COO. The stronger the perceptions of the COO, the easier it is to conclude contractual agreements in the same markets. This relationship highlights the possibility for the COO to valorize the company in the end market and the opportunity to appropriate this value within marketing channels. In the following sections, we describe cases in specific industries and markets to highlight the mutual relationships between some types of contractual agreements and the COO in an international context.

4.3   The Meaning of the Country of Origin in the Coffee Global Supply Chain

Coffee is one of the most marketed products and the most consumed drinks in the world (Morris, 2018). The coffee global supply chain includes a very long, complex set of interrelated steps, which can be represented by a chain of activities and phases that follow one another, integrating each other (Ton & Jansen, 2007). This chain is articulated in a sequence of production, transformation, and distribution activities necessary to obtain from the raw material of green coffee the finished product of roasted coffee, sometimes subjected to other processes such as decaffeination (Fig. 4.2).

The coffee supply chain usually involves a high level of internationalization due to the role of foreign trade in the main phases (Fig. 4.3). Direct relationships are often

Fig. 4.2 Coffee supply chain. Source: Authors' own figure

1. Agricultural coffee production	Main green coffee production countries
Growing, harvesting, processing, and classification of green coffee beans	Latin America, Africa, and Asia

2. Industrial coffee production	Main roasted coffee production countries
Selection and importing of green coffee, processing, and roasting	European Union (E.U.) (77% of world exports of roasted coffee)
	U.S., Canada, and few more countries (21.5%)
	Production countries (1.5%)

3. Coffee distribution and consumption	Main consumption countries (per capita)
Logistics and distribution, consumption, and post-use waste disposal	Northern Europe (Netherlands, Finland, Sweden, and Denmark); Central Eastern Europe (Germany, Slovakia, Serbia, and the Czech Republic); and North America (Canada and the U.S.)

Fig. 4.3 Global coffee supply chain and the main involved countries. Source: Translated and adapted from de Luca and Pegan (2015)

established between producers and roasters, but further players such as logistics operators and brokers can also be included. The supply chain operators manage the flow of materials connected to the product through various channels: farmers take care of the crops, which they sell to traders and processors, who, in turn, add value to the product, which is then sold downstream to the final consumers. In this long chain, the identity of the producing countries is still largely unknown to the end customer. In other words, producing countries, often characterized by very small companies, are not easily able to value the COO in the international markets and even less to appropriate that value.

In contrast, the COO plays a special role for those countries globally recognized for their unique coffee culture. The specific role of the COO, therefore, primarily emerges in the second and third phases of the coffee supply chain, along with a strong relationship between coffee consumption culture and distinctive technological skills in roasting. In the past century, important roasting companies have been growing in these phases through exports and direct investment or contractual agreements, with a view to downstream business integration. In this perspective, for example, we can consider the case of Italian roasting companies that are well known all over the world. Nevertheless, in recent years, some companies in coffee-producing countries have begun to invest in international markets with strong, meaningful COOs. Coffee, more than any other beverage, has been able to be integrated into different cultures, so much so that both roasting countries and producing countries have developed different ways of consumption and preparation based on local customs and traditions (Morris, 2018; Samoggia & Riedel, 2018). In this context, international agreements such as franchising, licensing, and strategic alliances play relevant roles in the valorization of the COO. In the following sections, some cases of coffee roasting companies based on secondary data are presented.

4.3.1   Role of the Country of Origin for Coffee Roasters: An Italian Case

Among roasting countries, Italy is an emblematic example of the particular relevance of coffee culture in the international consumption landscape. Made in Italy has a high symbolic value as a COO due to its ability to evoke the famous, appreciated Italian *dolce vita*. Coffee is a significant example of this lifestyle. Indeed, in Italy, coffee plays a relevant role in consumption culture and the agri-food industry. Italy, with its typical *caffè espresso* but also the bar as its traditional place of coffee consumption, is considered to be an "archetype of a coffee consuming nation" (Kjeldegard & Ostberg, 2007, p. 181). Italy has a large coffee-roasting industry and, in addition to its own domestic market, is an important supplier of both green and roasted coffee beans to other European countries and the US Lavazza dominates Italy's off-trade market. Other important Italian companies are Segafredo Zanetti, Kimbo, Illycaffè, Caffè Vergnano, and Pellini (CBI-Centre for the Promotion of Imports from developing countries, 2019). Most of these brands are well known around the world, especially in developed countries. This awareness also extends to on-trade channels primarily due to collaboration agreements in the destination markets.

Italian companies, even though they benefit from a very strong, positive COO effect, nevertheless are increasingly competing with global companies that might threaten even traditional leadership positions built in particular market niches. To understand this phenomenon, think, for example, of the strong competitive pressure exerted by the Nespresso brand of Nestlé in the espresso segment historically dominated by Italian brands such as Illy and Lavazza. From the perspective of coffee places, it is interesting to consider the entry of Starbucks in Milan, Italy, in 2018. As Howard D. Schultz—Chairman Emeritus of Starbucks—said, "we are not coming here to teach Italians how to make coffee. We're coming here with humility and respect to show what we've learned" (Purdy, 2018).

A global emblem of made in Italy, coffee, therefore, is a sector in which the dynamism and globalization of markets make internationalization, together with innovation, a fundamental strategic path for growing and consolidating one's presence abroad. Italian coffee faces many challenges to grow and consolidate in foreign markets. Exploratory research carried out using the netnographic method (de Luca & Pegan, 2012, 2014) has made it possible to gather the impressions of US consumers who have shared their interest in coffee online. From these studies (de Luca & Pegan, 2012, 2014) emerges a consumer who is generally fascinated by the Italian culture of coffee and often wants to come to Italy to try the real Italian espresso in its place of origin. The image of Italian coffee is predominantly positive and brands are often described as refined and prestigious. However, there is also much confusion about the product. The main problems are due to the questions of coffee storage and logistics. Many wonder if it is right to pay so much for coffee that is certainly good in Italy but, due to problems of storage and transport, may have already lost its freshness when it reaches the US consumer (de Luca & Pegan, 2012). For the Italian coffee shop chains, often developed in foreign markets through international contractual agreements such as franchising, we can highlight various opportunities such as new lifestyles and new preferences for quality espresso coffee but also threats such as attention to value for money. There are strengths connected to the Italian lifestyle and, therefore, the COO, and weaknesses, in this specific case derived from the limited presence in the USA and difficulties communicating with the reference targets. The chains also developed at an international level, especially through franchising, can contribute to the development of a virtuous circle, enhancing the COO abroad and, at the same time, being enhanced by the COO. In online discussions, however, anti-corporate attitudes have also emerged and fed the so-called Third Wave of Coffee. This movement born in the early 2000s among coffee lovers is led by a few small US producers searching for quality far from the large groups established in the mass market. Their offerings are essentially reminiscent of the traditional culture characterizing Italian coffee bars based on a mix of elements spontaneously originating in and from the territory. This customer experience is made up of familiar places, quality coffee, pleasant social relationships, and a welcoming atmosphere. How much can the Italian chains developed through contractual agreements be able to maintain and enhance abroad the experience of an authentic Italian coffee shop and, therefore, their COO? Here some meaningful examples are proposed, and developed using secondary data.

Illycaffè is a significant case in the global landscape of Italian coffee. This joint-stock company of the Illy Group S.P.A. in Trieste, Italy, has operated since 1933, producing and marketing high-quality coffee for on- and off-trade channels. Illycaffè offers a wide range of coffee products, including roasted, ground, beans, and coffee in special pods and capsules, along with coffee preparation machines, accessories, and designer cups. Currently, the company, still a family business, has more than 1200 employees, all over the world. Of its growing turnover, exceeding 400 million euros in 2018 (Illycaffè, 2019), about 35% comes from Italy and more than 65% from other countries (Seguso, 2019). Although Italy remains the main market, Illycaffè's international orientation has characterized the company from the outset. During the 1950s, with its first commercial branches, Illycaffè entered Germany and, in the following years, France, Holland, the USA, and other markets, reaching more than 140 countries on all continents (Illycaffè, 2019).

Initially directed at serving the horeca segments, offering on-trade consumption, the company then turned to the final consumer, first through the retail channel and more recently through the creation of a mainly contractual vertical system with the bar chain Espressamente Illy. The project started in 2003, and since then, more than 250 cafes have been opened in more than 30 countries on five continents. The locations of the Espressamente Illy chain, which has won several international awards, include Rome, London, Paris, Shanghai, Seoul, Tokyo, and Las Vegas. In the Far East, the chain is also present in Australia, China, Korea, Hong Kong, Japan, Malaysia, New Zealand, Taiwan, and Vietnam (Beverfood, 2008). In 2008, Illy enjoyed growth in turnover and profitability, with a consolidated turnover of 483 million euros (+3.5% compared to 2017) and net profit of 18.1 million euros (+39.1% compared to 2017). These results are mainly due to its performance in e-commerce (+78.9%) and foreign markets. In particular, incisive action was taken in the markets, the horeca core business, and portioned systems. The global development of the physical mono-brand retail channel also continued. In 2018, between franchising and ownership, the company had 259 points of sale in 43 countries: 179 Illy Cafès (17 directly managed and 162 franchised) and 80 Illy Shops, six directly managed and 74 franchised (Albricci, 2019). China is the market country with the highest growth (+12%), followed by the USA (+8%).

Geographical distance has led to the adoption of sophisticated, innovative techniques of product conservation and packaging. However, it is above all the cultural distance that presents an interesting challenge for future development, as, for example, in the case of the Chinese market where Illy—already in Asia since the first half of the 1990s—is developing successfully.

As Illy pointed out (Il Piccolo, 2005), the Gio Caffè in Shanghai, designed by Italian architect Luca Trazzi, was born from Illy's partnership with Chinese entrepreneur Wilson Zeng, a young lover of Italian-style coffee who decided to invest in the bar sector after managing a chain of Body Shops. Through the franchise chain Espressamente Illy in which the environment is enhanced by design and other multisensory stimuli, the company intends to interpret the culture of Italian coffee focused on the premium segment and transfer it to the Chinese consumer who is still not used to daily use of this drink. Moreover, coffee is a product consumed after a transformation process, as pointed out, so the company also considered it important to open China the University of Coffee in China. Indeed, in 2006, to grow in China where coffee is considered to be an elite drink, Illycaffè opened in Shanghai an international office of the University of Coffee, a training institute born and developed in Trieste, that aims to spread Italian coffee culture in the world. The opening of the Chinese headquarters under the name of China Coffee University, represented a completely new model of internationalization: instead of shifting production, the knowledge needed to appreciate the Italian product and, therefore, its COO was transferred.

This initiative is intended to transfer corporate knowledge to bar managers who have the difficult task of bringing to the final consumer a product designed according to the rules codified by the company. In a market such as China, it is important to have knowledge and training on the product not only in the final market but also in the intermediate one (Vianelli et al., 2012).

In addition, success in China was pursued with an alliance established in 2017 with Caffè de Coral Group, the largest fast food group in Hong Kong, with turnover of 457 million euros in the first half of 2018 (Albricci, 2019). The strategic partnership initially envisaged the development of Espressamente Illy in Hong Kong and Macao and then the expansion activities in the Chinese market. The basis of this collaboration is the management competence and market knowledge of the partners', on one hand, and the international success of the Espressamente Illy business model based on the excellence and culture of Italian coffee (Albricci, 2019).

The Illycafè Group has continued to open Espressamente Illy in India through collaboration with the Narang Group, which operates in the catering and distribution sector for premium brands in India. Illycaffè chose the Narang Group as the master franchisee to develop the opening of its new premises in the Indian subcontinent. The company is already a distributor of Illycafè products. The Narang family has been a pioneer in the airline catering sector and, for more than 30 years, in the horeca sector, working with high-end hotels, restaurants, and fast food outlets. The Narang Group is specialized in the distribution of premium consumer goods, including the well-known international brands Red Bull Energy Drink, Evian and Perrier mineral water, Russian Standard vodka, and Illycaffè. For Illycaffè, India is a key market because it has high potential for gourmet coffee, and the Illy blend is partially made with coffee beans grown in India (Beverfood, 2008).

The strong market orientation and business innovation of Illy (Halilem, Amara, & Landry, 2014; Küster & Vila, 2011) have led to a gradual transformation in the way of dealing with business-to-business customers, creating relationships mainly based on consulting and customer solution services (de Luca & Pegan, 2015). The internationalization process of Illy has been developed mainly through direct investments and collaboration agreements, particularly partnerships and franchising, always with the aim to spread and develop the culture and market of Italian espresso in the world. The collaboration agreements allow the cross-fertilization of different cultures, that is an important vehicle for the pursuit of the objective of transferring the culture of Italian espresso and the COO knowledge.

4.3.2   A Challenge for a Coffee-Producing Country: The Case of Ethiopian Coffee

Another case of COO in coffee that may be emblematic is Ethiopia as a producing country. Well known as the birthplace of coffee, Ethiopia is one of the largest coffee bean producers in the world. With production of more than 420,000 tons of coffee and exports of about four million bags in 2018–2019, Ethiopia is the largest producer of African coffee. In the country, people usually brew and drink coffee in elaborate ceremonies, often using crafting methods passed from generation to generation over the centuries (Dahir, 2018a). Nevertheless, Ethiopia, like other producing countries, has few locally produced brands. However, with the development of Ethiopian catering in the world and internal growth that has brought the country into the global economy, Ethiopian coffee has opportunities to take advantage of global consumer trends. Exporting the culture may require some adaptation to foreign markets (Chutel, 2019) that could be facilitated by contractual agreements. This entry mode could be a way for value creation and appropriation for this industry and/country.

In this context, entrepreneur Bethlehem Tilahun Alemu's idea to give to everyone the experience of hand-roasted Ethiopian coffee was born in 2016 with Garden of Coffee, a brand that uses artisanal methods to source, process, roast, and package Ethiopia's original beans (Chutel, 2019). The coffee shop could be the same anywhere in the world, but the women spreading beans over an open roaster in the slow, circular movements of Ethiopian coffee ceremony make it distinctively local. Using the words of Alemu, "Ethiopia coffee is big, but as an Ethiopian, I saw lot of green coffee beans sold to international brands" (Chutel, 2019). The Garden of Coffee also sells its own brand of single-source coffee produced in a small roastery with beans grown by a cooperative of female farmers. Alemu wants to spread her idea throughout the world by opening Garden of Coffee shops everywhere it is possible. Some might see in this initiative a risk for authenticity, but Alemu thinks that commercialization of this culture will not diminish its relevance. Furthermore, she believes that this commercialization will give Ethiopians opportunities in a global industry to which they already contribute (Chutel, 2019).

Garden of Coffee plans to open in Canada and China. Today, in Addis Abeba, 20 workers oversee the activity, roasting five types of coffee beans only for individual orders and shipping them to more than 20 countries, including Germany, Sweden, Russia, and the USA. In the opinion of Alemu, this personalized roasting creates a business model that values local manufacturing, contributes to preserving the quality of the coffee for the final consumer, and reduces the ecological footprint from factory roasting. In short time since the Garden of Coffee was launched in

China, it has developed a coffee culture in a tea culture market. The big plan is to open more than 100 café roasteries across China by 2022 using contractual agreements. In Alemu's words, "We are doing this not only because hand-roasting coffee is an ancient art that we strongly feel is worth preserving and promoting, but because we believe this method of coffee roasting is the key to unlocking Ethiopian coffee's true magical tastes" (Chutel, 2019). Through deploying traditional Ethiopian roasting methods at a global level, this initiative contributes developing the "fourth wave" of coffee evolution (de Luca, Pegan, & Vianelli, 2019), focusing on long-term sustainability.

Another brand, Tomoca, is famous in Addis Ababa as first experiment in commercializing the coffee culture. In 1953, Zewdu Meshesha bought a roaster from an Italian family and decided to retain the acronym Torrefazione Moderna Café (Tomoca). Tomoca has six outlets around Addis Ababa, and the design of each store reflects the changing city, including an office bar and a gallery space. It has not tried to copy the historic rituals but intends to present a distinctive flavor to the world offered in a globally recognizable style. Tomoca is opening three outlets in Japan and is looking at Sweden, other European countries, and the USA, where customers already buy bags of its roasted coffee. In Africa, Java House, East Africa's largest chain of coffee and dining shops, is entering China with coffee and tea (Dahir, 2018b), bringing the COO together with traditional products.

In these and similar cases, contractual agreements can be relevant tools for new COO value creation and opportunities of value appropriation.

4.4   The Prospective Relevance of Contractual Agreements to Creating Value in an Emerging Country: The Case of Italian Wine in India

Demographically significant countries in the process of economic growth are of great interest in the study on the process of internationalization. Among these countries, the so-called BRIC (Brazil, Russia, India, and China) nations should be mentioned. They present some common features but obviously also specific problems linked to the peculiarities of the individual countries and even subnational areas, given their considerable internal socioeconomic and cultural heterogeneity. These elements highlight the need for foreign manufacturers to develop innovative competitive strategies that can allow them to effectively penetrate these new markets.

The focus here is on the Indian market and a particular COO product such as wine (de Luca, Gallenti, & Penco, 2015; Pandey, 2017). Although wine in India has very ancient origins, a series of historical events, including prohibition, have eliminated it from the food tradition of the country. Considered a luxury good and not a necessity, wine is currently one of the most taxed products whose consumption is opposed by the constitution and made difficult by the central government through the definition of federal customs duties applied to imports. However, the various states and territories that make up the Republic of India have different rules. Some states encourage the development of the wine market, for example, by granting sales licenses to supermarkets, whereas others prohibit the sale of alcohol altogether, impose restrictive taxation policies, and ban advertising in the sector.

The Indian wine sector, therefore, is rather complex, and understanding it becomes a fundamental prerequisite for companies interested in successfully entering the Asian country. India, with 0.19 L of wine per capita per year (Pandey, 2017), has the lowest consumption in the world, but it is growing, even tenfold in the past decade. The potential for development is so high, considering that out of more than a billion people, only three million have so far tasted the product. To give an idea of the potential acceleration of domestic wine consumption, we must consider, for example, that in a generation, the percentage of women who consume wine in India has increased from 1 to 5% (Tesi, 2014). This increase is the result of a profound change in mentality because the consumption of wine has increased quantitatively due not only to increased income but also to social acceptance (Tesi, 2014). It, of course, is a market still in its infancy, and consumers' level of knowledge about wines, types, grapes, wine regions, and brands is very low. Consumers belonging to Generation Y, otherwise known as millennials, though, appear to be important. Of Indian wine consumers, 56% are younger than 35 years old, and living mainly in urban areas of the country, they drink wine, local and imported, at least once every 6 months. Although the discovery of wine by young people has been parallel to the discovery of other "new" beverages that are spreading, recent data (UIV-Unione Italiana Vini, 2018) indicate particular enthusiasm for wine among young people. Of the millennials interviewed by the researchers, 89% said that they enjoy experimenting with new and different wines, and many also showed a particular interest in increasing their knowledge of wine. Indian Millennials are also the largest consumers of wine in the on-trade channel, such as bars and restaurants (UIV, 2018).

The potential for growth has also been grasped by made in Italy, and a few years ago, it was highlighted that Italian institutions, in collaboration with the Indian ones, are increasingly committed to organizing events to promote knowledge and consumption of wine in India (de Luca et al., 2015). The Indian market shows a high rate of growth, but there are also negative signals. It seems that the wine culture has not yet been able to enter local traditions. Domestic production is very low, and imports are also quite limited. Half of the imported wine is destined for the horeca segment, although retail chains are beginning to dedicate space to quality wine. Unfortunately, the lack of knowledge of international brands, combined with high customs duties, push consumers toward local products. The decision to innovate the growth path through entry into new markets, therefore, can entail considerable risks for companies, which they need to face with adequate knowledge and awareness and the desirable support of business agreements. Despite the low consumption levels, it is possible to highlight the high quality of the products so far consumed and considered to be status symbols in the highest income segments.

4.4.1 Country of Origin Effect

Since the 1990s, India has been emerging from a period of protectionism and has encouraged the entry of foreign companies and new products from different parts of the world previously unknown to most of the population. Wine, which until now has not been part of the Indian food tradition, is a significant example. In this particular market, it is not clear what relevance the COO effect can have. In particular, the recognition of the importance of the product's COO as a variable capable of influencing the decision-making processes of consumers during the purchasing phase, has been the subject of numerous studies. These studies have agreed that the COO is one of the main extrinsic characteristics in the evaluation of product quality (Balabinis & Diamantoupulos, 2008; Chen, Wu, & Chen, 2011; de Luca & Marzano, 2012; Vianelli & Marzano, 2012). These studies have mainly been conducted in developed countries, but recently, work has also considered emerging and developing countries (Batra, Ramaswami, Alden, Steenkamp, & Ramachander, 2000; Bandyophadhayay & Banerjee, 2003; Essoussi & Merunka, 2007). Batra et al. (2000) focused on the COO perceptions of consumers in emerging countries and highlighted the various reasons that can motivate the purchase of foreign products by consumers in developing countries. For example (Batra et al., 2000; Hannerz, 1990), foreign products may be attractive due to their rarity and high price. The sense of insecurity and inferiority of developing countries relative to consumers in more developed countries may be filled with emulation of Western consumption patterns. Consumers might want to actively participate in the global consumer community, and elites who like to be considered cosmopolitan may want to show off their knowledge of different cultures through new products (Batra et al., 2000; Hannerz, 1990). In this frame of reference, regarding attitudes toward local and nonlocal goods among consumers in developing countries, Indian consumers' propensity to purchase foreign products emerges as a display of high social status in response to the strongly hierarchical structure of Indian society. These consumers thus express their desire to be considered part of the global economy through the purchase of products from various parts of the world and attribute to foreign-made products, often indicators of modernity and sophistication, a particular meaning in their domestic reality (Batra et al., 2000). Bandyophadhayay and Banerjee (2003), in a study on the COO effect of foreign products on Indian consumers, highlighted that when consumers evaluate a product without knowing its intrinsic characteristics, the COO is a more significant indicator of quality than price.

Based on these studies, the Indian consumer seems to have a strong predisposition for international products that can display conspicuous consumption. The need to show off wealth as a statement of social status is also demonstrated by the size of the luxury market in India, which was predicted to reach $30 billion by 2018–2019 versus $23.8 billion 2917–2018, CAGR 30% (Gupta, 2019). Eng and Bogaert (2010), in a study on the psychological drivers that induce the Indian consumer to buy Western luxury brands, showed how consumption of luxury products is conditioned by the social status induced by their possession. However, perceptions of luxury products are favored if the interactions between the traditional values of the national culture and the social prestige of the global culture of consumption can be grasped. It follows that Western luxury can also be considered to be luxury in India, especially if it is adapted to the local reality through an understanding of traditional customs and their fusion with Western ones (Eng & Bogaert, 2010). The COO concept is linked to the country image, understood as the set of beliefs, ideas, and impressions of people about a given country. A study by Dubois and Paternault (1997) examining the associations between seven countries and ten product attri-butes highlighted that the interviewees attributed the characteristics of design, style, and refinement in France and Italy and the characteristics of reliability, after-sales service, quality, and solidity in Germany. The role of the country's stereotype thus is highlighted, understood as an intangible attribute that associates particular qualities of the product with the COO. From this point of view, made in Italy seems to evoke, in particular, the characteristics of design, style, art, prestige, refinement, and good food (Dubois & Paternault, 1997).

With reference to the subject of the study, some contributions have highlighted the strong link between wine and the COO (D'Alessandro and Pecotich 2013; Lockshin, Jarvis, d'Hauteville, & Perrouty, 2006). According to Lockshin et al. (2006), the decision to purchase wine is determined by its price, brand, and COO. In particular, the country of production takes on a greater role if it is known and renowned for its wine production. D'Alessandro and Pecotich (2013) also stressed the significant influence of the COO on wine, pointing out that consumers who are not yet experts use the COO as the first quality indicator to evaluate wine.

4.4.2   Field Research on Italian Wine in India

To try to understand more deeply what the perceptions and attitudes toward Italian wine in the Indian market are, qualitative research with exploratory purposes was conducted in 2013–2014 after a first phase of desk research and collection of secondary data. Considering the particular difficulties to directly reach Indian consumers, it was decided to carry out interviews with a group of experienced operators in the market in question, primarily commercial intermediaries already operating in India and, therefore, able to provide adequate information (de Luca et al., 2019). The identification of potential interlocutors, which was especially long and complex, was achieved through subsequent contacts with various operators. First, the following organizations were contacted: institutions (the Italian–Indian Chamber of Commerce in Italy and India, with offices in New Delhi, Calcutta, and Mumbai); associations linked to the wine world (AIS and Slowfood); consortia and wine cooperatives; the chambers of commerce of the main wine-producing regions (in particular, Trentino Alto Adige, Tuscany, Piedmont, Marche, Veneto, Sicily, Abruzzo, Friuli, and Venezia Giulia); magazines specialized in the wine and food sector. Subsequently, based on the recommendation of these organizations, it was possible to identify various operators in both Italy and India, who were then contacted for interviews.

To carry out the study,[1] 96 potential subjects were identified: 20 Indians and 76 Italians in different sectors of the economy (e.g., production, services, and publishing). These subjects were contacted directly via email or telephone, but not all were willing to participate in this study for different reasons (e.g., they no longer operated in this market, and their email addresses were no longer valid). The questionnaire was then sent to 78 contacts (58 Italians and 20 Indians), of whom 21 (13 Italians and eight Indians) returned the completed questionnaire.

The set of the respondents to the interviews was composed of representatives of distributors, import/export companies, institutions, online magazines, hotel chains, consortia, cooperatives, wine companies, and associations. Of these, eight had operated in the Indian market for more than 3 years, five for 1–3 years, and seven for less than a year. The positions occupied by the interviewees varied from brand manager and commercial analyst to wine writer, sommelier, chief executive officer, and area manager. It was not possible to carry out face-to-face interviews at this stage, so it was decided to conduct online interviews using a semi-structured questionnaire with general questions on the interviewees and the three areas of interest for the research (the wine market, consumer behavior, and the COO effect). The structured questions, which included multiple or dichotomous answers, emerged from the first phase of desk research (market data and reference literature), while the unstructured questions with free answers were essential to obtain information that only operators could provide. The most delicate aspect of the questionnaire design was developing clear questions while reducing the risk of obtaining vague and inaccurate answers.

The questionnaire was administered through SurveyMonkey and carried out in Italian and English. For the Italian contacts, the operational phase of the survey was preceded by a telephone portion in which availability to complete the questionnaire was requested, and the scope and purpose of the work were specified. The access link to the survey was forwarded by email. The elaboration and analysis of the data followed the methodology of framework analysis, a process to elaborate texts related to interviews that is particularly suitable for qualitative research with explorative purposes (Srivastava & Thomson, 2009). The familiarization phase of the data analysis allowed highlighting the main aspects that emerged from reading the collected data. The identification of the thematic framework was based on the previous identification of the study areas chosen for the formulation of the question-naires. These areas were gradually refined through analysis of the individual answers to specific questions. The following areas of study were identified: the wine market in India; consumer and consumption models; consumer perceptions and product positioning; the COO effect and the situation of made-in-Italy wine in India; and the entry modes into Indian market. The questions whose topics served as codes allowed

----

[1]This phase of empirical research was conducted with the contributions of Eleonora Vanello, who today works at the Italian Chamber of Commerce and Industry in the UK.

filtering and sorting the information needed to move on to the next stage. The cataloguing led to the creation of tables sorted by case (with cases in the rows and themes in the columns). For each case, four tables corresponding to the different thematic frames were created.

To develop the tables, Microsoft Excel was used to make immediate and continuous comparison between the different cases and between the different themes within the same case. Organizing the data in an orderly manner made it possible to gain an aggregate view of the various answers to the research questions. The number of responses to the questionnaires sent, the nature of the various economic intermediaries, and the years of their presence in the Indian market were examined. The phase of mapping and interpretation of each table previously produced was then begun. In this stage, the answers to the survey questions were critically analyzed to identify the main associations and trends found in the various cases.

To further deepen the subject, some in-depth interviews were carried out with three operators in the sector with different experiences and professions who, for various reasons, had entered the new Indian market:

- An Italian oenologist who had worked in India for several years as a winemaker consultant for a company specializing in wines from Italian vines.
- A top manager of an important company in the Italian wine market.
- A marketing consultant and wine critic specializing in the promotion of Italian wines and foods in export markets.

The interviews conducted in May 2015 allowed further confirming the picture of the current situation, bringing out some relevant aspects summarized in the following sections. The main research results are presented in discursive form, broken down into the areas of study focusing on the Indian wine market, COO effect, and entry modes through contractual agreements.

4.4.3   The Wine Market in India

Almost all the respondents point out that there is a constant and continuous increase in the Indian market due to improvement in income, tourism, and lifestyles. According to some operators, the growth rate is 20–30% per year, while according to others, the real development is yet to come. The main obstacles to the development of the sector are tariff barriers, followed by cultural and legislative ones. For operators, the greatest impediments to the consumption of wine products are the high costs, which make them available only to a few, followed by the difficulty of finding them.

The areas of greatest consumption are identified as metropolises (e.g., New Delhi, Mumbai, Bangalore, Chennai, and Hyderabad) and tourist areas (e.g., the states of Goa and Punjab and areas of Pradesh), where the frequency of wine consumption for about 45% of the respondents is higher than once a week. The most influential factors in the purchase of wine are the COO and the price, considered a conditioning element for the choices of the majority of the interviewees. So far, the main recommended way to enter the market has been direct participation with local distributors and importers to avoid bureaucratic and cultural difficulties, but joint ventures and other forms of contractual agreements are also particularly interesting solutions.

4.4.4   Country of Origin Effect in India

The origin of the wine has "enough" effect for some Indians and "a lot" of effect for others in their purchasing choices. Currently, Italian wine ranks third among imported wines in India (de Luca et al., 2015), and its growth is undeniable, although it encounters various difficulties caused by tariff barriers, limited promotion and management, and not particularly effective and efficient by Italian intermediaries. For these reasons, greater use of contractual procedures for entry into the country could be especially advantageous. In fact, although Italian wine has considerable potential, it still needs to be supported by strategic marketing policies aimed at enhancing the binomial enology-gastronomy and spreading the wine culture of the so called "beautiful country" (Corsi, Marinelli, & Alampi Sottini, 2013).

The interviewees were asked to identify the best strategy to promote made-in-Italy wine in the Indian market. Their conclusion is the fundamental importance of promoting the land, culture, and cuisine, in combination with wine, to increase consumer awareness. It is extremely important to develop a strong brand for made in Italy. In this regard, a commercial analyst interviewed states that "the Italian wine industry must create a 'central base' capable of adopting a global Italian strategy that pays attention to the positive signals of the market. It is necessary to build an overall image of Italian wines, making consumers more aware and training restaurateurs, sommeliers, and sales agents." From this point of view, it is clear that these objectives can also be pursued through collaboration agreements suitable for generating that cultural fusion which, through the creation of strategic alliances and co-marketing, can facilitate a more effective meeting of tastes and traditions. Numerous other interviewees highlight the importance of training local professionals capable of advising customers and increasing their knowledge. It is also suggested companies to adopt more aggressive marketing policies linked to price and advertising and to host more tastings, or food and wine dinners, focusing on launching new wines and increasing consumer awareness.

4.4.5   Relevance of Contractual Agreements in a Complex Market

The interviewees' statements reveal the complexity of the country: "India is an enormous nation, with differences between extremely important states." "India is a confederation of states in which each has its own laws that it applies autonomously." "India is the most complex market of all, the one in which it is possible to find the right solution." "India, where everyone hopes, and then the numbers remain insignificant or almost insignificant."

The difficulties for Italian companies also arise from protectionist barriers of various kinds. In fact, as the interviewees point out, "in some countries, there is a monopoly that manages sales, while in others, the task is entrusted to distributors who represent a very powerful lobby." Moreover, for imported wines, nonrepayable grants are provided for expenses related to the promotion of wine abroad, such as participation in trade fairs, tastings in restaurants, and simple advertising.

Another important aspect is the role played in product development by large hotel chains and restaurants in tourist areas. As the interviewees state, "at the moment, the work is concentrated in Delhi and Mumbai and tourist areas. The market is that of large hotels and restaurants for tourists." "Targeted tastings should be made in hotels and restaurants through collaboration with various importers." "In my experience, I have seen a lot of interest in wine from both the large hotel chains and from wine clubs, such as those already present in Delhi, Mumbai, Kolkata, and other places." In fact, apart from the consumption of wine in tourist facilities, in the Indian population, the consumption of wine remains substantially limited, displayed as a status symbol and used to celebrate special occasions of a social nature, such as weddings, cocktails, and a few dinners and business lunches. Wine consumption is not yet widespread in the everyday life of meals.

Moreover, the dimensional problem of Italian small companies should be considered. As some interviewees point out, "it takes human and financial resources that small companies do not have (it is not the bi-tourist journey that counts), and the return on investment is often non-existent." Moreover, it is not believed that today, India can be "a relevant market for small companies. The return on investment of time and financial resources is not in the short term." The positive aspect is that imported wines tend to be considered to be better than national wines, even if local "canons of appreciation are rather distant from ours," and "we still need to educate the Indian market about the knowledge of wine to the extent of how to combine wine with Indian food, not easy for very spicy dishes."

In the current economic and competitive scenario, can Italian wineries regard India as a promising, new outlet market? The research carried out has collected interesting although not generalizable information. Its qualitative nature based on interviews with operators in the sector allows highlighting various aspects of the Italian wine in India, substantially shared by all the respondents in the two phases of field research.

India is a very large country with a big population and, for wine, represents an emerging market that is of great interest to operators but is still characterized by considerable uncertainty about its actual potential for development. Market interest in the product is growing but very slowly, mainly due to significant cultural and legislative obstacles. Distribution is mostly concentrated in large cities and is substantially controlled by big hotel and restaurant chains, especially in areas with greater tourist industries.

Internationally known wines such as some Italian brands certainly have more possibilities than others, but the small size of the Italian wine system does not encourage entry and development in a market such as India, where it is necessary to invest significant resources, especially in market research and communication, not easily accessible to small businesses. For this reason, collaboration agreements are especially important. In their various possible forms such as franchising, licensing, and strategic alliances, they can allow easier access to resources, especially information resources, and, therefore, the achievement of objectives in specific foreign markets.

4.5 Conclusion

This chapter focuses on the relationship between the COO and contractual entry modalities, particularly licensing, franchising, and strategic alliances. These agreements are close to the marketing and sales area and, as mentioned, are frequently used, above all, to enter more complex foreign markets where agreements with local operators can allow overcoming cultural distances and legal limitations. The link between the COO and contractual agreements can be twofold: on one hand, contractual agreements are an important tool for the valorization of the COO in the foreign market, and on the other hand, the strong image of the COO can favor the possibility of concluding agreements in the target markets.

These aspects have been studied through the use of specific product–market cases in the food and beverage sector in both developed and emerging markets where collaboration agreements have played and are likely to play important roles. The case of the coffee global supply chain has highlighted the role of the COO in both roasting countries and countries producing green coffee. The former historically has been able to appropriate much of the value generated, as in the example of Italy. The latter only recently have sought to valorize and appropriate of their COOs. Wine, whose COO is a fundamental component of value, has been analyzed in an emerging country, India, where contractual agreements can play a fundamental role in the entry and valorization of this product that so far has had a very low level of consumption.

The long-term economic sustainability of these initiatives is based on the ability to develop contractual agreements that can enhance the product and brand in the final market and overcome cultural distances. These same contractual agreements become easier as adequate marketing initiatives strengthen the image of the COO in the country of destination.

References

Aiello, G. (2013). *Davanti agli occhi del cliente. Branding e retailing del made in Italy nel mondo.* Roma: ARACNE Editrice.

Albricci, P. (2019, April 30). *Illy festeggia la crescita del consumo di caffè in Cina.* Tratto il giorno june 10, 2019 da Class - China Economic Information Service. http://www.classxhsilkroad.it/news/azienda-manifatturiero/illy-festeggia-la-crescita-del-consumo-di-caffe-in-cina-201904301947376632

Alon, I., Jaffe, E., Prange, C., & Vianelli, D. (2016). *Global marketing: Contemporary theory, practice and cases.* New York: Routledge.

Balabinis, G., & Diamantoupulos, A. (2008). Brand origin identification by consumers: A classification perspective. *Journal of International Marketing, 16*(1), 39–71.

Bandyophadhayay, S. K., & Banerjee, B. (2003). A country of origin analysis of foreign products by Indian consumers. *Journal of International Consumer Marketing, 15*(2), 85–109.

Batra, R., Ramaswami, V., Alden, D. L., Steenkamp, J. B., & Ramachander, S. (2000). Effects of brand local and nonlocal origin on consumer attitudes in developing countries. *Journal of Consumer Psychology, 9*(2), 83–95.

Beverfood. (2008, April 10). *Espressamente Illy Sbarca In India In Partnership Con Narang Group.* Retrieved June 08, 2019, from Beverfood: https://www.beverfood.com/espressamente-illy-sbarca-india-partnership-narang-group-wd1870/

Bursi, T., & Galli, G. (2012). *Marketing internazionale.* Milano: McGraw-Hill.

CBI-Centre for the Promotion of Imports from Developing Countries (2019, April 10). *Exporting coffee to Italy.* Retrieved June 30, 2019, from CBI: https://www.cbi.eu/market-information/coffee/italy

Chen, L. S. L., Wu, Y. J., & Chen, W. C. (2011). Relationship between country of origin, brand experience and brand equity: The moderating effect of automobile country. In *First international technology management conference* (pp. 638–642). San Jose, CA: IEEE.

Chutel, L. (2019, February 28). *Ethiopia already exports coffee beans-exporting its culture will be the next big step.* Retrieved June 28, 2019 from Quartz: https://qz.com/africa/1560013/ethiopias-coffee-ritual-is-being-exported-to-china-japan/.

Corsi, A. M., Marinelli, N., & Alampi Sottini, V. (2013). Italian wines and Asia: Policy scenarios and competitive dynamics. *British Food Journal, 115*(3), 342–364.

D'Alessandro, S., & Pecotich, A. (2013). Evaluation of wine by expert and novice consumers in the presence of variations in quality, brand and country of origin cues. *Food Quality and Preference, 28*(1), 287–303.

Dahir, A. (2018a, October 22). *This Ethiopian homegrown coffee brand is opening 100 cafés in China.* Retrieved June 28, 2019, from https://qz.com/africa/1432178/ethiopias-garden-of-coffee-to-open-100-cafes-in-china/

Dahir, A. (2018b, August 17). *East Africa's largest coffee shop chain is taking Kenyan tea and coffee to China.* Retrieved June 20, 2019, from Quartz: https://qz.com/africa/1361547/kenya-based-coffee-chain-java-to-export-coffee-tea-to-china/

de Luca, P., Gallenti, G., & Penco, P. (2015). Nuovi clienti in nuovi mercati: prospettive e criticità per il vino italiano in India. In P. de Luca (Ed.), *Le relazioni tra innovazione e internazionalizzazione. Percorsi di ricerca e casi aziendali* (pp. 71–96). Trieste: EUT.

de Luca, P., Marzano F. C. (2012). L'effetto country of origin sull'intenzione di acquisto del consumatore: un'analisi metodologica. Working paper series - Dipartimento di Scienze economiche, aziendali, matematiche e statistiche "Bruno de Finetti", N. 3, Trieste: EUT. pp. 1–26. Trieste.

de Luca, P., & Pegan, G. (2012). La percezione del Made in Italy sui mercati internazionali: primi risultati di una ricerca "netnografica" sulle comunità online di consumatori di caffè. *Atti del IX Convegno Annuale della Società Italiana Marketing*, Benevento, 20–21 settembre 2012, 1–14.

de Luca, P., & Pegan, G. (2014). The coffee shop and customer experience: A study of the U.S. market. In F. Musso & E. Druica (Eds.), *Handbook of research on retailer-consumer relationship development*. Hershey, PA: IGI Global.

de Luca, P., & Pegan, G. (2015). Relazioni tra innovazione di business e internazionalizzazione: prime evidenze empiriche nel settore italiano del caffè. In *P. de Luca (a cura di). Le relazioni tra innovazione e internazionalizzazione. Percorsi di ricerca e casi aziendali* (pp. 33–53). Trieste: EUT.

de Luca, P., Pegan, G., & Vianelli, D. (2019). Customer experience in the coffee world. Qualitative research on the U.S. market. In F. Musso & E. Druica (Eds.), *Handbook of research on retailing techniques for optimal consumer engagement and experiences*. Hershey, PA: IGI Global.

Dubois, B., & Paternault, C. (1997). Does luxury have a home country? An investigation of country images in Europe. *Marketing and Research Today: The Journal of the European Society for Opinion and Marketing Research, 25*, 79–85.

Eng, T. Y., & Bogaert, J. (2010). Psychological and cultural insights into consumption of luxury Western brands in India. *Journal of Customer Behaviour., 9*(1), 55–75.

Essoussi, L. H., & Merunka, D. (2007). Consumers' product evaluationsin emerging markets. Does country of design, country of manufacture, or brand image matter? *International Marketing Review, 24*(4), 409–426.

Google Arts & Culture. (2019). *Made in Italy*. Retrieved July 2, 2019, from https://artsandculture.google.com/project/made-in-italy.

Gupta, A. (2019, January 14). *What to expect from India's luxury industry in 2019. Luxury society*. Retrieved August 8, 2019, from https://www.luxurysociety.com/en/articles/2019/01/indian-luxury-outlook-2019/.

Halilem, N., Amara N., & Landry R. (2014). Exploring the relationships between innovation and internationalization of small and medium-sized enterprises: A nonrecursive structural equation model. *Canadian Journal of Administrative Sciences, 31*(1), 18–34.

Hannerz, U. (1990). Cosmopolitans and locals in world culture. In M. Featherstone (Ed.), *Global culture* (pp. 237–251). London: Sage.

Il Piccolo. (2005). *Illycaffè apre a Shanghai un «concept bar»*. Retrieved July 10, 2019, from http://ricerca.gelocal.it/ilpiccolo/archivio/ilpiccolo/2005/02/10/NZ_06_ILLY.html

Illycaffè. (2019). Retrieved July 27, 2019, from www.illycaffe.com

ITPI, Istituto Tutela Produttori Italiani. (2019). *100% Made in Italy*. Retrieved July 4, 2019, from https://madeinitalycert.it

Keegan, W., & Green, M. (2008). *Global marketing*. Upper Saddle River, NJ: Pearson Prentice Hall.

Kjeldegard, D., & Ostberg, J. (2007). Coffee grounds and the global cup: Glocal consumer culture in Scandinavia. *Consumption Markets and Culture, 10*(2), 175–187.

Küster, I., & Vila, N. (2011). The market orientation-innovation success relationship: The role of internazionalization strategy. *Innovation: Organization and Management, 13*(1), 36–54.

Kwok, D. (2010, May 6). *McDonald's aims to expand franchise trial in China*. Retrieved July 20, 2019, from Reuters: http://www.reuters.com/article/2010/05/06/us-mcdonalds-china-idUSTRE6451W420100506

Il Piccolo. (2005, February 10). *Illycaffè apre a Shanghai un concept bar*. Retrieved June 20, 2019 from http://ricerca.gelocal.it/ilpiccolo/archivio/ilpiccolo/2005/02/10/NZ_06_ILLY.html

Lockshin, L., Jarvis, W., d'Hauteville, F., & Perrouty, J. P. (2006). Using simulations from discrete choice experiments to measure consumer sensitivity to brand, region, price, and awards in wine choice. *Food Quality and Preference, 17*(3), 166–178.

Morris, J. (2018). *Coffee. A global history*. London: Reaktion Books.

Pandey, A. (2017, July 21). *Laws regulating production of wine in India*. Retrieved June 26, 2019 from ipleaders: https://blog.ipleaders.in/laws-regulating-production-wine-india/

Purdy, C. (2018, November 24). *Starbucks' bid to conquer Italy has begun*. Retrieved July, 10, 2019, from Quartzy: https://qz.com/quartzy/1473903/starbucks-opens-more-outlets-in-italy-following-debut-in-milan/

Samoggia, A., & Riedel, B. (2018). Coffee consumption and purchasing behavior review: Insights for further research. *Appetite, 129*, 70–81.

Seguso L. (2019). Illycaffè chiude il 2019 con un utile netto di 18,1 milioni di euro, MarkUp, may, 2nd. Retrieved August 2, 2019, from https://www.mark-up.it/illycaffe-2018-utile-netto-181-milioni-euro/

Srivastava, A., & Thomson, S. B. (2009). Framework analysis: A qualitative methodology for applied policy research. *Journal of Administration & Governance, 4*(2), 72–79.

Tesi, S. (2014). *L'India vi sorprenderà*. Retrieved July, 15, 2019, from Unione Italiana Vini.te

Ton, G., & Jansen D. (2007). *Farmers' organisations and contracted R&D services: Service provisioning and governance in the coffee chain*. Markets, Chains and Sustainable Development Strategy & Policy Paper, 4, Wageningen.

UIV. (2018, November 14). *India il vino è cosa da generazione Y*. Retrieved June, 14, 2019, from UIV: http://www.uiv.it/india-il-vino-e-cosa-da-generazione-y/

Vescovi, T. (2011). *Libellule sul drago. Strategie di marketing e modelli di business per le imprese italiane in Cina*. Padova: Cedam.

Vianelli, D., de Luca, P., & Pegan, G. (2012). *Modalità d'entrata e scelte distributive del Made in Italy in Cina*. Milano: Franco Angeli.

Vianelli, D., & Marzano, F. (2012). L'effetto country of origin sull'intenzione d'acquisto del consumatore: una literature review. Working paper series – Dipartimento di Scienze economiche, aziendali, matematiche e statistiche "Bruno de Finetti", N. 2, Trieste: EUT.

Zeidman P. F., & Xu T. (2012). *China updates its franchise filing and disclosure rules: A mixed bag*. Retrieved August 5, 2019, from DLA Piper: https://www.dlapiper.com/it/italy/insights/publications/2012/03/china-updates-its-franchise-filing-and-disclosur/.

Zhou, N., & Belk, R. W. (2004). Chinese consumer readings of global and local advertising appeals. *Journal of Advertising, 33*(3), 63–76.

Chapter 5
From Country of Origin Effect to Brand Origin: Challenges in International Direct Marketing Channels

Abstract Direct investments are an entry mode that increases business risk but allows a high level of control of the international marketing channel. Control means to be able to exploit and defend one's own competitive advantages and to operate personally in the production and commercial activities. This chapter is aimed at investigating the ways in which greenfield direct investments can facilitate manufacturers' value creation process for the market through the COO and value appropriation process. In the COO perspective, a representative office can oversee the foreign market by controlling implementation of the company's branding strategy, suggesting possible adaptations, and maintaining close relationships with distribution partners. This chapter analyses what, from companies' perspective, the role of the concept of manufactured-in has in the associations drawn between the country and the specific brand.

The relationship between the country of manufacturing and the country of brand is also explored, giving voice to some companies that have entered directly through greenfield investment types in China and the USA operating in the food, furniture, and fashion sectors. Knowing how to adapt product attributes by rereading the made-in and its relationship with the brand to match local market needs is one of the main challenges to compete effectively in foreign markets.

5.1 Introduction

The company that decides to invest directly in the foreign market faces greater risks but is able to better control the international marketing channel, increasing its chances of success abroad. In fact, in Chap. 2, it has been highlighted that to control means to exploit and defend one's own competitive advantages and to operate personally in productive and commercial activities (Vianelli, de Luca, & Pegan, 2012). It also means being able to better manage the synergies between the COO and the brand, facilitating the company's processes of value creation through the COO for the market and value appropriation. The choice to operate through greenfield direct investments requires that the company be able to reinterpret the made-in, especially in relation to the brand, using a new language capable of dialoguing even with very distant cultural contexts.

The aim of this chapter is to deepen the theme of the different dimensions of the COO and its dynamics with the brand, enriching the theory with the experiences of some companies that have invested directly with subsidiaries and DOS in specific product contexts and foreign markets. In the following sections, after a summary of the contributions of the literature on the relationship between the COO and brand, the main challenges, opportunities, and criticalities encountered by the companies participating in the research are illustrated.

5.2 Country of Origin Effect and Brand

During the purchasing decision-making process, consumers perceive and process a wide range of information that influences their buying preferences and choices. The abundant offerings of domestic and foreign products push people to adopt simplified decision-making strategies, using extrinsic cues such as brand and COO to infer and evaluate the quality of products (Han, 1989; Oberecker & Diamantopoulos, 2011).

To better understand the relationship between the COO and the brand, it is important to briefly mention the role the brand plays in the decision-making process of the individual in general. The brand fulfils a number of fundamental functions for the consumer. First, it identifies the product's attributes and benefits and facilitates choice by guiding the consumer through the myriad of products in the market. Second, the brand reduces the consumer's perceptions of risk (Solomon, Bamossy, Askegaard, & Hogg, 2006) by offering a long-term quality guarantee. The brand also allows customization of the company's value proposition, giving the consumer the ability to communicate to others the desired personal image (Kapferer & Thoening, 1991; Olivero & Russo, 2013). The brand tells stories and builds possible worlds in which consumers can recognize themselves (Semprini, 1996). The brand plays the role of mediator, a sort of a cognitive bridge between the worlds of products and consumers (Keller, 2003) through the common ground of values, defined as conditions judged as desirable by the individual (Dalli & Romani, 2001). The brand does not create its own values but appropriates socially existing ones by making them its own. In a world governed by confusion and the collapse of strong beliefs, consumers are increasingly asking brands, as the protagonists of the economic system, to share their values and contribute to the well-being of society, embracing important social causes. Branded product purchasing thus become a tool to reduce consumer anxieties about the world inequalities. Brands thus can fill the gap often left by governments and institutions (Edelman Earned Brand, 2018; Kotler, Hermawan, & Iwan, 2017; Kotler, Kartajaya, & Setiawan, 2010). In the global comparison space where local products coexist with foreign and hybrid products, and the consumer may be disoriented trying to understand the actual quality of alternative purchases, the brand makes a promise of value (also social value) that reassures and facilitates consumer choice.

Several authors have studied the relationship between the COO and the brand to understand which of the two plays a dominant role in influencing the consumer's process of buying products and have arrived at divergent conclusions. Han and Terpstra (1988), Wall, Liefeld, and Heslop (1991), Tse and Gorn (1993), and Darling and Arnold (1988) concluded that the COO has greater influence than the brand on perceptions of product quality. Other scholars supported the opposite thesis, considering the brand effect to be the most important (Hui & Zhou, 2003; Srinivasan, Jain, & Sikand, 2004; Ulgado, 2002; Verlegh & Steenkamp, 1999).

The links between the COO and the brand have been analyzed more recently from a new point of view, embracing, as mentioned in Chap. 1, the perspective of the association strategy. This approach considering the association's customers make among the product, brand, and COO shifts the focus of research on the COO effect from production to consumption (Andehn & Berg, 2011). The importance of the place where a product is manufactured, designed, or assembled—subject to analysis instead of the perspective of the deconstruction strategy, which aims to investigate the influence of the different components of the COO, such as country of manufacture, assembly, and design, on final purchasing decisions (Ahmed & D'Astous, 1996; Allred, Chakraborty, & Miller, 2000; Chao, 1993; Han & Terpstra, 1988)—diminishes in favor of focusing on the customer's perceptions and identification of the COO (the country of association). In other words, the difficulty encountered in the hyperconnected global scenario of knowing how to precisely identify the country of production (Chao, 1993) has led scholars to focus on the consumer's perception of the product origin in relation to associations with the brands (Thakor & Lavack, 2003; Usunier, 2011).

Some authors have pointed out that it is not always important to dwell on the company's exact place of origin because it is possible that the consumer is not fully aware of it and, instead, bases choices on personal beliefs resulting from direct or indirect experiences with the product and its brand (Andehn & Berg, 2011; Hamzaoui, Merunka, & Bartikowski, 2011). Thakor and Kohli (1996) previously coined the term *brand origin*, defining it as "the place, region or country where a brand is perceived to belong to its target consumers" (p. 26). These two scholars argued that this perception may differ from the place where the product to which that particular brand is linked was built or even where the company is based. Thakor pointed to a number of underlying causes for the perceptual distortion of consumers: "Consumer perceptions may differ from reality due to ignorance, lack of salience of information about the origin of a particular brand or deliberate obfuscation by companies to avoid negative reactions from consumers to an unfavourable origin" (p. 26). According to categorization theory, daily consumers categorize brands in a fairly incidental way in a specific COO (Hutchinson & Alba, 1991; Markman & Ross, 2003). According to this theory, consumer attitudes and preferences, therefore, are more influenced by categories stored in memory than by authentic COO information (Hutchinson & Alba, 1991).

Consequently, there is a problem of consumer awareness about the COO that companies can exploit to their advantage (Balabanis & Diamantopoulos, 2008; Samiee, 2010; Samiee, Shimp, & Sharma, 2005). Marketers, in fact, can create appropriate communication policies aimed at strengthening the association between superior product quality and brand image, marginalizing the effect of the country of manufacturing (Clarke, Owens, & Ford, 2000). As mentioned, several tools can be used to strengthen this association beyond the classic label of made-in (Insch & Florek, 2009; O'Shaughnessy & O'Shaughnessy, 2000), the inclusion of strong suggestions about the company's origin in the brand name, such as the names of many companies in the air transport sector (Thakor & Lavack, 2003; Usunier & Cestre, 2007); the adoption of images that symbolize a particular country in the collective imagination, such as the colors and stylized shapes of flags (Insch & Florek, 2009); the choice in the brand name of a particular language that quickly recalls the country and geographical area of reference (Harun, Wahid, Mohammad, & Ignatius, 2011). Some effects of origin can be spontaneously evoked by consumers through the natural associations between certain productions and specific countries traditionally and culturally perceived as linked (e.g., pasta and pizza with Italy and sushi and manga with Japan) without the need for any effort on the part of the marketing operator (Usunier & Cestre, 2007).

Recent studies have further developed the concept of brand origin by presenting a more evolved paradigm in the evaluation of the COO effect, called the culture of brand origin (COBO). This approach focuses on the linguistic and cultural factors (phonetic, morphological, and semantic) applied to the brand to stimulate positive perceptions in those who come into contact with it (Harun et al., 2011; Lim & O'Cass, 2001) and indicate the product origin to the consumer (Li & Shooshtari, 2003; Thakor & Lavack, 2003). The brand image, therefore, seems to be able to generate and transmit to consumers associations linked to the origin of the product regardless of the place of production (O'Shaughnessy & O'Shaughnessy, 2000; Papadopoulos & Heslop, 1993; Samiee, 1994).

5.3   Rereading the Meaning of the Country of Origin to Create Value in Greenfield Investments

In the very dynamic international competitive arena where small and large companies face each other and compete without barriers at a global level (Wright & Dana, 2003), it is essential to know how to innovate a business to create not only new things but also new value for the customer (de Luca, 2015; de Luca & Pegan, 2014; Pegan & de Luca, 2015; Sawhney, Wolcott, & Arroniz, 2006). The question then arises: how can a company create new value in foreign markets?

Certainly, a direct presence in the foreign market due to the greater proximity to the segments of foreign customers who the company wants to serve can allow the company to develop effective value propositions for the market superior to those of its competitors. For companies, knowing and fully understanding the specificity of foreign consumers is more crucial now than ever. Indeed, one paradox in the globalized economy, which offers new spaces for comparisons between very distant cultures, is precisely to accentuate the perception of local differences (Dana, Etemad, & Wright, 1999). The defense of one's own local identities, on one hand, and the desire to westernize by purchasing products and brands that express and evoke these cultures, on the other hand, are the basis of many oriental consumption styles, as, for example, happens in China (Vianelli, de Luca, & Pegan, 2012). The presence in the branch of managers with intercultural skills capable of intercepting the specific and often contradictory needs of foreign consumers more than ever is considered to be a successful driver of the internationalization of the company (Dana, Etemad, & Wright, 2008). In this way, it becomes easier for the company to adapt the attributes of the product, the meaning of the COO, and the brand values according to local needs, creating superior value for the foreign market (Pegan, de Luca, & dal Pont, 2015).

The difficulty of adapting the company's product offerings, even in its COO-related attributes to its articular business context, seems to be the basis of the failures experienced by some SMEs, especially in very geographically and psychologically distant markets such as India and China (Bertoli & Resciniti, 2012; Vianelli, de Luca, & Pegan, 2012). This difficulty may also emerge in cases in which companies, regardless of size, can count on a strong, positive country image that facilitates initial entry into the foreign market (e.g., Italian food companies; de Luca et al. 2015; Khanna, Palepu, & Bullock, 2010; Pegan et al., 2015). In fact, larger companies, even if they have more skills and resources for internationalization, may not be able to grow due to strong competition from domestic players better rooted in the local community (Alon, Jaffe, Prange, & Vianelli, 2016). These competitors base their market power on their high presence in the distribution channel and their offerings of products and brands tailored to the wishes of local consumers who may end up preferring them to foreign ones.

The ability to adapt is closely related to the level of control the company can exert in the outlet market, which is maximized by direct investments. The relationship between high business risk and the benefits of increased market control, as analyzed in Chap. 2, depends on the type of direct investment pursued. The size and weight of the product, quality and transferability of knowhow, and complexity of the product category from a commercial point of view, are also essential aspects that influence the types of investment the company decides to make (Alon et al., 2016; Andersen & Kheam, 1998). As pointed out, perceptions of the product origin can be influenced by its brand and country of brand, even if these perceptions may differ from the product's real place of production, the country of manufacture, and the headquarters of the company due to a lack of consumer awareness (Thakor & Kohli, 1996).

As mentioned in Chap. 2, companies that choose hierarchical modes can use greenfield investments to strengthen their presence in retail with investment in directly operated stores (DOS). From a manufacturer's perspective, DOS are configured as a brand narrative in which companies can create consumer-centered communication interfaces, encouraging the end customer's active participation in all dimensions of the shopping experience. The aim is to provide a physical space capable of recreating the universe of the brand and its values (de Luca & Pegan, 2014). Brand values are more credible if conveyed at real points of sale (Semprini,

1996). In this perspective, the company is able to create a customer experience based on the values of the brand and the COO, directly managing the relationship with foreign customers and thus monitoring the perceptions of the value proposals distributed in the market. The customer experience (Hirschman & Holbrook, 1982; Pine & Gilmore, 1999) is considered to be a key factor in creating value for the customer and a key element in any company's competition (Smith & Wheeler, 2002). The customer experience can be defined as the result of a set of emotions, feelings, and behaviors that arise throughout the decision-making and consumption process through a series of integrated relationships among people, objects, processes, and atmospheres (Pine & Gilmore, 1999). The customer experience is especially important in the retail sector where the shop atmosphere is a basic multisensory communication vehicle (Donovan & Rossiter, 1982; Kotler, 1973; Machleit, Eroglu, & Powell, Mantel, 2000). The importance of the ability to offer a customer experience that is authentic to the brand and its COO but at the same time respectful of the geographical and cultural context of reference is a real challenge for companies with high national typicality (de Luca & Pegan, 2014).

For companies that choose other types of greenfield investments, it is crucial to understand the effects of the choices of production relocation and commercial subsidiaries on the perceptions of product quality and the brand image held by the intermediate and final foreign customers. It, therefore, is important to investigate what relationships link the evolution of the COO construct in the particular dimensions of the country of manufacture and the country of brand and the choices to enter abroad through subsidiaries.

5.4   Relevance of the Country of Manufacture, Country of Brand, and Brand Origin: Insights from Companies in Traditional and New Foreign Market

As pointed out, studies aimed at analyzing the link between the COO and the brand have favored the consumer's perspective, leaving a gap on the perceptions of companies. Therefore, it is important to understand how the dynamics between the COO and the brand are managed by companies, especially SMEs that have product offerings with high national typicality but scarce financial resources and make some greenfield direct foreign investments. In particular, the aim of the research was to investigate whether to create value in foreign markets, these companies focus mainly on promoting the value of the country of production or chose to invest more in the brand, considering it to be a vehicle for the creation of a culture of the brand origin (Vianelli, Pegan, & Micoli, 2014).

Table 5.1 Characteristics of the companies

Company	Industry	Country of manufacturing			Country of brand	Directly operated store (DOS)		
		Italy	USA	China	Italy	Italy	China	USA
1	Food (wine)	Y	N	N	Y	N	N	N
2	Food (wine)	Y	N	N	Y	N	N	N
3	Food (wine)	Y	N	N	Y	N	N	N
4	Food (ham)	Y	Y	Y	Y	N	N	N
5	Food (cheese)	Y	N	N	Y	N	N	N
6	Food (dessert)	Y	Y	N	Y	N	N	N
7	Food (coffee)	Y	N	N	Y	Y	N	Y
8	Food (coffee)	Y	N	N	Y	N	N	N
9	Apparel	N	N	Y	Y	Y	N	Y
10	Apparel	N	N	Y	Y	N	N	N
11	Apparel (shoes)	N	N	Y	Y	N	N	Y
12	Furniture	Y	Y	Y	Y	Y	N	Y
13	Home/furniture	Y	N	N	Y	N	N	N
14	Furniture	Y	N	Y	Y	Y	N	Y

Source: Compiled by authors

5.4.1 Reasons for Focusing on a Particular Product–Market Contexts

To fill the gap on the perceived relationship between the brand and its COO from the company's perspective, as mentioned in Chap. 1, we have carried out a qualitative research on Italian SMEs operating in both the US and Chinese markets through subsidiaries and, in some cases, DOS. The methodological choices were justified by a number of key considerations (see Table 5.1).

First, several authors (Bertoli & Resciniti, 2012; Bursi, Grappi, & Martinelli, 2012; Marino & Mainolfi, 2010) have highlighted that the COO can be an important element in developing a distinctive positioning in international marketing strategies, especially when perceptions of the attributes of the country's image and the product category are consistent and positive (Hamzaoui & Merunka, 2006; Roth & Romeo, 1992). In the case of made in Italy, a strong link with this local dimension rich in symbolic connotations carries a unique identity that is the result of traditions and historical skills rooted in these particular territories. This link endows the product with new meanings and enriches it with added value perceived by the consumer (Golinelli, 2012; Marino & Mainolfi, 2013). The globalization of markets seems to have contributed to the spread of new instances of immaterial consumption in which the product's territorial origin plays an important role in supporting the consumer to develop and communicate personal identity (Bursi et al., 2012; Pegan & Vianelli, 2013). The desire to express one's uniqueness through the purchasing process increases in the eyes of the consumer the value of production specialization and the real or perceived strengths of a particular territory of origin. In this perspective, it seems that one effect of globalization has been to give a competitive advantage to the local identity of the product made in Italy (Pegan & Vianelli, 2016). Hence, the declination of the COO in made in Italy can represent a competitive advantage for both the country of production and the country of the brand.

Second, for SMEs, exploiting the advantage of the COO effect, which acts as a driver for differentiating the company's offerings, maybe cheaper from a financial point of view than investing in the brand. Third, even if SMEs invest in the brand, they can choose to use the image of the COO (Roth & Diamantopoulos, 2009) as an element to enrich the strategic positioning of the brand (Pastore, Ricotta, & Giraldi, 2011). Following the logic of co-branding, a country's image can be used to strengthen the brand image (Aiello, Donvito, Godey, & Pedersoli, 2008; Busacca, Bertoli, & Molteni, 2006), so the final value transferred to the market could be higher (Bursi et al., 2012).

The choice made for this research to focus on the specific foreign countries for entry, the USA and China, was motivated by the following reasons. As noted in Chap. 3, for Italian companies, the USA is their most important commercial partner outside the European Union, has long-term relationships, and continues to offer them significant opportunities for growth. Made-in-Italy brands are very popular in the USA, especially in traditional industries such as food, fashion, and furniture. These, in fact, constitute the three macro-sectors of excellence of made in Italy: the so-called *bello e ben fatto* (Bbf) products, which are medium-high goods with high symbolic value for international consumers. While Bbf is increasingly exported to new markets, the USA also continues to absorb this category of products. A traditional market for the internationalization of Italian products, the US market also has the highest number of Italian-sounding and fake products in the world (de Luca & Pegan, 2013). This phenomenon raises the problem of the foreign consumer's lack of knowledge, which hinders companies' ability to effectively take possession of that intrinsic value (often merely symbolic) present in the product made in Italy. To fill this knowledge gap, Italian companies have gradually increased direct investment in recent years, often due to the difficulty of controlling distribution networks, in addition to exports. The development of sales and production branches has allowed greater rapprochement between Italian products and US consumers, increasing brand penetration not only through greater adaptation to the market but also through effective management and increased control of distribution channels (Aiello, 2013).

China continues to present an important business partner of Italy and a growing market.[1] However, it offers numerous challenges to Italian SMEs that have found or continue to encounter difficulty growing due to both geographical and cultural distances. In fact, there are many unsuccessful cases in this market, which all

---

[1]In 2018, Italy confirmed its position as the fourth largest supplier to China among European countries, with exports of 13.2 million euro. In addition, with 30.7 million euro, Italy ranked fourth among European customers of China (Source: http://www.infomercatiesteri.it/paese.php?id_paesi=122#slider-6, accessed May 05, 2019.

teach that it is necessary to know how to reread the company's product offerings and the meaning of made in Italy, adapting them to Chinese market's specificities (Aiello, 2013; Vianelli, de Luca, &, Bortoluzzi, 2012; Vianelli, de Luca, & Pegan, 2012). Table 5.1 summarizes the main characteristics of the companies interviewed; for privacy reasons, all firms have requested not to be revealed and are therefore identified by a number.

As can be seen in Table 5.1, the sample examined is composed of Italian companies belonging to the so-called 3 F industries (fashion, furniture, and food), which are perceived by the foreign market as historically and typically linked to the Italian production system. In other words, customers perceive the attributes of the country image (Italy image) and the product country image (e.g., fashion product) as coherent, the positive effect of made in Italy on consumers purchasing choices should be strong (Hamzaoui & Merunka, 2006; Roth & Romeo, 1992; Vianelli & Pegan, 2014). In addition, the companies manage production and sales subsidiaries in both the Chinese and the US markets, and some of these companies have DOS in the USA. As mentioned in Chap. 1, in-depth semi-structured interviews were conducted (Yin, 2011) with export and marketing managers who had direct responsibility for the markets analyzed and were strongly involved in the strategic decisions of their subsidiaries in recent years. The aim was to investigate the relationship between the brand and the COO by deepening the relationship between the country of manufacture and the country of branding and the dynamics characterizing this relationship. This phase of the study was also aimed at understanding the role of the brand in relation to its country of manufacture and branding. The results of the interviews[2] as discussed in the following sections, provide an interesting overview of the importance of the country of production compared to the country of the brand as a distinctive element in the international marketing strategies of the companies analyzed. Additionally, these stories describe the interviewed companies' perceptions of the relationships among the brand, the country of production, and the country of the brand.

5.4.2   Dynamic Relationships Between the Country of Manufacture and the Country of Brand in International Marketing Strategies

The voice of the companies from different sectors enabled obtaining an articulated overview of the different weights given in their international marketing strategies to the two dimensions of the COO: the country of manufacture and the country of brand. These voices, although not generalizable, offered perspectives and

---

[2]Many of the original quotations extracted from the interviews, which are reported in this chapter, have already been published in a previous work by Vianelli and Pegan (2014).

interpretations based on the specific sector of activity consistent with the overall evaluation of the phenomenon studied.

In the fashion industry, the great luxury brands that once distinguished themselves by highlighting their craftsmanship in local production linked to the peculiarities of a territory now want to distinguish themselves through different tools. Some companies, for example, claim that it is not the place where a company produces but perceptions of a company's brand origin that makes it distinctive in the market. In this sense, the role of retailing is emphasized as a primary vehicle for the diffusion of the image of a country and, therefore, the brand linked to the country. This awareness is expressed in the statements by the owner and vice-president of one company analyzed:

> Does it really matter where the product is made? If we want to communicate the Italian origin, we must work on the design of both the garments and the shops. Italian products can be found almost everywhere. The same cannot be said of the real Italian shops. (Company 10)

The idea that the relevance attributed to the country of manufacture in the fashion sector is perhaps taken for granted is expressed by several companies analyzed. For example, a respondent points out the lack of attractiveness of the country of production in describing the partnerships that his/her company is building in the US market to strengthen brand awareness:

> Our consumers do not care if the product was manufactured in Italy or not. To the contrary, we are following the tendency to collaborate with the American large-scale retail trade. In fact, an important new phenomenon is emerging. It is defined as "mass privilege," i.e., the possibility of purchasing a luxury object that, in the eyes of the consumer, appears unique but is not accompanied by the added value of real made in Italy. For example, our lines that we make available in Target were made in Japan and with different materials from our other products. (Company 9)

These arguments also appear to be valid in the Chinese market. Here, appreciation for the made-in-Italy brand is high, but at the same time, purchases are determined primarily by the perceptions of the origin of the brand. In a country where all that matters is that "consumers feel that they are wearing a garment that embodies the Italian style" (Company 10), the value shifts from the qualities linked to production in the territory of origin to the COO of the perceived brand.

Similar opinions also emerge from the reports of companies operating in the other sectors examined. For example, those who work in the furniture sector recognize a segment of consumers who want authentically Italian products. However, the growth potential of this type of product in foreign markets is marginal. The manager of an Italian company based in Shanghai states:

> My customers buy some of the parts we produce in the Italian factory. However, afterward, they ask me to produce them here again at lower prices, exactly the same in all respects as the products made in Italy. What really matters is the Italian style brand made in China, not the real product made in Italy. (Company 14)

Many Italian companies in China also export the made-in-Italy brand and, at the same time, produce in the Chinese market models successful due to the strong bond with Italy. The Asian manager of a well-known Italian furniture brand reports:

As far as our image is concerned, the double relationship between the export of European brands and the on-site production of our Chinese brands in China is working well. In order to sell brands produced directly in China, in fact, we focus on factors such as design and quality. A local brand of our company, for example, is translated into Chinese with an expression similar to "German friend." The aim is to convey the idea of the German brand synonymous with quality and innovation. Another brand, on the other hand, turns into something like "beautiful Italian cuisine," focusing on Italian design and lifestyle. (Company 3)

Turning to the food sector, the interviewees reveal several interesting aspects concerning the product's country of production. In this sector, the success of many Italian-sounding products highlights how much (symbolic) value the declination of the COO in made in Italy has in itself. At the same time, however, it highlights that the consumer often lacks the competence to recognize authentic Italian products.

Indeed, many companies surveyed underline the limited knowledge of the final consumer, who can rarely recognize and appreciate the true origin of products. This problem also applies to markets such as the wine market, where the origin should be an essential element in product evaluation. Several managers, such as that of a well-known company in the wine sector, emphasize this critical situation:

Everything that is Italian is always one step ahead of all other products in the market. However, it makes me smile when I see on the American market products made in Italy that have actually been produced in Canada or the United States. Unfortunately, the American consumer who lives along the coast—cities like New York and San Francisco—is the only one who knows Italy well enough. On the competition front, if we move to the central states of the United States (where 90% of the wine is purchased), the consumer is not informed at all and, therefore, mixes the made in Italy with everything that is proposed in this way. (Company 2)

This quotation suggests that even in the case of companies operating in sectors that can benefit from the high potential intrinsic value of the COO, the positive effects of the COO on the foreign consumer should never be taken for granted due to the typicality of their product offerings. To the contrary, companies should always monitor the needs of the foreign market, even traditional foreign outlets such as the US market, to understand the different degrees of product expertise matured by different segments of demand.

Competitiveness is another problem reported by businesses. A dominant theme in all the interviews with food companies is that the main competitors of Italian companies are Italian companies in the USA and generally European companies in China. The managers' experience often highlights the critical issue of consumers' lack of knowledge of actual product origins. There are many Italian products in the market, so Italian managers rightly argue that differentiation by the country of production has become difficult. Similar issues arise in China, where competition is increasing year by year, and companies from individual European countries are often aggregated in consumer perceptions into the undifferentiated made in Europe. Companies, therefore, should be aware of this lack of general expertise in products and origins and try to fill this gap with targeted communication activities.

An issue that concerns various industrial sectors is the need to ensure high levels of service. The importance of bringing the company's value proposition to the end market highlights the importance of sales, logistics, and after-sales services. It is precisely from these aspects, however, that criticalities linked to the conception of the COO in the sense of the country of manufacture can arise. These criticalities concern the actual value of the product perceived in the foreign market.

The export managers of two well-known coffee companies point out that:

> What really matters is to associate the intrinsic quality with an equally high perceived quality, which depends only in part on the place of manufacture of the product. In selling coffee, the size of the service is very important because the coffee is a semi-finished product until it is poured into a cup of coffee. In this way, an excellent semi-finished product can be transformed into a finished product, into a can in case we can't teach our barmen the Italian way to prepare good coffee. I would say that producing it in Italy or here in the United States doesn't really make a difference. What matters is the service we offer here to our bartenders. (Company 8)

> You can focus your efforts only on production in your country of origin, focusing on technologies that can reduce the difficulties that a foreign barman often faces in preparing coffee. However, the risk is that you increase the quality of the coffee cup but create a negative effect on "romanticism," which is the pride of the bartender to be recognized as an "artist" of Italian coffee. To say that coffee is produced in Italy is very important, but it is much more important if it is perceived as "born" from the hand of the local American or Chinese bartender. (Company 7)

In some cases, the concept of the country of manufacture is even more complicated: the country of production can assume negative connotations due to excessive geographical distance from the country of consumption. Indeed, geographical distance may raise doubts about the reliability of logistics. The importance of direct investment through the realization of a new production establishment in a foreign country is clearly expressed by the director of an Italian food company:

> They only came to us because we produce here. Many Italian restaurant chains recognize the value of manufactured-in, but they are afraid. They prefer local suppliers because they don't want to take risks with logistics. (Company 6)

The experience of those who have decided to operate in China is similar. The difficulty of remotely managing marketing channels without constant, on-site supervision emphasizes the strategic importance of making greenfield direct investments by relocating production to the Chinese market. In this regard, the manager of a furniture company states:

> Italians expect to come here with the catalogue, give it to the distributor, saying "buy" and without giving any kind of help. Once you sell it, it's "bye bye bye bye," and they don't want to have anything to do with the problems. If a piece breaks, there is no one here; then it is a disaster. There is no assistance because the company is not present, and the local partner is not able to provide it. For this reason, I'm investing in relocating production here to China. (Company 13)

However, it is interesting to point out that in the different perspectives of the managers, the constant monitoring of the foreign market and the ability to redefine the concept of the COO based on local consumers' specificities are critical success factors. If it is true that, in general, the relevance of the country of manufacture cannot be taken for granted, it is also true that the border between the country of manufacture and the country of brand can be dynamic and change depending on the specific product and market considered. The experience of the manager of one of the three furniture companies effectively explains it:

> The American market seems to perceive positively a product of our brand even if it is made in Europe but does not seem to be able to accept made in China. On the other hand, a possible sofa of our brand made in the USA is appreciated. In the latter case, the possibility of improving the service through a reduction of logistical costs and fast, efficient delivery, which is particularly appreciated by the American consumer, could reward the non-manufacture in Italy. (Company 12)

As explained in the following, the decision to invest directly through DOS allows the company to constantly understand the trends in foreign customers' tastes, their degree of satisfaction, and the dynamic relationship between the sub-concepts of the country of manufacture, country of brand, and brand origin effect. In fact, this relationship is not static but constantly evolving and, therefore, should be reread in the different product–market contexts in which the company decides to invest.

5.4.3 Need to Invest in Branding

In the dynamic relationship between the country of manufacture and the country of brand, the companies interviewed agree that the role of the brand should be regarded as strategic. Beyond the specific product–market context considered in the interviews, in the global scenario in which small and large companies compete in the same space, the brand is confirmed to be a protagonist in international marketing strategies in both the US and Chinese markets.

Some companies stress the need to invest in a brand because they believe that it is the only way to differentiate themselves from other brands not made in Italy, even if presented as such. They also emphasize the importance of the brand name, which, in addition to having a denotative function identifying and recognizing their product, communicates the image of the product and its benefits and values. The owner of a famous winery reports:

> At first, the label of our bottle for American supermarkets had "prosecco" written in large letters. Currently, there are about forty brands of different companies on the shelves, from Ciao [Hello] to Primo Amore. We had to change the label by writing our name in large letters to differentiate ourselves. Our worst "enemies" are Italians abroad, and only by investing in our brand can we increase our differentiation to become more competitive with respect to other Italian brands. (Company 3)

Regarding the importance of the evocative, strategic function of the brand name, the head of a US subsidiary of a famous food company states:

> If you look at the brand image developed by Amano Artisan Chocolate, an American company based in Utah, you immediately realize that the first step to success is to invest in the brand. The word "amano" comes from the Italian translation "by hand" and "love," which is the way the company describes its chocolate. In other words, by investing in the brand, the company is able to create a strong association with the country of production and the (non-existent) Italian origins for consumers. (Company 5)

Paradoxically, companies such as those operating in the wine sector where the product origin must be able to guide the image of the product are among those who state that company needs to invest in the brand if it wants to grow:

> If we add the two parameters to 100%, for us, the brand counts for 70%, and the origin for 30%. The strategy of the whole group is to enhance the brand more than the origin: the origin is a consequence because then when we talk about our brand, it is closely linked to Tuscany and Italy. All the policies we implement create value through brand focus. We implement global projects, [and] we localize them for different markets, and importers give us suggestions to improve the results. (Company 1)

The companies consider the brand to be one of the main tools to increase perceived quality. The companies' perspectives affirm the role of the brand as a promise of the quality, worth, and value of their product offerings. It is clear to the companies that the brand represents a bridge between the worlds of products and consumers.

The creation of a physical bridge between these two worlds that makes the company's promise of value a reality explains why several companies analyzed have adopted today's very popular trend of taking risks, investing with integrations at the bottom of the channel through DOS and in the US market. In this way, these companies can constantly monitor the behaviors and especially the changes in the desires of the various targets of foreign customers. An emblematic experience of the importance of the manufacturer's downstream integration of the marketing channel is that of furniture companies. In this sector, given the complexity of the product, many consumers' purchasing decisions are made with the help of retailers' advice. It, therefore, is strategic for a furniture manufacturer to have a direct link that allows it to communicate the essence of the brand and its functional and symbolic benefits. Guaranteeing an experience focused on product typicality then becomes easier, and it is easier to convey the intrinsic value of the COO and ensure that it is transformed into the perceptions of real value among the final users. The relevance of this aspect is reflected in the words of one company:

> We have become increasingly aware of the opportunity to develop a consumer-centered communication interface within the store, encouraging the active participation of the end customer in all dimensions of the shopping experience. (Company 12)

The strategic importance of DOs also clearly emerges with great force in the fashion sector, where the symbolic components of the product acquire particular importance in the eyes of the final consumer. A fashion company interviewed states:

> Our stores are ambassadors in the world of our brand, its essence, its origins, its distinctive value. (Company 9)

The importance of investing in physical places where consumers can enjoy shopping experiences based on the authenticity of the COO and its dynamics with the brand also arises in the coffee sector.

> Our flagship is a meeting point for discovering Italian excellence in the world. (Company 7)

However, the complexity and, above all, the dynamism of the relationship between the COO and the brand from the operational viewpoint of managers emerges in statements by the companies.

According to some firms, it does not always really matter if the product is made in Italy or another country. One manager interviewed confirms that:

> Our products are made in Italy, and many of us think that this is important to ensure better quality control. I know both the American and Chinese markets, and I know this is not the case for them. It's quality that counts. On the market, the factor of authenticity in the equation "Parmigiano = Italy" is not a critical factor for success, but the brand is. And our problem is the lack of credibility of a quality label that is still in its infancy. Being Italian counts, but we can only do that if we communicate through a known brand. (Company 5)

Communicating through the brand also means building a bridge with a foreign market, which requires developing associations that attract the domestic market and approach the country served. This is very important in countries like China, where the appreciation of Western styles coexists with a strong attachment to local cultures. The director of a Chinese food company states:

> Italian managers and their target consumers are concerned about authenticity, controlled designation of origin, and the link with the territory. But the buyers are Chinese buyers and their customers, and after a difficult start, we realized that they do not consider it essential to buy a product that is truly Italian but rather a product of Italian identity, ideally adapted to their market. Identity is created exclusively through marketing. For example, we replaced the historic logo of the company's bell with a panorama of the Alps in the background for our sausages produced in China with a Venetian image marked "Marco Polo," which evokes the relations of Italy with China. (Company 4)

In addition, some companies argue that investing in the brand helps exploit the brand made in Italy, emphasizing only its positive aspects and avoiding its negative dimensions. One director reports:

> Made in Italy is reinforcement and offers a greater margin than its competitors. As an Italian, you have a certain charm, but then you have to be able to keep your promises. The food scandals (Botox, buffalo, ethanol, Parmalat) have been destructive: they have had a devastating impact on the image of made in Italy for all Italian companies abroad. Our company is proud to be Italian, but we realize that it is important to invest in the brand also by disconnecting it from the Italian flag. (Company 6)

The interviewees reveal another important element in relation to the brand. The presence of international players is not always seen as a threat but can also be an opportunity for SMEs that decide to invest in the brand image. In fact, large competitors invest in advertising with budgets completely inconceivable to SMEs, and these huge investments can also to spread knowledge of the product and country on which Italian companies can capitalize and use to highlight the characteristics of their brands:

> Direct comparisons with financially powerful competitors like Starbucks would be a waste of capital. Their presence should instead be seen as an opportunity. In fact, the market must, first of all, be aware of the peculiarities of the product itself to be receptive to a company that offers a product like Italian expresso. Leaving Starbucks to invest in the concept of Italian products allows our company to go directly from the image of the territory to invest in the brand, to propose itself as a brand of superior quality. Indeed, the country of production and the role of origin marking are mainly reinforced by the investment in the brand. (Company 7)

Finally, the importance that consumers and retailers attach to a brand requires strong marketing investments. Italian companies must be able to create an image that goes beyond the concept of made in Italy and can still be competitive with other European and even Chinese companies. The chief executive officer of a fashion company notes:

> Italian shoes are beautiful; if they're expensive, that's fine. Actually, it is even better, but in China, if the brand is not known, no one will buy them, even if they are the best shoes on earth. It doesn't matter. Nobody's gonna buy it. This is a concept that Italians do not seem to understand. (Company 11)

5.5 Conclusion

This qualitative analysis on Italian SMEs that operate with direct investments in the USA and China has provided a multifaceted overview of the strategic relevance of the brand and its dynamic relationship with its COO. In the experience of these managers, the country to which the brand belongs assumes a primary strategic role.

The voices of the interviewees show that in the company's global marketing strategy, the country of brand plays a more important role than the country of manufacture. In the fashion sector, the country of manufacture is considered to be of little importance, both in the USA and China. However, the companies interviewed argue that it is the perceptions of where the brand originates that influence the process of consumer choice. In this context, particular importance is given to the role of retail, seen as a primary tool for spreading the image of a country, an Italian style, and, consequently, the country of brand.

This trend is confirmed in the furniture sector where niche consumers demand the original made in Italy, thus enhancing the country of manufacture. However, we must point out that this segment is completely marginal: an entrepreneur, for example, states that, given the supplies of original pieces, large quantities of copies with the same aesthetic characteristics but made at a lower price in China are often requested. Similarly, a company highlights that exporting some of its brands from Italy with the Italian country of manufacture can enhance its production in China by offering products with the Chinese country of manufacture but associated with the Italian image of its other original brands.

In the food sector, the association of the country of brand with the country of manufacture is confirmed by the Italian-sounding phenomenon, especially in the USA. Many of the interviewees state that consumers have poor knowledge of product origins, even in the case of wine whose origin should be seen as a distinctive factor. This statement once again highlights the lower relevance of the country of manufacture than the country of brand.

The competitive context of reference should also be mentioned. In China, for example, European companies (e.g., those from Germany and France) are the main competitors of Italian products, and it is difficult to make differentiations based on the country of manufacture, which is generally associated with European production.

The country of brand then becomes the only real distinctive element, but strengthening the image of the Italian brand requires significant investments.

Thoughts can be offered in relation to services. Many companies underline that, in fact, it does not matter if an Italian brand is produced in Italy, the USA, or China: what matters is the ability to enhance it locally, making it born or offered from the hands of an American or Chinese partner and ensuring high reliability through a network of local services that oversee the after-sales phase. If in the consumers' evaluation of a product is the country of brand that prevails on country of manufacture, when brand and COO are compared, it is the strength of the brand to have the supremacy in the customers' evaluation.

Regarding the relevance of the brand in global marketing strategies, the firms interviewed agreed that the brand has a primary role over the COO (Vianelli et al., 2014). Investment in the brand is seen as necessary to counter the competitors that play on the positive effect of the Italian sounding. In this perspective, some companies' decisions to invest directly through the DOS are very important to be able to communicate effectively to the final market the authenticity of the brand and its COO. The DOS represents a place where companies can constantly monitor and understand the need trends of their foreign targets.

Even in sectors such as wine in which the origin should have strong impacts on the consumer, companies highlight the fundamental importance of investing in the brand to make it possible to associate it, but only secondarily, to a country of reference. The brand is seen as an indispensable tool to improve perceived quality and as the first factor in success: having a strong made in Italy is important, but it is even more important to have a strong brand that enables communicating the made-in, enhancing its positive aspects and mitigating any negative elements. The managers interviewed also consider the brand to be an important tool to link the foreign origin of the product and the need for localization as an approach to local culture.

Finally, it is interesting to note the competitive dynamics in relation to investment in the brand. In some cases, it is precisely foreign competitors that invest to associate their product with the culture of the country considered most favorable; think of the made in Italy in the case of the culture of espresso. This can be considered to be an opportunity because it allows Italian SMEs that may have limited financial resources to invest in the already fertile ground where the value of the COO is already recognized and to focus on brand differentiation in product quality (Vianelli et al., 2014).

In sum, however, it is important to underline that the relationship between the COO and its sub-components—country of manufacture, country of brand, and brand origin—is very dynamic and constantly evolving. Companies, therefore, must invest time and resources to monitor foreign market trends without ever taking anything for granted.

References

Ahmed, S. A., & D'Astous, A. (1996). Country-of-origin and brand effects: A multi-dimensional and multi-attribute study. *Journal of International Consumer Marketing, 9*(2), 93–115.

Aiello, G. (2013). *Davanti gli occhi del cliente*. Rome: Aracne.

Aiello, G., Donvito, R., Godey, B., & Pedersoli, D. (2008). An international perspective on luxury brand and country-of-origin effect. *Brand Management, 16*(5/6), 323–337.

Allred, A., Chakraborty, G., & Miller, S. J. (2000). Measuring images of developing countries: A scale development study. *Journal of Euromarketing, 8*(3), 29–49.

Alon, I., Jaffe, E., Prange, C., & Vianelli, D. (2016). *Global marketing: Contemporary theory, practice and cases*. New York: McGraw-Hill.

Andehn, M., & Berg, P. O. (2011). *Place-of-origin effects: A conceptual framework based on a literature review* (Working paper). Stockholm University School of Business. Retrieved from http://www.docstoc.com/docs/94544381/.

Andersen, O., & Kheam, L. S. (1998). Resource based theory and international growth strategies: An exploratory study. *International Business Review, 7*(2), 163–184.

Balabanis, G., & Diamantopoulos, A. (2008). Brand origin identification by consumers: A classification perspective. *Journal of International Marketing, 16*(1), 39–71.

Bertoli, G., & Resciniti, R. (Eds.). (2012). *International marketing and the country of origin effect*. Cheltenham, UK: Edward Elgar.

Bursi, T., Grappi, S., & Martinelli, E. (2012). *Effetto country of origin: Un analisi comparata a livello internazionale sul comportamento d'acquisto della clientela*. Bologna: Il Mulino.

Busacca, B., Bertoli, G., & Molteni, L. (2006). Consumatore, marca ed effetto made in: Evidenze dall'Italia e dagli Stati Uniti. *Finanza Marketing e Produzione, 2*(2), 5–32.

Chao, P. (1993). Partitioning country of origin effects: Consumer evaluation of a hybrid product. *Journal of International Business Studies, 24*(2), 291–306.

Clarke, I., Owens, M., & Ford, J. B. (2000). Integrating country of origin into global marketing strategy. *International Marketing Review, 17*(2), 114–126.

Dalli, D., & Romani, S. (2001). *Il comportamento del consumatore*. Milano: FrancoAngeli.

Dana, L. P., Etemad, H., & Wright, R. W. (1999). The impact of globalization on SMEs. *Global Focus, 11*(4), 93–105.

Dana, L. P., Etemad, H., & Wright, R. W. (2008). Toward a paradigm of symbiotic entrepreneurship. *International Journal Entrepreneurship and Small Business, 5*(2), 09–126.

Darling, J., & Arnold, D. (1988). The competitive position abroad of products and marketing practices of the United States, Japan, and selected European countries. *Journal of Consumer Marketing, 59*(1), 61–68.

de Luca, P. (2015). (a cura di). *Le relazioni tra innovazione e innovazione e internazionalizzazione. Percorsi di ricerca e casi aziendali*, Università di Trieste: ed EUT.

de Luca, P., & Pegan, G. (2013). La percezione dei prodotti agro-alimentari made in Italy nel mercato Usa: primi risultati di una ricerca netnografica. In G. Aiello (Ed.), *Davanti agli occhi del cliente. Branding e retailing del Made in Italy nel mondo* (pp. 215–234). Roma: Aracne.

de Luca, P., & Pegan, G. (2014). The coffee shop and customer experience: A study of the U.S. market. In F. Musso & E. Druica (Eds.), *Handbook of research on retailer-consumer relationship development* (pp. 173–196). Hershey, PA: IGI.

de Luca, P., Pegan, G., & Fazio, M. (2015). Innovazioni di canale nell'arredamento made in Italy. In P. de Luca (Ed.), *Le relazioni tra innovazione e innovazione e internazionalizzazione. Percorsi di ricerca e casi aziendali* (pp. 150–171), Università degli Studi di Trieste: EUT ed.

Donovan, R. J., & Rossiter, J. R. (1982). Store atmosphere: An environmental psychology approach. *Journal of Retailing, 58*, 34–57.

Edelman Earned Brand. (2018). Brand take a stand. Retrieved from: https://www.edelman.com/sites/g/files/aatuss191/files/2018-10/2018_Edelman_Earned_Brand_Global_Report.pdf

Golinelli, G. (Ed.). (2012). *Patrimonio culturale e creazione di valore. Verso nuovi percorsi*. Bologna: CEDAM.

Hamzaoui, L., & Merunka, D. (2006). The impact of country of design and country of manufacture on consumer perceptions of bi-national products' quality: An empirical model based on the concept of fit. *Journal of Consumer Marketing, 23*(3), 145–155.

Hamzaoui, L., Merunka, D., & Bartikowski, E. (2011). Brand origin and country of manufacture influences on brand equity and the moderating role of brand typicality. *Journal of Business Research, 64*, 973–978.

Han, C. M. (1989). Country image: Halo or summary construct? *Journal of Marketing Research, 26* (May), 222–229.

Han, C. M., & Terpstra, V. (1988). Country of origin effects for uni-national and bi-national products. *Journal of International Business Studies, 16*(4), 235–256.

Harun, A., Wahid, A. N., Mohammad, O., & Ignatius, J. (2011). The concept of culture of brand origin (COBO). A new paradigm in the evaluation of origin effect. *International Journal of Academic Research in Business and Social Sciences, 1*(3), 282–290.

Hirschman, E. C., & Holbrook, M. B. (1982). Hedonic consumption: Emerging concepts, methods and propositions. *Journal of Marketing, 46*, 92–101. https://doi.org/10.2307/1251707.

Hui, M. K., & Zhou, L. (2003). Country of manufacture effects for known brands. *European Journal of Marketing, 37*(1/2), 133–153.

Hutchinson, J., & Alba, J. (1991). Ignoring irrelevant information: Situational determinants of consumers learning. *Journal of Consumer Research, 18*, 325–346.

Insch, A., & Florek, M. (2009). Prevalence of country of origin association on the supermarket shelf. *International Journal of Retail and Distribution Management, 37*(5), 453–471.

Kapferer, J. N., & Thoening, J. C. (1991). *La marca.* Milan: Guerini e Associati.

Keller, K. L. (2003). *Building, measuring and managing brand equity.* New York: Prentice Hall.

Khanna, T., Palepu, K. G., & Bullock, R. J. (2010). *Winning in emerging markets: A road map for strategy and execution.* Boston: Harvard Business Press.

Kotler, P. (1973). Atmospherics as a marketing tool. *Journal of Retailing, 49*, 48–64.

Kotler, P., Hermawan, K., & Iwan, S. (2017). *Marketing 4.0. Dal tradizionale al digitale.* Milano: Hoepli.

Kotler, P., Kartajaya, H., & Setiawan, I. (2010). *Marketing 3.0: From products to customers to the human spirit.* New Delhi: Times.

Li, F., & Shooshtari, N. H. (2003). Brand naming in China: Sociolinguistics implications. *Multinational Business Review, 11*(3), 3–22.

Lim, K., & O'Cass, A. (2001). Consumer brand classifications: An assessment of culture-of-origin versus country-of-origin. *Journal of Product and Brand Management, 10*(2), 120–136.

Machleit, K. A., Eroglu, S., & Powell Mantel, S. (2000). Perceived retail crowding and shopping satisfaction: What modifies this relationship? *Journal of Consumer Psychology, 9*, 29–42. https://doi.org/10.1207/s15327663jcp0901_3.

Marino, V., & Mainolfi, G. (2010). Made in Italy e country branding: strategie di marca per il sistema Italia. *Esperienze d'impresa, 17.*

Marino, V., & Mainolfi, G. (2013). *Country brand management.* Milano: Egea.

Markman, A., & Ross, B. (2003). Category use and category learning. *Psychological Bulletin, 129* (4), 592–613.

Oberecker, E. M., & Diamantopoulos, A. (2011). Consumers' emotional bonds with foreign countries: Does consumer affinity affect behavioral intentions? *Journal of Marketing, 19*(2), 45–72.

Olivero, N., & Russo, V. (2013). *Psicologia dei consumi.* Milano: McGraw Hil.

O'Shaughnessy, J., & O'Shaughnessy, N. J. (2000). Treating the nation as a brand: Some neglected issues. *Journal of Macromarketing, 20*(56), 56–64.

Papadopoulos, N., & Heslop, L. A. (1993). *Product and country images: Research and strategy.* New York: Haworth Press.

Pastore, A., Ricotta, F., & Giraldi, A. (2011). Innovare l'offerta attraverso le caratteristiche estrinseche del prodotto. Il ruolo creativo del country of origin. In L. Pilotti (Ed.), *Creatività innovazione e territorio. Ecosistemi del valore per la competizione globale* (pp. 629–650). Bologna: Il Mulino.

Pegan, G., & de Luca, P. (2015). Innovation and internationalisation: Evidences from the Italian furniture industry. *International Journal of Management Cases, 17*(4), 188–207.

Pegan, G., de Luca P., & dal Pont M. (2015). Innovazione di business e adattamento al mercato: il caso Luxottica in Asia. In P. de Luca (Ed.), *Le relazioni tra innovazione e innovazione e internazionalizzazione. Percorsi di ricerca e casi aziendali* (pp. 106–123). Università degli Studi di Trieste: EUT ed.

Pegan, G., & Vianelli, D. (2013). Il ruolo degli importatori nella valorizzazione del country of origin: un'indagine qualitativa sul vino italiano nel mercato statunitense. In *Atti del X Convegno Annuale della SIM—Società Italiana di Marketing*. Milano.

Pegan, G., & Vianelli, D. (2016). L'identità territoriale come risorsa per creare valore nei mercati esteri. Una ricerca qualitativa sul ruolo della distribuzione nel comparto del Prosecco in USA. In M. R. Napolitano & V. Marino (Eds.), *Cultural Heritage e Made in Italy. Casi ed esperienze di marketing internazionale* (pp. 297–325). Napoli: Editoriale Scientifica.

Pine, J. B., II, & Gilmore, J. H. (1999). *The experience economy*. Boston: Harvard Business School Press.

Roth, K. P., & Diamantopoulos, A. (2009). Advancing the country image construct. *Journal of Business Research, 62*, 726–740.

Roth, M. S., & Romeo, J. B. (1992). Matching product category and country image perception: A framework for managing country-of-origin effects. *Journal of International Business Studies, 23*(3), 477–497.

Samiee, S. (1994). Consumer evaluation of products in a global market. *International Business Studies, 25*(3), 579–604.

Samiee, S. (2010). Advancing the country image construct—A commentary essay. *Journal of Business Research, 63*, 442–445.

Samiee, S., Shimp, T. A., & Sharma, S. (2005). Brand origin recognition accuracy: Its antecedents and consumers' cognitive limitations. *Journal of International Business Studies, 364*, 379–397.

Sawhney, M., Wolcott, R. C., & Arroniz, I. (2006). The 12 different ways for companies to innovate. *Sloan Management Review, 47*(3), 28–34.

Semprini, A. (1996). *La marca*. Milan: Lupetti Editore.

Smith, S., & Wheeler, J. (2002). *Managing the customer experience: Turning customers into advocates*. Harlow, UK: Prentice Hall.

Solomon, M., Bamossy, G., Askegaard, S., & Hogg, M. K. (2006). *Consumer behaviour. A European perspective*. London: Prentice Hall.

Srinivasan, N., Jain, S. C., & Sikand, K. (2004). An experimental study of two dimensions of country-of-origin (manufacturing country and branding country) using intrinsic and extrinsic cues. *International Business Review, 13*(1), 65–82.

Thakor, M. V., & Kohli, C. S. (1996). Brand origin: Conceptualization and review. *Journal of Consumer Marketing, 13*(3), 27–42.

Thakor, M. V., & Lavack, A. M. (2003). Effect of perceived brand origin association on consumer perceptions of quality. *Journal of Product and Brand Management, 12*(6), 394–407.

Tse, D., & Gorn, G. (1993). An experiment on the salience of country of origin in the era of global brands. *Journal of International Marketing, 1*(1), 57–76.

Ulgado, F. (2002). Country of origin effects on e-commerce. *Journal of American Academy of Business, 2*(1), 250–253.

Usunier, J. C. (2011). The shift from manufacturing to brand origin: Suggestions for improving COO relevance. *International Marketing Review, 28*(5), 486–496.

Usunier, J. C., & Cestre, G. (2007). Product ethnicity: Revisiting the match between products and countries. *Journal of International Marketing, 15*(3), 32–72.

Verlegh, P. W. J., & Steenkamp, J. B. E. M. (1999). A review and meta-analysis of country of origin research. *Journal of Economic Psychology, 20*(5), 521–546.

Vianelli, D., de Luca, P., & Bortoluzzi, G. (2012). Distribution channel governance and value of made in Italy products in the Chinese market. In G. Bertoli & R. Resciniti (Eds.), *International marketing and the country of origin effect* (pp. 133–150). Cheltenham, UK: Edward Elgar.

Vianelli, D., de Luca, P., & Pegan, G. (2012). *Modalità d'entrata e scelte distributive del made in Italy in Cina*. Milan: Franco Angeli.

Vianelli, D., & Pegan, G. (2014). Made in Italy brands in the US and China: Does country of origin matter? *Journal of Euromarketing, 23*(1 & 2), 57–73.

Vianelli, D., Pegan, G., & Micoli, C. (2014, September 18–19). Dal country of origin al country of brand: Quali sfide per le imprese del made in Italy? In *Atti del XI convegno annuale SIMktg: Food marketing: Mercati, filiere, sostenibilità e strategie di marca* (pp. 1–6). Rome: SIM.

Wall, M., Liefeld, J., & Heslop, L. (1991). Impact of country of origin cues on consumer judgments in multi-cue situations: A covariance analysis. *Journal of the Academy of Marketing Science, 19* (1), 105–113.

Wright, R. W., & Dana, L. P. (2003). Changing Paradigms of International Entrepreneurship Strategy. *Journal of International Entrepreneurship, 1*, 135–152.

Yin, R. K. (2011). *Qualitative research from start to finish*. New York: Guilford Press.

Chapter 6
The Role of Country of Origin in Foreign Retailers' Strategies

Abstract The success of companies in foreign markets depends not only on how they enter and manage international distribution channels but also on their ability to influence the choices of retailers that include products from domestic and foreign companies in their assortments. The role of retailers, in fact, is fundamental because they constitute the link with final consumers and can decide whether to place products in their portfolios. An empirical analysis was carried out in the US market. The main aim of the analysis reported in this chapter was to investigate the influences of the COO on retailers' choices to determine the product portfolios in their stores. In addition, a comparison was made among three countries of origin: made in Italy, made in China, and made in USA. The relationship between attention to the COO and the store experience was also investigated. Finally, this study focused on the impacts of the COO in connection with the Italian-sounding phenomena to understand how US retailers deal with the alternative between a real COO and a COO based on the foreign-sounding brand.

6.1 Introduction

Marketing functions are not only played by producers: the entire environment, including wholesalers and retailers, has impacts on perceptions of brand value. For this reason, it is important to consider retailers as part of the marketing system. Good management of all relationships, in this case with retailers, can in fact significantly affect the profitability of companies. To efficiently leverage retailing contracts, therefore, manufacturers have to study the behaviors of these intermediaries, understand their needs, and create synergies based on mutual benefits.

In recent years, markets have become dynamic, changeable, and globalized: brands from emerging countries are entering foreign markets with new products whose price advantages are hardly attainable for Western companies. Differentiation is complex, especially in industries where the products are homogeneous, and innovation is limited. For these reasons, manufacturers have to act in different

---

This chapter was written by D. Vianelli and M. Balzano.

© Springer Nature Switzerland AG 2020

G. Pegan et al., *International Marketing Strategy*, International Series in Advanced Management Studies, https://doi.org/10.1007/978-3-030-33588-5_6

ways. They not only have to develop marketing strategies to target foreign consumers, but they also have to deal with retailers, for example, to leverage the COO of their products. The role of retailers is fundamental because they constitute the link with final consumers and can decide whether to place products in their portfolios. In fact, a positive COO can significantly influence the image of products, communicating value for money, performance, quality, and reliability to both retail buyers and consumers (Reardon, Vianelli, & Miller, 2017).

Focusing on the origin of products can serve as a way to strengthen the brand value and brand loyalty. In fact, the COO presents an extrinsic, emotional cue that can become part of the brand strategy and positioning of companies entering foreign markets, especially in the case of premium and high-involvement products. For these products, emotional differentiation is a source of value that, if recognized by consumers and retailers, generates higher margins and more sales.

When retailers select products to display in their assortments, they implicitly decide what will and what will not appear on their shelves, giving them the power to create a barrier between product suppliers and end consumers. Furthermore, they have the power to decide to maintain relationships with foreign manufacturers or give them up in favor of other suppliers, sometimes from other countries. Communicating a positive COO associated with quality and value for money thus can not only influence purchase intention but also create the basis for long-term manufacturer–retail buyer supply relationships (Reardon et al., 2017). For this reason, it is important to interpret retailers' behavior and analyze their choices from a COO perspective.

In this chapter, an ad hoc research is presented to gain greater awareness of how retailers perceive the COO variable in the purchasing process and how this value is managed. Most of the analysis, particularly the quantitative analysis, was carried out in the US market, but relevant examples of the COO in the retailing context of other countries such as China were also included in the analysis. In the quantitative analysis, the sample of almost 200 retailers, reported in Table 6.1, included retailers of different sizes and in industries such as food, furniture, and fashion in which the COO plays a significant role in consumers' and retailers' choices.

The main goal of the data collection process was to examine the effects of the COO from a holistic perspective and to investigate the actual influences of the COO on retailers' choices to determine the product portfolios in their stores. In addition, a comparison was made of perceptions of products with three COOs: made in Italy, made in China, and made in USA. Furthermore, the relationship between attention to the COO and the store experience was also investigated. Finally, this study focused on comparisons between perceptions of real COOs and foreign-sounding US brands. To understand how retailers deal with these alternatives, Italian-sounding brands were taken into consideration due to their diffusion in the US market.

Table 6.1 Sample characteristics

Industry (NAICS)	Valid N = 196	# of stores	Valid N = 180
442—Furniture	39 (19.9%)	Under 10 stores	55 (30.6%)
443—Electronics and appliances	8 (4.3%)	11–50 stores	30 (16.7%)
444—Building materials and garden supplies	6 (3.1%)	51–200 stores	28 (15.6%)
445—Food and beverages	46 (23.5%)	201–500 stores	23 (12.8%)
446—Health and personal care	4 (2%)	501–1000 stores	12 (6.7%)
448—Clothing	54 (27.6%)	1001–2000 stores	12 (6.7%)
451—Sporting goods	7 (3.6%)	Over 2000 stores	11 (6.1%)
452—General merchandise	24 (12.2%)		
453—Miscellaneous	6 (3.1%)		
454—Non-store retail	2 (1%)		
Nonresponse	9 (4.4%)		25 (12%)

Source: Table compiled by authors

6.2 Focus on Retailers

The success of domestic companies in foreign markets is affected by more than their choices about entry modes described in previous chapters. The capabilities of companies to influence retailers' choices may also be crucial. Although it may be argued that retailers are naturally segregated to the function of intermediaries, it is worth pointing out that they are an essential component in the chain that links the producers to the final buyers of products.

The COO effect is one of the most debated topics in the international marketing literature (Alon, Jaffe, Prange, & Vianelli, 2016). As pointed out in the first chapter, the contemporary literature does not provide a common, generally accepted framework of retailers' behavior in relationship to the COO. In recent years, the main focus of the academic literature has been on final customers, while intermediaries' perceptions of the origins of products have been considered to be a marginal part of the background.

Retailers play the role of gatekeepers: their behaviors substantially impact the market and the buying choices ultimately made by customers. Indeed, if retailers decide not to insert items in their assortments, individual customers probably will have neither access to those products nor available information to access them at reasonable prices. It, therefore, becomes important to highlight the possible influences and the actual impacts of the COO on retailers' choices to determine their portfolios of products. In fact, retailers can substantially determine the performance of companies, in particular, foreign firms that have lower market awareness than domestic companies.

In this scenario whose complexity is increasing over time, having a good awareness of the behavioral models that drive the choices of retailers can present a competitive advantage for manufacturers relative to others in the same industry. In fact, retailers are able to manage worldwide and everyday large flows of stocks and accept or reject putting items in their portfolios of products, selecting what is available to consumer markets. In other words, if retailers refuse to include specific items in their assortments of products, it is a significant barrier to producers desiring to enter new markets.

However, it is not easy to determine whether and to which extent the choices of retailers impact the choices of final customers. Although it might be argued that retailers usually try to align their portfolio preferences with their costumers' choices, the decision-making process of retailers can be driven by several factors often ignored by final users of products. For this reason, it is important to analyze what factors affect retailers' choices in order to form the basis for a behavioral model from the perspective of the COO effect.

6.3 Influences of the Country of Origin on Retailer Buyers' Decisions

The human mind is broadly defined as a set of cognitive faculties. Its decision processes take into consideration a multitude of key factors and conduct heuristic evaluations. Ceteris paribus, the COO may be a driver in the final choices of retailers, but unlike consumers, retailers' main goal in creating their assortments is to maximize their turnover and the gross margin return on their investments.

Turnover depends on prices and sales volume, so the COO is an important cue to be taken into consideration in the following cases:

- If the COO increases the value perceptions of the product or service, allowing the retailer to increase the final price.
- If the COO is relevant to product or service differentiation, thus affecting consumer preferences and satisfaction and, thereby, leading to higher retailers' sales.
- If the COO can reinforce the store image affecting the attractiveness of the store and improve the experiential dimension of the shopping experience.

At the same time, margins depend on the costs of the goods sold and the efficiency of the transaction process. Consequently, the following aspects of the marketing channel have to be considered:

- If the higher price paid by the retail buyer to the manufacturer of a product or service with a strong COO can be compensated by with a higher sell-out price.
- If the COO is taken into consideration in supply chain decisions and has impacts on the efficiency of the supply chain.

In Fig. 6.1, it is possible to identify the main dimensions involved in the relationship between the COO and the retailers.

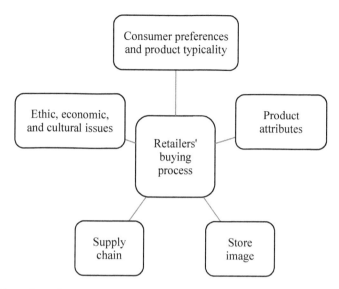

Fig. 6.1 Dimensions of the country of origin in the analysis of retailers' buying behavior. Source: Authors' own figure

6.3.1 Consumer Preferences and Product Typicality

It is well established in the literature that retailers compose their assortments taking into consideration consumer preferences (Levy, Weitz, & Grewal, 2019). Matching the requests and tastes of consumers can affect store loyalty and customer satisfaction and increase the number of store visits, thus improving the sales volume. Final customers tend to classify products according to ex ante mental structures based on their previous experience. They often rely on their previous ideas concerning the quality of specific products of a particular country and extend these ideas to other items from the same country (Hong & Wyer, 1989). Product typicality has been defined as "the degree to which an instance is a good example of a category" (Yi & Gray, 1996). In other words, a product can be considered to be "typical" of its COO if it can be matched and directly linked to that specific country. Aboulnasr (2006) concluded that the COO effect influences the choices of many end users of items because they rely on some characteristics associated with a country and extend them to any product directly related to that country. For this reason, it is important to understand whether retailers experience the same effect of typicality as consumers. More specifically, the theory of Hong and Wyer (1989) provides an additional step: the more product typicality is linked to a country, the more human minds associate the key characteristics of that country with its products. If we consider that consumers use the COO as a heuristic to determine preferences, retail buyers may directly appeal to these preferences by buying goods from countries that consumers prefer (Reardon et al., 2017). For example, retailers in China know that some Chinese consumers like European products, even in the food industry that is

Fig. 6.2 Country of origin in a Chinese store. Source: Authors' own figure

culturally distant from Western culture, and that France is one of the more appreciated European countries. For this reason, the presence of French products is
highlighted in stores. For example, in Fig. 6.2, the French COO is clearly pointed
out by the biscuit brand Lu. In this case, "made in France" is used as a direct appeal
to consumers' COO cues.

Managers and policy makers can take great advantage of the positive relationship
between product typicality and retail buyers' intention to buy and develop ad hoc
strategies to successfully penetrate foreign markets and develop long-term relationships with distributors. If retail buyers' purchase intentions increase when products
fit the stereotype of the COO, export managers can influence the probability that
retail buyers will stock brands in their portfolios by developing marketing strategies
and operative actions that reinforce the match between particular product categories
and the COO. Successful approaches by manufacturers can include:

- Investing in relationships with retail buyers to make them aware that if consumers
  associate the product with its category, they will view a brand more favorably.
- Supporting retailers' marketing strategies to strengthen the match of consumers'
  perceptions of the COO and the typicality of the product.

Marketing strategies that can enhance perceptions of product typicality can be
developed through:

- Advertising that emphasizes the origin of the product and creates a match
  between the product category and the COO.
- Packaging that evokes colors, images, and language related to the products
  typical of a specific country.
- Product labelling with information about the COO of the product.
- In-store marketing strategies developed with retailers to create a store experience
  that enhances the winning relationship between the COO and the product
  category.

- Collaboration with trade organizations and other institutions that promote a particular country and its products in foreign markets to reinforce the image of the COO in business-to-consumer and business-to-business trade fairs and events.

Typicality has different impacts for high- and low-involvement goods. In the first case, the consumer is looking for more information, and the decision-making process is longer. The consumer or, in our case, the retailer making decisions about its assortment makes decisions more rationally and evaluates all the product characteristics, not only the COO. In contrast, for products with lower involvement, the COO can influence the buying process more because the consumer's decision-making process is more emotionally based, and less time is dedicated to buying these products. Nevertheless, Ahmed, Johnson, Yang, Fatt, Teng, and Boon (2004) found that the COO is an influencing variable for low-involvement goods, but its impacts are weakened when extrinsic cues such as price and brand are taken into consideration.

6.3.2 Product Attributes

As pointed out in Fig. 6.1, consumer preferences for product origin are not the only variable taken into consideration by retail buyers, which may use the COO in multiple ways depending on their goals or considerations. Indeed, we can suppose that theories underlying the COO effect can also be applied to retail buyers, which may use COO cues as a heuristic to categorize quality, price, and other product attributes just as consumers do. More specifically, there is a significant relationship between COO perceptions and their potential influences on risk attitudes, product evaluations, and buying intention. Thus, to create appealing assortments, retail buyers might use the COO both as a direct appeal to consumers' desires and a heuristic in their own decision-making process.

First, it is worth analyzing whether cue utilization theory, described in the first chapter, can also be applied to retailers' decision-making process. Based on this theory, when intrinsic cues are not available, consumers rely heavily or exclusively on extrinsic cues (Magnusson, Westjohn, & Zdravkovic, 2011) such as price, brand, and COO (Olson & Jacoby, 1972). Extrinsic cues such as COO allow individuals, in this case, retailers, to reduce cognitive demands and expedite the decision-making process when other information is not present.

Second, the halo effect and the summary construct model, described in the first chapter, can be useful to describe retailers' decision-making process. In fact, when the degree of familiarity with a specific product is low—in other words, its intrinsic factors are not available—the country's image and key attributes are automatically transferred to the item considered (the halo model). Conversely, if the level of perceived familiarity with a specific country is high, then each item from that country is considered with the same main attributes of its COO (the summary construct model).

6.3.3   Store Image

Another variable that can be taken into consideration in relation to retail buyers is the COO's contribution to reinforcing the store image, in particular, the product assortment and the shopping experience. In fact, experiential marketing in the retailing context, especially for premium products that require congruence between product selection and store image, can have significant relevance to moving the consumer along the purchase process due to the satisfactory shopping experience.

Over the decades, retailing research has established the pivotal role of store image management (Baker, Parasuraman, Grewal, & Voss, 2002; Shankar, Inman, Mantrala, Kelley, & Rizley, 2011). Research has also suggested an interdependency between the store environment and the consumer's evaluation of the store (Titus & Everett, 1995) and has analyzed how various combinations of design, ambient, and social factors in the store environment influence consumers' inferences about merchandise and service quality and thereby the store image (Baker et al., 2002; Reardon, Miller, & Coe, 2011). This influence can also be determined by the COO that characterizes the store environment.

6.3.4   Supply Chain Management

The analysis of supply chain management can be seen from different perspectives. The first one is related to the length of the channel. When the distribution channel is long, the manufacturer faces the issue of price escalation. Table 6.2 presents the case of a coffee company selling in a domestic market and the USA. The price in the foreign market increases significantly (+40.3%) when the company has to use different intermediaries to penetrate foreign countries, even if they give up part of the manufacturer margin (50% in the USA versus 70% in the domestic market). The higher price has to be justified, and the COO can be an emotional cue that creates higher value and justifies a higher price to retailers and, consequently, final consumers.

The problem of price escalation in the supply chain is not the only issue that can be related to the COO. In fact, the country where retail buyers source a product can affect the efficiency and efficacy of the buying process. Retailers use a significant number of decision criteria to select a supplier (i.e., a manufacturer) from among the many potential vendors. In this context, as pointed out by Reardon et al. (2017), retailers can use the COO as a useful cue to categorize countries, thus simplifying the complex decision-making process in relation to not only consumers but also supply chain management in general. In fact, time is scarce for retail buyers' to manage store operations and for consumers to make decisions, so they are likely to use heuristics to simplify decision making, speeding the process and decreasing research costs. For example, a buyer might perceive certain countries as less inefficient in the supply chain, hence impacting the performance of the retail business. Many different

Table 6.2 Price escalation of an Italian company selling to the USA

	Italy Domestic channel with retailer (*Manufacturer margin: +70%*)	USA Foreign channel with importer and retailer (*Manufacturer margin: +50%*)
Manufacturer's cost	**5.00**	**5.00**
Manufacturer's margin (%)	+70%	+50%
Manufacturer's margin ($)	3.5	2.5
= Manufacturer's price	8.50	7.50
+ Insurance, shipping cost, export documentation (2%)	–	0.15
= Landed cost	–	7.65
+ Tariff (20%)	–	1.53
= Importer's cost	–	9.18
+ Importer's margin (30% on cost)	–	2.75
= Wholesaler's cost	–	–
+ Wholesaler's margin (30% on cost)	–	–
= Retailer's cost	8.50	11.93
+ Retailer's margin (40% on cost)	3.40	4.77
= Consumer's cost (=retailer's price)	11.90	16.70
Price escalation over domestic		**+40.34%**

Source: Adapted from Alon et al. (2016)

scholars have emphasized that customers tend to prefer products from their own country over other countries and to favor brands from developed countries over emerging countries. The main factors affecting such choices have been identified as commercial barriers, economic stability, and higher levels of risk in less developed countries, as well as physic distance, which can affect the quality of the relationships between sellers and buyers (Alon et al., 2016). All of these factors can be included in the definition of the macro COO. Retailers also can consider these factors in their decision-making process, especially when they take into consideration the influences of the macro and micro dimensions of the COO (macro- and microimage) on the perceived quality of products and the efficacy and efficiency of commercial transactions.

6.3.5   Ethical, Cultural, and Economic Issues for Retailers

From another point of view, in light of recent developments related to food scarcity, product safety issues, and sustainability, COO cues have become an increasingly significant topic to many people worldwide. While COO cues were long considered to be a marginal variable by many consumers, rapid, recent environmental changes have raised awareness of the importance of this factor in the context of globalization. The salience of the COO is shared across fields from ethical debates to the economical approaches of companies. Furthermore, between consumers and companies, we find the figure of the retailer examining the different alternatives from the previous step of the supply chain (producers) and deciding what main criteria drive its own choices. We maintain that the COO of products is a critical variable in retailers' decisions for various reasons.

From an ethical perspective, a fair retailer should care about offering complete information and transparency to its clients. It has to be clear about from where the products in its assortment come. At the same time, good knowledge of the offerings from different COOs can give a competitive advantage over competitors and contractual leverage with suppliers (manufacturers). Furthermore, important issues in ethical debates are related to ethnocentric behavior (Shrimp & Sharma, 1987), as well as the sentiments of cosmopolitanism (Hannerz, 1990), nationalism (Keillor, Hult, Erffmeyer, & Barbakus, 1996), and animosity, especially against certain countries (Klein, Ettenson, & Morris, 1998). The term *ethnocentrism* (Shimp, 1984) refers to consumers' beliefs "about the appropriateness, indeed morality, of purchasing foreign-made products" (Shrimp & Sharma, 1987, p. 280). Retail buyers are expected to be more rational than consumers. Nevertheless, non-ethnocentric consumers consider it important to evaluate foreign products based on objective information such as product quality (Brodowsky, 1998), even while the attitudes and choices of highly ethnocentric consumers are influenced by emotional, moral, and economical motives (Suh & Kwon, 2002). The same behavior can be found in retailers if we hypothesize an analogy with consumers. In addition, the academic literature has demonstrated that cosmopolitanism has an important role in its predictive power for foreign product purchases (Riefler & Diamantopoulos, 2009). The cosmopolitan attitude can be defined as willingness to "entail relationships to a plurality of cultures understood as distinctive entities" and to "include a stance toward the diversity itself, toward the coexistence of cultures in the individual experience" (Hannerz, 1990, p. 239). Cosmopolitan consumers actively consume cultural differences (Caldwell, Blackwell, & Tulloch, 2006; Thompson & Tambyah, 1999; Yoon, Cannon, & Yaprak, 1996) and manifest empathy and interest in other cultures, revealing a distinct ethical orientation toward selfless, worldliness, and communitarianism (Skrbis, Gavin, & Woodward, 2004). Similarly, this openness toward other cultures, strengthened by the globalization process (Cannon & Yaprak, 2002), can be found in retailers that tend to appreciate and insert in their assortment products typical of foreign countries.

An antecedent of consumer ethnocentrism is the sentiment of national identity, defined as "the set of meanings owned by a given culture that sets it apart from other

Fig. 6.3 National identity
and patriotism in the product
assortment of a Chinese
retailer. Source: Authors'
own figure

cultures" (Keillor et al., 1996: p. 58). A strong sense of national uniqueness is manifest when people identify themselves with the religious, historical, cultural, and social aspects of their country (Keillor et al., 1996), exhibiting a feeling of belonging that can significantly involve their general behavior through giving cultural significance to their overall experiences (Arnold & Wallendorf, 1994; Thelen & Honeycutt, 2004) and influencing the purchase experience. For example, in an analysis of Chinese consumers, Ishii (2009) concluded that patriotism is a component of ethnocentrism. For retailers, it is possible to predict love for the country and national values, making the sentiment of national identification a strong predictor of domestic product purchases in the creation of store assortments. For example, the product assortment sold in the store of a famous Chinese retailer is exclusively made of Chinese brands whose clothes state "proud to be Chinese," as seen in Fig. 6.3. This approach is a clear way to create value by taking advantage of the sentiments of patriotism and national identity.

Considering retailers' behavior, domestic product purchasing can be realized by focusing on products from local producers or, where the COO can influence the brand value, buying local products with foreign-sounding brands. Especially in some countries such as the USA and China, foreign-sounding products are widely diffused, so it is interesting to investigate the purchasing behavior and preferences of local retailers in relation to these brands. For example, in Fig. 6.4 it is possible to see the example of Stella® Cheese, where different types of US cheese are presented under the Italian-sounding name Stella, which is a domestically produced version of Italian cheese.

Fig. 6.4 Italian-sounding brands in a US supermarket. Source: Authors' own figure

6.4   Purchasing Behavior and Country of Origin: An Analysis of US Retailers

Working with the sample described in Table 6.1 in the beginning of this chapter, US retailers were first asked to provide an assessment of the images of three distinct COO: the USA, Italy, and China. The USA was included in the analysis of US retailers because it was their domestic country. Italy has a wide manufacturing base with diverse product offerings, and its COO perceptions are extremely favorable for some products and unfavorable for others. Furthermore, Italian-sounding products are diffused throughout the world. China is an example of a value product maker with cheap products and weak COO.

In this evaluation, US retailers were asked to take into consideration aspects linked to the general image of the country (the macro image) and its manufacturing production (the micro image). The survey distinguished between the variables of the country of manufacture and the country of brand, highlighting the possible differences in perceptions of goods actually produced in a particular country or simply by a brand from that particular country. The actual purchase intent of retailers was also assessed by proposing different hypothetical product combinations based on the country and brand of origin and the relationships of consumer attention to the COO and product typicality. Furthermore, an in-depth analysis of store image and COO was conducted. Finally, the phenomenon of foreign-sounding brands was considered to analyze retailers' buying behavior for foreign products and domestic products with foreign-sounding brands. In the following sections, the main results are presented, distinguishing between value products and premium products, because it can be supposed that the COO can play different roles in value creation depending on the product characteristics.

The construct measures for this research were mostly derived from the literature (Table 6.3). Three dimensions of the COO were drawn from the literature: macro country image (Martin & Eroglu, 1993; Hamzaoui-Essoussi, Merunka, & Bartikowski, 2011), micro country image (Pappu, Quester, & Cooksey, 2007), and country-of-brand image (Balabanis & Diamantopoulos, 2011). The concept of product typicality was drawn from Loken and Ward (1990), and operational measures of store image from Reardon et al. (2011). Consumer attention to the COO was measured based on four items introduced and tested in our empirical research. Both high (premium) and low (value) involvement products were included, and the endogenous variable of intent to trial a product from Italy was introduced. To evaluate whether the relative difference between the two variables (low and high involvement products) was captured for each respondent, a t-test of them was conducted as a simple manipulation check to ensure that the respondents interpreted them differently ($t = 4.342$, df $= 204$, $p < 0.001$) (Reardon et al., 2017).

The reliability of the construct scales was established using composite reliability found to have values of "respectable or better"—that is, greater than 0.70 (De Vellis, 2003). The scales were examined with confirmatory factor analysis (CFA) using LISREL 8 (Jöreskog & Sörbom, 1993) and the R package Lavaan. The results indicated an acceptable fit of the CFA model, and some standard operational measures suggested that the model had acceptable explanatory power and fit.

Considering the empirical analysis, different methods were used. Some data are presented using descriptive statistics for all three countries. The hypotheses were tested using structural equation modelling, but the data on China were not significant, so only US and Italian products were included in the analysis.

6.5   Country Macro Image

To understand the reasons underlying retailers' COO effect analysis, we consider it to be interesting to look at their general ideas about different countries. In fact, even before evaluating products from certain countries, people build mental constructs to evaluate the countries themselves. In other words, ex ante experience leads to the association of some attributes to a country. As pointed out, the data collected concerned the USA, Italy, and China, which were expected to have completely different COO perceptions in the sample of US retailers. Figure 6.5 exhibits the overall judgments of these three countries as reported by retail buyers.

The sample of domestic US retailers tends to consider its own country to be economically stable (5.2/7), with high levels of industrialization (5.9/7) and technological development (6.2/7), high standards of living (5.9/7), and a good level of economic development (5.2/7). US retailers tend to consider Italy to be a relatively economically stable country (4.2/7), with good levels of industrialization (4.8/7) and technological development (4.7/7), high standards of living (5.2/7), and a fair level

Table 6.3 Construct/Items for the analysis of the influence of COO on retailers' behavior

Country macro image
(Hamzaoui-Essoussi et al., 2011; Martin & Eroglu, 1993)—Semantic Differential 7 point scale
Please describe the image you have of US/Italy/China on each of these characteristics:
    1. Economically unstable ... Economically stable
    2. Less industrialized ... Highly industrialized
    3. Low standard of living ... High standard of living
    4. Low level of technological research ... High level of technological research

Country micro image
(Pappu et al., 2007 from Nagashima, 1970–77)—Semantic Differential 7 point scale
Products made in US/Italy/China are...:
    1. Technically backward ... Technically advanced
    2. Imitative ... Innovative
    3. Unreliable ... Reliable
    4. Accessible ... High status
    5. Poor finish ... Excellent finish

Country of brand image (COB)
(Adapted from Balabanis & Diamantopoulos, 2011) Likert 7 point scale
My consumer considers brands from US/Italy/China as having...
    1. Good value for money
    2. High reliability
    3. High performance
    4. High quality

Product typicality
(Loken & Ward, 1990) Likert 7 point scale
The line of merchandise that I am responsible for is
    1. Representative of US/Italy/China
    2. Typical of US/Italy/China
    3. A good example of brands from US/Italy/China

Consumer attention to COO
Likert 7 point scale
    1. When choosing a product, my consumers first look at the made-in labelling.
    2. The country of manufacture is important to my consumers.
    3. My consumers judge products by where they are made.
    4. My consumers care about the country of origin of most of the products that I stock.

Store image
Adapted from Reardon et al., 2011)—Semantic Differential 7 pt
Please circle which best describes your planned store image.
Our store positions itself as ...
    1. Value oriented products ... Highest quality products
    2. Generic ... Up-scale atmosphere
    3. Accessible... Exclusive positioning
    4. Self-service approach... High service oriented
    5. Untrained sales personnel... Highly qualified sales personnel

Italian sounding
7 point scale (least likely.... Most likely)
Please indicate what would be the likelihood to examine/trial/purchase a PREMIUM/VALUE
Italian sounding brand (for example Frappuccino, Starbucks) made in USA by a US company for
inclusion in your line.

(continued)

Table 6.3 (continued)

Endogenous variable manipulations
7 point scale (least likely.... Most likely)
    1. Trial high involvement—how likely would you be to examine/trial/purchase a PREMIUM Italian brand made in US/Italy?
    2. Trial low involvement—how likely would you be to examine/trial/purchase a VALUE Italian brand made in US/Italy?

Source: Adapted from Reardon, Vianelli, and Miller (2017) and Vianelli et al. (2017)

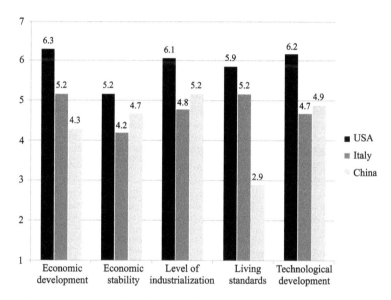

Fig. 6.5 Macro images of the USA, Italy, and China. Source: Authors' own figure

of economic development (5.2/7). In contrast, they consider China to be a country with low standards of living (2.9/7) but fair levels of industrialization (5.2/7) and technological development (4.9/7), a good degree of economic stability (4.7/7), and a medium economic development (4.3/7).

Although it is difficult to unambiguously and objectively measure each of these five variables, this simple graph (Fig. 6.5) demonstrates that all the retailers in the sample were ready to formulate judgments on these parameters. Furthermore, individuals often tend to hold similar evaluations based on subjective considerations, which leads to the conclusion that marketing scholars should study these convergences to maximize the effects of new marketing campaigns. Based on the data collected and analyzed, it is interesting to point out that there are in general more positive evaluations of the domestic country, in this case, the USA.

Products made in

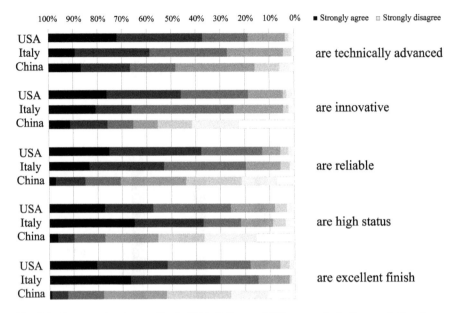

Fig. 6.6 Country micro images for the USA, Italian, and Chinese products. Source: Authors' own figure

6.6   Country Micro Image

The comparison of the different countries also considered the micro image connected to their products. In this case, the domestic country also received more positive evaluations in most of the dimensions (Fig. 6.6).

In general, products made in the USA are perceived as more technically advanced, innovative, and reliable. Nevertheless, Italian products are more appreciated for their association with high status and excellent finish. Chinese products received negative evaluations for most characteristics. When considering the products of these three countries, it is thus clear that US retailers experience the COO effect.

Taking into consideration the overall perceptions of products, it is possible to observe different attitudes toward the three countries in relation to characteristics such as high- and low-status products. As Fig. 6.6 shows, product perceptions point to significant changes in the perceived reliability, technological development, innovation, etc. if a different COO is considered.

Indeed, when transmitting the idea of a high-status product (Fig. 6.7), the COO parameter influences retailers' choices. If products come from China, retailers generally assign them to an accessible status rather than a higher status. In contrast, premium products manufactured in Italy enjoy a stable, high reputation among US retail buyers, with an average score of 5.9 of 7. Although US products have a slightly lower than average score than Italian products, US products also seem to have attributes linked to high-status perceptions.

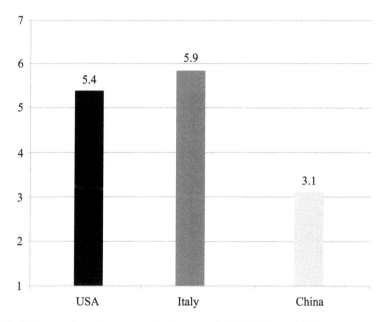

Fig. 6.7 Differences in product perceptions between the USA, Italy, and China. Source: Authors' own figure

6.7 Country-of-Brand Image

As explained throughout this book, stereotypes and heuristics can have strong influences on human behaviors. In our survey, a set of questions was dedicated to investigating the country-of-brand effect, which is one of the components of the COO and probably has the highest impact on retailers' intention to buy.

In Fig. 6.8, it can be seen that value for money is not different among the three countries, although Chinese brands on average have lower prices than US and Italian brands. The COO is strongly perceived in the analysis of the other dimensions. US and Italian products are definitely considered to have higher reliability and performance than Chinese products. This difference is especially strong when product quality is taken into consideration, with Chinese products receiving the lowest evaluations.

The analysis of the country of brand becomes especially interesting when the distinction between premium and value brands is introduced, and the country of manufacturing is taken into consideration to investigate the possibility of inclusion of the products in the retailer's assortment. As pointed out in Fig. 6.9, the COO does not play a role in the following situations:

- If a premium Italian or US brand is manufactured in China
- If a value Italian or US brand is manufactured in Italy or in China

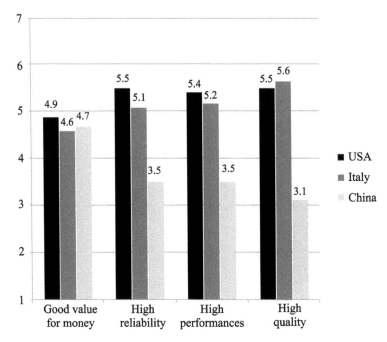

Fig. 6.8 Country of brand: attributes commonly associated with brands from the USA, Italy, and China. Source: Authors' own figure

Vice versa, the COO affects retailers' purchases in the following situations in different ways:

- Retailers are more likely to include Italian premium brands manufactured in Italy than US premium brands manufactured in Italy; the association between country of brand and country of manufacturing thus creates value for target retailers.
- If production is in the USA, retailers prefer both premium and value US brands; thus, from the empirical analysis, it seems that Italian brands tend to lose value if produced in the USA, if compared with local brands in the USA.

Another trend that can be considered to analyze is how the COO affects retail buyers' propensity to trial new products. Retailers characterized by lines of merchandise highly typical of the USA were asked if they were ready to try new Italian value products. Although their assortments are not typical of Italy, we used this way to investigate whether the COO effect influences retail buyers' decisions to trial new products to include in their assortments. Figure 6.10 clearly shows that US retail buyers who manage assortments mainly made of local products nevertheless are quite attracted to Italian value brands manufactured in both Italy and the USA (these two countries of manufacture have average scores for intention to try of 4.3 and 5.1 of 7, respectively). However, they prefer the USA as a country of manufacture. In other words, with value products, a strong COO such as made in Italy influences intention to buy, but domestic production (the USA) is preferred over foreign (Italy).

Please indicate which of the following product combinations you would be
most likely or unlikely to examine/trial/purchase for inclusion in your line.
If the brand and the company are

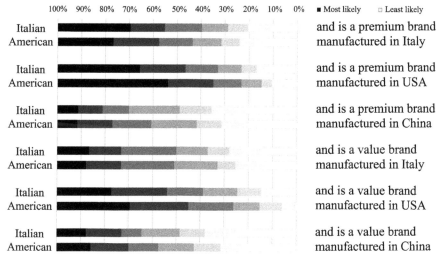

Fig. 6.9 Value and premium Italian and US brands manufactured in different countries. Source:
Authors' own figure

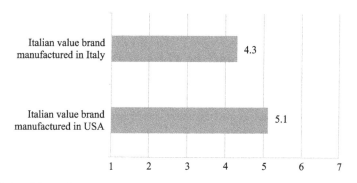

Fig. 6.10 Retail buyers' propensity to include value products. Source: Authors' own figure

This result is consistent with the literature. In fact, it was found that ceteris paribus,
people are more likely to prefer items manufactured domestically than abroad (Han,
1988). Han (1989) stated that the emotion of patriotism often plays a significant role
in buying choices and for this reason customers tend to evaluate their own country's
products more favorably than those of foreign nations. Moreover, Han (1988) found
that the effect of product evaluation bias can be offset by lower prices and other
factors that many customers may recognize as superior in specific foreign countries.
These empirical results, supported by the literature, open the door to analysis of
intention to buy foreign-sounding products instead of original foreign brands.

Fig. 6.11 Giada Casa: An Italian-sounding furniture store in China. Source: Authors' own figure

6.8   Country of Origin and the Foreign-Sounding Effect on Retailers' Propensity to Trial New Products

Although it would be fair to also consider the phenomenon of foreign-sounding products from a moral perspective, reality tells us that an increasing number of companies are adopting products that sound like they are from one country but are actually manufactured in another, particularly Italian-sounding products. This phenomenon is especially diffused in the food industry, but also in fashion and furniture many local producers and retailers are taking advantage of Italian-sounding products, as seen in Fig. 6.11 where a Chinese retailer is selling furniture under the store name "Giada."

According to a study by Assocamerestero (2018), in the global food industry, total sales of Italian-sounding products reached 90 billion euros, with a constant growth of more than 70% in the past 10 years. More specifically, the sales value of Italian products abroad is only one third that of Italian-sounding products. In US supermarkets, for example, it is common to see Italian original brands of tomato sauce such as Barilla close to US Italian-sounding brands such as Prego (Fig. 6.12).

When retailers are ready to include in their merchandise lines value brands, preferring those manufactured domestically, they can opt to characterize their

Fig. 6.12 Italian-sounding products on a supermarket shelf in the US Source: Authors' own figure

assortments with a strong foreign COO, especially if their products are typical of a specific foreign country. As pointed out in Sect. 6.6 with the case of Italian value brands manufactured in the USA, the choices made by retailers imply that they implicitly admit that there is a fit between made in Italy and some positive attributes consumers associate with products. Consequently, if Italian brands have higher attractiveness, the choice to insert brands that are not Italian but are perceived as Italian (i.e., with Italian-sounding names) can be a profitable alternative, especially for value products.

As pointed out, the standard definition suggests that the Italian-sounding phenomenon can be broadly defined as the creation by manufacturers of names, images, and colors to imitate Italian styles because Italy is often associated with a tradition of manufacturing excellence in several industries, especially food and beverages. Although it might be argued that such imitations have no real, direct connection to Italy, many foreign customers may be attracted to the appearance of these items. Similar to this phenomenon, products manufactured in Italy, linked to the machinery industry and the electronics industry, usually gain concrete benefits when they have German-sounding names.

Based on our research results, we have already pointed out that US retailers are ready to adopt Italian brands in their assortments even if the products are not manufactured in Italy. It is also interesting to analyze the impacts of this effect in connection with the Italian-sounding phenomenon to understand how US manufacturers try to exploit the potential benefits from the COO effect to increase their domestic market share. Retailers with positive domestic COO images (the USA), in

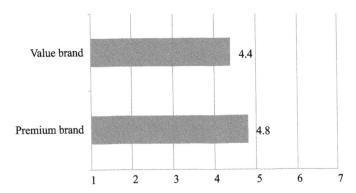

Fig. 6.13 Italian-sounding brands made in the USA by US companies: average values. Source: Authors' own figure

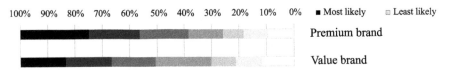

Fig. 6.14 Italian-sounding brands made in the USA by US companies: percentage values. Source: Authors' own figure

particular, might be more attracted to Italian-sounding products manufactured in the USA than value products manufactured in Italy.

Figure 6.13 presents the average results of the answers to the item "Please indicate what is the likelihood of examining/trialing/purchasing an Italian-sounding brand made in U.S.A by a U.S. company for inclusion in your line (for example, Frappuccino, Starbucks)." This question clearly addresses the Italian-sounding phenomenon to investigate whether it is true that US manufacturers and retail buyers adopt attributes usually associated with Italy by inserting products made in the USA by US companies in distribution channels with the aim to make these products more appealing to a segment of lovers of made in Italy.

The results are significant. In general, US retailers consider the possibility of including Italian-sounding products, both premium and value (4.8 and 4.4 of 7, respectively). These results mean that the probability of such inclusion is considerably high. These results are even more impressive when considering the percentages of the different answers (Fig. 6.14): in this case, it is possible to see that US retailers are most likely to insert Italian-sounding brands made in the USA in their assortments, especially for premium products.

From a marketing perspective, a significant level of awareness of the made-in concept can be a critical success factor for many domestic manufacturers because retailers seem to favorably accept local products with foreign-sounding COOs. In our analysis, the distinctiveness of a brand and its resemblance with its COO make it recognizable to the target consumers even if the product is only typical of a specific country—Italy, in our analysis—but is neither manufactured nor branded by an Italian company.

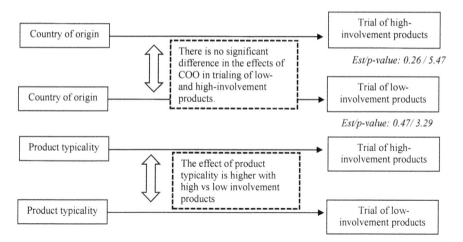

Fig. 6.15 Impacts of COO on retailers' intention to try new products. Source: Authors' own figure

6.9 Country of Origin and Intention to Buy Low- and High-Involvement Products

To carry out an in-depth analysis of the behavior of retail buyers in the choice of foreign and domestic products to include in their assortments, Italian and US products were taken into consideration, and the linkages between variables were estimated with structural equation model. More details of this analysis were published by Reardon et al. (2017).

In our analysis, summarized in Fig. 6.15, we were able to highlight that the COO has a direct effect on retail buyers' intent to try goods, with no differences between high- and low-involvement products, probably because other product characteristics are considered by retailers, weakening the relative importance of the COO in the buying process. In addition, product typicality influences intention to try foreign products with a strong COO for both high- and low-involvement goods, but the effect is stronger for high-involvement products.

This result is interesting and can be explained by the fact that when retail buyers are responsible for a specific line of an assortment or manage stores with product lines specialized in a single product category, sourcing in one country or another can make the difference in terms of perceived quality, depending on whether the product line for which they are responsible is more or less typical of the specific foreign market. The finding of a stronger effect for high-involvement products probably can be explained by retailers' perceptions that if consumers are buying premium products, different COOs can differentiate brands' image. However, for low-involvement products, even foreign-sounding products can probably satisfy final consumers, and in this case, retailers can create their assortment considering only the price variable. In addition, high-involvement products have a long buying process but can

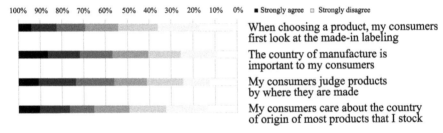

100% 90% 80% 70% 60% 50% 40% 30% 20% 10% 0%   ■ Strongly agree   ▫ Strongly disagree

When choosing a product, my consumers first look at the made-in labeling

The country of manufacture is important to my consumers

My consumers judge products by where they are made

My consumers care about the country of origin of most products that I stock

Fig. 6.16 Retailers' perceptions of consumer attention to COO. Source: Authors' own figure

guarantee higher margins to retailers, which consequently are more concerned about final consumers' evaluation of the COO.

Considering consumer attention to the COO, it is interesting to analyze retailers' perceptions. As pointed out in the literature (Berman, Evans, & Chatterjee, 2017) retail managers make decision about their product portfolio based on their expectations of consumers' choices. A further aspect to explore when studying the relationship between the COO and retail buyers' intention to buy, therefore, is their opinions on consumer attention to the COO. It is imperative to understand whether buyers change their buying strategy based on this variable.

Consumer attention to the COO was considered in the analysis as a moderating variable, and the moderating effect was relevant only for high-status products. However, as seen in Fig. 6.16, retailers generally do not seem to think that consumers give much attention to the COO. This finding can explain why there is a significant relationship only when premium/high-involvement products are taken into consideration.

6.10   Country Image, Country of Brand, and Store Image

The COO effect, as pointed out, can be analyzed from different perspectives that all can be useful to characterize perceptions of product origins that usually are not univocal. An example is represented by hybrid products (Hamzaoui & Merunka, 2006), that are not characterized by a unique COO: the country where the product is manufactured or designed and the COO of the brand can be different. From this perspective, it is also important to distinguish the country of manufacture from the country of brand (Chen et al., 2011; Thakor & Lavack, 2003; Ulgado, 2002) in the analysis, especially when considering the effect of delocalization strategies. It is also worth considering the country's image (Papadopoulos & Heslop, 1993; Pappu et al., 2007) and its different dimensions: the general image of a country (macro image) and the general image of its products (micro image). All these dimensions, as pointed out, can influence retailers when they include new products in their assortments. Considering the image of the country as a whole (country macro image) and the country-of-brand image, which is useful for product evaluation in assortment decisions, we decided to test the following hypotheses (Vianelli, Gregori, & Valta, 2017):

- Country macro image has positive impacts on retailers' intention to buy premium products (H1a) and value products (H1b).
- Country of brand (COB) has positive impacts on retailers' intention to buy premium products (H2a) and value products (H2b).

Considering consumer attention to the COO, we carried out another analysis distinguishing between country macro image and country of brand. We hypothesized that retail buyers care more about the made-in dimension when their target consumers are especially interested in this variable. Therefore:

- Consumer attention to the COO mediates country macro image (H3a) and country-of-brand image (H3b).
- Consumer attention to the COO is a mediator when considering the intention to buy premium products (H3c) and value products (H3d).

The findings reported in Table 6.4 indicate that in most cases, country macro image does not affect retailers' intention to buy. However, the country-of-brand image has strong positive impacts on retailers' intention to buy and is mediated by store image and consumer attention to the COO. However, consumer attention to the COO is a mediator when considering premium products. The model holds true when a different COO is considered for both domestic and foreign products with strong COOs, as in the case of made in Italy. Consumer attention to the COO mediates the relationship between country-of-brand image and intention to buy value products only in the case of national brands (i.e., made-in-US products).

These results suggest that foreign companies should invest in country-of-brand perceptions only if they are selling premium products to upscale retailers. In the case of value products, retailers' choice are price based, favoring national brands.

Store image was also analyzed to evaluate the link of the COO with retailers' buying decisions. In fact, store image might influence consumers' attitudes toward products, inducing a mediating effect between attitude and intention to buy. Buyers that trial high-involvement products and pay more attention to product quality, store environment, customer service, and personnel competence should carefully examine distinctive product features, including the COO. However, the relationship between COO and intention to buy is weak or nonexistent when the buyer does not care about store image, which likely is the case when considering buying value products. The following hypotheses were tested:

- Store image mediates consumer attention to the COO (H4a).
- Store image mediates consumer attention to the COO when considering intention to buy premium products (H4b).
- Store image does not mediate consumer attention to the COO when considering intention to buy value products (H4c).

The results point out that store image mediates the relationship between country-of-brand image and retailers' intention to buy. However, similarly to consumer attention to the COO, the store image is a mediator when considering premium

Table 6.4 Structural parameter estimates and goodness-of-fit indices

Hypotheses	Path	Made in Italy		Made in USA	
		Est/p value	Hypotheses results	Est/p value	Hypotheses results
H1a H1b	CMI → Buy premium CMI → Buy value	−0.11/ −0.52 0.40/ 1.85*	H1a rejected H1b supported	0.21/1.15 0.23/1.21	H1a rejected H1b rejected
H2a H2b	COB → Buy premium COB → Buy value	0.49/ 2.21** 0.43/ 1.9*	H2a supported H2b supported	0.40/3.32** 0.45/2.94**	H2a supported H2b supported
H3a H3b	CMI → ConAtt COB → ConAtt	0.16/ 1.00 0.40/ 2.34**	H3a rejected H3b supported	−0.06/−0.35 0.48/3.62**	H3a rejected H3b supported
H3c H3d	ConAtt → Buy premium ConAtt → Buy value	0.33/ 2.61** 0.17/ 1.33	H3c supported H3d rejected	0.31/2.92** 0.19/1.74*	H3c supported H3d supported
H4a	ConAtt → STO	0.64/ 7.46**	H4a supported	0.63/7.46**	H4a supported
H4b H4c	STO → Buy premium STO → Buy value	0.40/ 3.44** 0.10/ 0.85	H4b supported H4c supported	0.29/2.89** 0.09/0.90	H4b supported H4c supported
H5a H5b	CMI → (med.) Buy premium CMI → (med.) Buy value	0.15/ 0.32 0.11/ 0.98	H5a rejected H5b rejected	−0.05/−0.35 −0.04/−0.35	H5a rejected H5b rejected
H6a H6b	COB → (med) Buy premium COB → (med.) Buy value	0.36/ 2.23** 0.28/ 2.2**	H6a supported H6b supported	0.39/2.28** 0.33/3.22**	H6a supported H6b supported
		Goodness of fit statistics chi² = 232.46, 128df p = 0 RMSEA = 0.067, p = 0.025 NFI = 0.91; NNFI = 0.95; CFI = 0.96; IFI = 0.96; RFI = 0.89		Goodness of fit statistics chi² = 228.84, 128df p = 0 RMSEA = 0.069, p = 0.014 NFI = 0.90; NNFI = 0.94; CFI = 0.95; IFI = 0.95; RFI = 0.89	

products. The importance of the COO for retailers managing assortments of premium products was confirmed by another analysis we have conducted on retailers' behavior. Only retail buyers that consider their stores to be in high-positioned market segments and consequently are more oriented to premium brands than value ones (only scores more than 4 of 7 on the store image scale) were taken into consideration. The analysis considered the probability that this subsample of retailers included in their product lines brands from Italy and China with products manufactured in one of

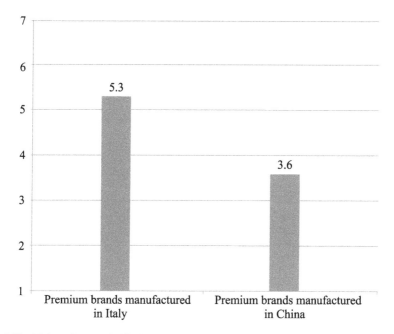

Fig. 6.17 COO preferences in highly positioned stores. Source: Authors' own figure

these two countries. As easily seen from Fig. 6.17, the COO effect seems to have considerable influence.

Indeed, ceteris paribus, the respondents that consider their stores to be highly positioned explicitly increase their attention to the COO, preferring premium brands manufactured in Italy over brands manufactured in China. On average, preferences score 5.3 of 7 for premium brands manufactured in Italy and only 3.6 of 7 for premium products manufactured in China. The noticeable difference in the two scores means that if the other variables stay constant, retailers manifest a clear preference for products manufactured in one country over another and transmit and extend the values and attributes of that specific country to products manufactured in another country. Through such behavior, it seems that retail buyers expect the COO to yield higher positioning, with the heuristic association linking the good attributes of a positive COO to brands manufactured in that country.

6.11   Conclusion

This analysis of the role of the COO effect in retailers' assortment strategies has clearly shown that the COO can affect retailers' choices. The success of companies entering foreign markets thus depends not only on the ways in which they target final consumers but also the ways in which they manage international distribution channels and their ability to influence the choices of retailers that include products of domestic and foreign companies in their assortments. Manufacturing companies must study retailers' behavior, understand their needs, and create synergies based on mutual benefits because they have a fundamental role in the link with final consumers and can decide whether to include products in their portfolios. These analysis results can inform manufacturers about the types of marketing investments they should make to create value for retailers to enhance the COO effect and convey positive perceptions of brand image to final consumers.

References

Aboulnasr, K. (2006). Country of origin effects: The role of information diagnosticity, information typicality and involvement. *Marketing Management Journal, 16*(1), 1–18.

Ahmed, Z. U., Johnson, J. P., Yang, X., Fatt, C. K., Teng, H. S., & Boon, L. C. (2004). Does country of origin matter for low-involvement products? *International Marketing Review, 21*(1), 102–120.

Alon, I., Jaffe, E., Prange, C., & Vianelli, D. (2016). *Global marketing. Contemporary theory, practice, and cases.* New York: McGraw-Hill.

Arnold, E. J., & Wallendorf, M. (1994). Market-orientated ethnography: Interpretation building and marketing strategy formulation. *Journal of Marketing Research, 31*(November), 484–504.

Assocamerestero. (2018). https://distribuzionemoderna.info/primo-piano/italian-sounding-ma-quanto-mi-costi

Baker, J., Parasuraman, A., Grewal, D., & Voss, G. B. (2002). The influence of multiple store environment cues on perceived merchandise value and patronage intentions. *Journal of Marketing, 66*(2), 120–141.

Balabanis, G., & Diamantopoulos, A. (2011). Gains and losses from the misperception of brand origin: The role of brand strength and country-of-origin image. *Journal of International Marketing, 19*(2), 95–116.

Berman, B. R., Evans, J. R., & Chatterjee, P. M. (2017). *Retail management: A strategic approach.* Harlow, Essex, UK: Pearson Education.

Brodowsky, G. H. (1998). The effects of country of design and country of assembly on beliefs about automobiles and attitudes toward buying them: A comparison between low and high ethnocentric consumers. *Journal of International Consumer Evaluative Marketing, 10*(3), 85–113.

Caldwell, M., Blackwell, K., & Tulloch, K. (2006). Cosmopolitanism as a consumer orientation: Replicating and extending prior research. *Qualitative Market Research, 9*(2), 126–139.

Cannon, H. M., & Yaprak, A. (2002). Will the real-world citizen please stand up! Many facets of cosmopolitan consumer behavior. *Journal of International Marketing, 10*(4), 30–52.

Chen, Y.-M., Su, Y.-F., & Lin, F.-J. (2011). Country-of-origin effects and antecedents of industrial brand equity. *Journal of Business Research, 64*(11), 1234–1238.

De Vellis, R. F. (2003). *Scale development: Theory and applications* (2nd ed.). Thousand Oaks, CA: Sage.

Hamzaoui, L., & Merunka, D. (2006). The impact of country of design and country of manufacture on consumer perceptions of bi-national products' quality: An empirical model based on the concept of fit. *Journal of Consumer Marketing, 23*(3), 145–155.

Hamzaoui-Essoussi, L., Merunka, D., & Bartikowski, B. (2011). Brand origin and country of manufacture influences on brand equity and the moderating role of brand typicality. *Journal of Business Research, 64*(9), 973–978.

Han, C. M. (1988). The role of consumer patriotism in the choice of domestic versus foreign products. *Journal of Advertising Research, 28*(3), 25–31.

Han, C. M. (1989). Country image: Halo or summary construct? *Journal of Marketing Research, 26* (May), 222–229.

Hannerz, U. (1990). Cosmopolitans and locals in world culture. *Theory, Culture and Society, 7*(2), 237–251.

Hong, S., & Wyer, R. (1989). Effects of country-of-origin and product-attribute information on product evaluation: An information pro-cessing perspective. *Journal of Consumer Research, 16*(2), 175–187.

Ishii, K. (2009). Nationalistic sentiments of Chinese consumers: The effects and determinants of animosity and consumer ethnocentrism. *Journal of International Consumer Marketing, 21*(4), 299–308.

Jöreskog, K., & Sörbom, D. (1993). *LISREL 8: Structural equation modeling with the SIMPLIS command language.* Chicago: Scientific Software.

Keillor, B. D., Hult, T. M., Erffmeyer, R. C., & Barbakus, E. (1996). NATID: The development and application of a National Identity Measure for use in international marketing. *Journal of International Marketing, 4*(2), 57–73.

Klein, J. G., Ettenson, R., & Morris, M. (1998). The animosity model of foreign product purchase: An empirical test in the people's Republic of China. *Journal of Marketing., 62*(1), 89–100.

Levy, M., Weitz, B. A., & Grewal, D. (2019). *Retailing management.* New York: McGraw-Hill Education.

Loken, B., & Ward, J. C. (1990). Alternative approaches to understanding the determinants of typicality. *Journal of Consumer Research, 17*(2), 111–126.

Magnusson, P., Westjohn, S. A., & Zdravkovic, S. (2011). Further clarification on how perceived brand origin affects brand attitude: A reply to Samiee and Usunier. *International Marketing Review, 28*(5), 497–507.

Martin, I. M., & Eroglu, S. (1993). Measuring a multi–dimensional construct: Country image. *Journal of Business Reviews, 28*(3), 191–210.

Nagashima, A. (1970). A comparison of Japanese and U.S. attitudes toward foreign products. *Journal of Marketing, 34*(1), 68–74.

Olson, J., & Jacoby, J. (1972). Cue utilization in the quality perception process. In *Proceedings of the Third Annual Conference of the Association for Consumer Research* (pp. 167–179). Chicago, IL: Association for Consumer Research.

Papadopoulos, N., & Heslop, L. (1993). *Product-country image: Impact and role in international marketing.* London: International Business Press.

Pappu, R., Quester, P. G., & Cooksey, R. W. (2007). Country image and consumer-based brand equity: Relationships and implications for international marketing. *Journal of International Business Studies, 38*, 726–745.

Reardon, J., Miller, C., & Coe, B. (2011). Applied scale development: Measurement of store image. *Applied Business Research, 11*(4), 85–93.

Reardon, J., Vianelli, D., & Miller, C. (2017). The effect of COO on retail buyers' propensity to trial new product. *International Marketing Review, 34*(2), 311–329.

Riefler, P., & Diamantopoulos, A. (2009). Consumer Cosmopolitanism: Review and replication of the CYMYC scale. *Journal of Business Research, 62*(4), 407–419.

Shankar, V., Inman, J. J., Mantrala, M., Kelley, E., & Rizley, R. (2011). Innovations in shopper marketing: Current insights and future research issues. *Journal of Retailing, 87*, 29–42.

Shimp, T. A. (1984). Consumer ethnocentrism: The concept and a preliminary empirical test. In T. C. Kinnear (Ed.), *Advances in consumer research* (Vol. 11, pp. 285–290). Provo, UT: Association for Consumer Research.

Shrimp, T. A., & Sharma, S. (1987). Consumer ethnocentrism: Construction and validation of the CETSCALE. *Journal of Marketing Research, 24*(August), 280–289.

Skrbis, Z., Gavin, K., & Woodward, I. (2004). Locating cosmopolitanism between humanist ideal and grounded social category. *Theory, Culture & Society, 21*(6), 115–136.

Suh, T., & Kwon, I. G. (2002). Globalization and reluctant buyers. *International Marketing Review, 19*(6), 663–680.

Thakor, M. V., & Lavack, A. (2003). Effect of perceived brand origin associations on consumer perception of quality. *Journal of Product and Brand Management, 12*(6), 394–407.

Thelen, S. T., & Honeycutt, E. D., Jr. (2004). Assessing National Identity in Russia between generations using the National Identity Scale. *Journal of International Marketing, 12*(2), 58–81.

Thompson, C. J., & Tambyah S. K. (1999). Trying to be cosmopolitan. *Journal of Consumer Research, 26*(3), 214–241.

Titus, P. A., & Everett, P. B. (1995). The consumer retail search process: A conceptual model and research agenda. *Journal of the Academy of Marketing Science, 23*(2), 106–119.

Ulgado, F. (2002). Country of origin effects on E-commerce. *Journal of American Academy of Business, 2*(1), 250–253.

Vianelli, D., Gregori, M., & Valta, M. (2017). The mediating effect of store image and consumer attention to COO on the relationship of COO and retailers' intention to buy. *Marketing di successo. Imprese, enti e persone* (pp. 1–6). ISBN:978–88–907662-9-9.

Yi, Y., & Gray, K. C. (1996). Revisiting attribute diagnosticity in the context of product typicality. *Psychology and Marketing, 13*, 605–633.

Yoon, S.-J., Cannon, H. M., & Yaprak, A. (1996). Evaluating the CYMYC cosmopolitanism scale on Korean consumers. *Advances in International Marketing, 2*, 211–232.

Chapter 7
Online Channels and the Country of Origin

Abstract This chapter focuses on the relationship between the online channel and the COO. Indeed, the online channel is rapidly assuming a growing role in the international distribution, but studies on the relationships between the online channel and the COO not yet seem to have a consolidated framework. In the context of marketing channels, it is relevant to explore what role the online channel can play in creating value for the market through the COO. The online channel allows conveying the COO and has become crucial to presence and competitiveness in international markets. Moreover, the COO can serve as an important research reference for online customers who recognize the value of certain products. Against this background, this chapter explores the current and potential roles of the online channel in the valorization of the COO from the perspective of omnichannels, taking into account specific experiences in international markets. In particular, based on abundant data collected through a digital method approach, this study primarily considers the US food and beverage sector, including olive oil and wine products.

7.1 Introduction

Today, the online channel is rapidly assuming a growing role in the system of marketing channels, but studies on the relationships between the online channel and the COO do not yet seem to have developed a consolidated framework. The online channel refers to transactions of products (goods and services) carried out through computer networks (the Internet or other systems). The new frontiers of the online channel are mobile commerce and social commerce. The former is based on the use of mobile devices (e.g., smartphones, tablets, and smart speakers), while the latter is based on social networks (e.g., Facebook, YouTube, Twitter, and Google+). Both continue to evolve rapidly. Furthermore, the online channel can refer to both business-to-business and business-to-consumer areas along with the entire marketing channels system, from entry modes to the final market, as highlighted in Fig. 1.2. The growing diffusion of connectivity can be considered to be the biggest revolution in marketing history (Kotler, Kartajaya, & Setiawan, 2017).

© Springer Nature Switzerland AG 2020

G. Pegan et al., *International Marketing Strategy*, International Series in Advanced Management Studies, https://doi.org/10.1007/978-3-030-33588-5_7

Table 7.1 Key digital statistical indicators (millions), 2017

	Total population	Internet users	Active social media users	Unique mobile users	Active mobile social users
World	7593	4021	3196	5135	2958
China	1412	751	911	1396	911
Europe	843	674	448	1106	376
USA	327	287	230	341	200
Italy	59	43	34	76	30

Source: Adapted from secondary data (WeAreSocial & Hootsuite 2018)

The available data show a rapidly developing phenomenon in whose current picture, however, destined to quickly change, indicates that more half (4.021 billion) of the world's population of more than 7.5 billion are Internet users (WeAreSocial & Hootsuite, 2018). Penetration rates differ across the multiple media available (e.g., the Internet, mobile, and social media) and across countries (Table 7.1; WeAreSocial & Hootsuite, 2018).

Regarding Internet users (WeAreSocial & Hootsuite, 2018), at the end of 2017, China had the most, with more than 751 million Internet users, approximately 19% of the world's total. China is followed by Europe, with 674 million users (17%), and the USA, with 287 million users (7%). Italy and its 43 million Internet users account for about 1% of the total. These countries maintain the same relative positions in active social media users, unique mobile users, and active mobile social users (WeAreSocial & Hootsuite, 2018).

In this context, advanced Internet connection technologies have made e-commerce extremely pervasive. Consumers can quickly obtain information and purchase products (physical and digital goods and services) on online channels. In addition to offline channels, today's companies can—or must—stay in touch with customers through different online modes managed and integrated into complex marketing channels using different devices and platforms, such as the Internet, mobile devices (e.g., smartphones, tablets, and smart speakers) and social networks (e.g., Facebook, YouTube, Twitter, Instagram, Pinterest, and Google+). At the same time, even for online companies, it has become important to maintain and develop relationships with customers through physical channels.

Against this background, what role can the online channel play in perceptions of the COO? The online channel allows conveying the COO and has become crucial to presence and competitiveness in international markets. Moreover, the COO can serve as an important research reference for online customers who recognize the value of certain products. This chapter explores the current and potential roles of the online channel in the valorization of the COO from the perspective of omnichannels, taking into account specific experiences and cases in international markets.

7.2   Connectivity and Interactions in Marketing Channels

In such an interconnected world, there is a clear need to integrate online and offline elements in the commercial environment to offer a complete customer experience and successfully compete at the global level (Kotler et al., 2017). Integration is necessary because in a world increasingly pervaded by technology, the human element can present a significant tool for differentiation. Moreover, from a multi-touch point perspective, interactions that take place offline can be made richer and more engaging through the use of an appropriate high-tech interface.

Regarding the first perspective on the role of the human element, consider how the human factor plays a fundamental role in many fields dominated by online channels, such as tourism and hospitality. In the world outside the home, the Internet is increasingly central. According to TradeLab research performed for Host Milano (2016), consumers use the web for various reasons: to get information on premises (61.5% of the interviewees), check price levels (69%), examine other consumers' comments (60.3%), and learn about the types of cuisine and offerings (59.9%). However, the most important element, in final judgments about tourism and hospitality services, is still the human factor—that is, the welcome, smile, and kindness from staff members—that is, the priority for 45.3% of the participants (Host Milano, 2016). The offline channel can also offer advantages for digital-born companies. In an interesting example, Amazon has an idea to create a network of supermarkets for both offline shopping and collecting online purchases (Green, 2017). In Project Como, Amazon intends to expand into the large-scale retail trade, following the same path as opening its first physical store, a bookshop, in Seattle in 2015 (Griswold, 2016).

The digital dimension, in turn, has an important role in offline interactions, especially in supporting the customer experience through greater customer involvement. For example, multimedia kiosks and interactive windows have enriched the customer experience for years. Today, the Internet-of-Things technologies and new analysis tools such as analytics and big data have enabled developing new forms of customer interactions, of which there are already many examples.

In the agri-food sector, new potentials have opened up with blockchain technology (Bellini, 2017), which guarantees the safe traceability of the supply chain to both protect health and enhance the COO. Think, for example, about the problem of Italian sounding and unfair competition for made-in-Italy products and the potential of blockchain technology to guarantee products' authenticity. In the fashion sector, new technologies have contributed to increasingly rich, interactive customer experiences. The use of quick response code readers and radio-frequency identification readers that recognize garments can provide information on the available models, sizes, and colors, significantly expanding the showroom. Mirrors in fitting rooms can be sophisticated touch displays, allowing personalized navigation of collections. In the most advanced cases, superimposition of product images on customers' silhouettes permits them to virtually wear as much as they want, even if the items are not physically available at the point of sale.

New technologies such as multimedia, augmented reality (AR), virtual reality (VR), three-dimensional scanning, and interactive touch displays, among other innovative tools, assist companies in developing original business storytelling solutions, especially those that effectively enhance the COO. Two examples in the valorization of the COO through storytelling come from the Mad in Italy and Italia Caput Mundi projects (Cito & Paolo, 2014). For some years, Milc, an Italian communication agency, has promoted made in Italy through two connected projects. First, Mad in Italy aims to promote valuable entrepreneurial ideas made in Italy by giving space to all those who have stories to tell about their "mad" ideas for enterprises. Second, Milc initiated Italia Caput Mundi in collaboration with the University of Siena's master in business communication program and under the patronage of the Ministry of Economic Development. Launched in 2014, this initiative supports and raises awareness of the excellence of Italian industry. Crossing the data in the Fortis-Corradini dossier shows that Italy has a wealth of thousands of companies and ranks first in production in 250 product categories. In the AIDA database (*Analisi Informatizzata Delle Aziende Italiane*), which has information on more than 700,000 companies, Italia Caput Mundi has identified more than 4500 Italian companies with turnover of more than five million euros in the 250 product categories in which Italy holds world leadership. These product categories are collected in an interactive map of excellence on Italia Caput Mundi's website and illustrated with a series of video clips made by Milc in collaboration with Moviement HD and Ninja Marketing. The videos are posted on the YouTube MadeinItaly channel, and the series can be followed on social networks with the official hashtag #ItaliacaputMundi.

The potential of new technologies is fully exploited in the case of so-called d-commerce, a term used "to delineate companies that create digital products and services that are marketed, delivered, and supported completely online. Examples include ebooks, online education, virtual membership communities, downloadable software, web hosting, and software as a service" (Digital Commerce Institute, 2018). Technological innovation, therefore, is revolutionizing the ways in which users buy and consume amid the growing integration of traditional trade and online commerce. Such integration is becoming an important key factor in the distribution sector, where speed and quality are the significant differentiating elements. Following this logic, we are witnessing the growing phenomenon of alliances between large digital-born operators and traditional operators.

7.3 Omnichannel Retailing: Toward the "Phygital" Era

In a short time, increasing connectivity has the led to the strong, rapid development of online channels, followed by a rapid shift to multichannels, and, more recently, the emergence of the new frontier of omnichannel perspectives (Brynjolfsson, Hu, & Rahman, 2013; Gao & Su, 2017; UPS, 2016). Devices provide the means to access channels, and each type of device affords different channels. Some channels are

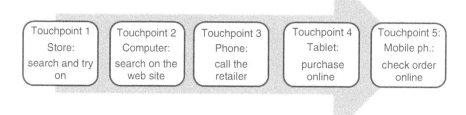

Fig. 7.1 Example of the customer journey through different touchpoints (Source: Authors' own figure)

device specific (e.g., mobile websites and mobile and smartwatch apps), while other channels function across multiple devices. In this new context, the customer journey becomes a succession of interactions through different touchpoints of contact between users and organizations (Fig. 7.1). With the rapidly growing connectivity in today's world, the consumer journey from product discovery to purchase often involves multiple channels. The customer can search for products at the point of sale and then place an order online, and vice versa, the customer can search for product information online and then complete the purchase at a physical point of sale (Brynjolfsson et al., 2013; Gao & Su, 2017).

A kind of ubiquity emerges due to the ability to be in multiple places at the same time. This phenomenon is also known as store-to-web and web-to-store shopping. In the first type, the customer preselects items at the point of sale and then buys them online with the certainty of making the right purchase in terms of size, color, and other factors. In the second type of purchasing behavior, the consumer searches for information online before making a purchase in a physical store. According to the available data (Ahmed & Kumar, 2015), 84% of consumers appreciate new technologies, but not all use them in the same way. For example, 43% of Internet users use their mobile phones while shopping at the point of sale, and 70% of consumers go to physical stores to see items before buying online (Ahmed & Kumar, 2015). Consumers have become cross-channel consumers and can operate in opportunistic ways. They thus expect retailers to make additional channels available to them during their shopping trips. In summary, consumers can search for information online, check feedback on social networks, and decide to buy at the point of sale or on any other available channel (Ahmed & Kumar, 2015). These consumers prefer the so-called anytime, anywhere, any device (ATAWAD) approach to purchasing (Digitas Study & Wincor-Nixdorf, 2012).

Amid these rapid technological and commercial evolutions, various channel players such as manufacturers and distributors are moving from traditional, single-channel, and multichannel sales systems to more complex, integrated omnichannel models (UPS, 2016). The concept of the omnichannel, which first appeared about

Fig. 7.2 Omnichannel
perspective (Source:
Authors' own figure)

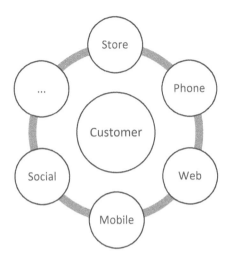

2010, remains somewhat unclear in the literature (Beck & Rygl, 2015; Klaus, 2013; Rigby, 2011). The first contributions on the subject state that the omnichannel consumer who uses multiple channels simultaneously in an integrated logic represents an evolution of the multichannel consumer who uses multiple parallel channels (Parker & Hand, 2009). Omnichannel retailing is described as "an integrated sales experience that melds the advantages of physical stores with the information-rich experience of online shopping" (Rigby, 2011, p. 4). Others have defined omniretailing "as a coordinated multichannel offering that provides a seamless experience when using all of the retailer's shopping channels" (Levy et al., 2013, p. 67). Omnichannel models use both physical and online channels to deliver a seamless shopping experience (Lazaris & Vrechopoulos, 2014). The integrated, continuous shopping experience based on the use of all channels, therefore, has strong relevance in marketing management.

Omnichannel marketing refers to strategies that integrate all the available channels to create an ongoing shopping experience that increases convenience, engagement, and commitment throughout the customer journey (Bettucci, D'Amato, Perego, & Pozzoli, 2015). This evolution requires the use of new platforms (retail transaction interface platforms) capable of conveying to consumers offerings from businesses (manufacturers and distributors) independent of the channel visited. A common circular representation of the omnichannel world (Fig. 7.2) overcomes the parallel channel management vision typical of the multichannel model.

The case of Alibaba, which began in e-commerce, is an interesting example of this new model (Bassi, 2018). In 1999, Jack Ma founded Alibaba Group Holding Ltd. in China. It began with e-commerce activities and, in less than 20 years, became an articulated system of companies operating on a wide scale in the digital field. Listed on the Wall Street Stock Exchange in 2014, Alibaba is worth more than $450 billion and is Amazon's main competitor. Both are racing to reach half of $1 trillion in capitalization. In 2014, to extend its business offline, Alibaba acquired a stake in the

Intime Retail Group Co. department store chain, which markets luxury brands in the Chinese market. Alibaba's goal is to expand its sales from online to physical stores. With a recent offer for further companies acquisition, Alibaba is expected to increase its stake in the retail chain to around 74% (Bassi, 2018). Alibaba, Auchan Retail S.A., and Ruentex Group have announced a strategic alliance combining their experiences in offline and online commerce to build a new food store in China. This venture follows the logic of new, increasingly integrated retail from a "phygital" perspective. Once the transaction is complete, the three groups should hold 36.16, 36.18, and 4.67% of capital in Sun Art, respectively. Their interest in Sun Art is easily understandable: it is a leader in multiformat food distribution in China, and in mid-2017, it operated in 29 locations with hundreds of hypermarkets, superstores, and local shops with a total area of approximately 12 million square meters (Bertoletti, 2017). The strategic alliance aims to redesign future trade through digital transformation. Physical shops are fundamental to the consumer journey, but in the digital age, they must be enriched by services enabled by new digital technologies with different applications. By completely combining the online and offline channels, it is possible to offer consumers an original, pleasant, personalized, integrated, quality shopping experience in the new phygital retail (Bertoletti, 2017).

In contrast, Ikea, born, and spread offline with huge stores in extra-urban areas, has recently aimed to open new, smaller urban stores and to develop online shopping. Ikea has experimented with new sales formats and services to meet the needs of digital consumers in urban areas less interested in car travel to large, crowded shopping areas in suburban areas. One such experiment is a pop-up store, a new distribution format characterized by smaller stores in city centers offering services with higher added value such as consulting, refined environments, entertainment initiatives, and greater integration of offline and online channels. An even-newer initiative consists of temporary stores. Since the first test carried out at Expo 2015 in Milan, Ikea has opened temporary stores in Rome, Stockholm, Madrid, Paris, London, and New York. Another field of investment of Ikea is omnichannel retailing, which marks a radical change oriented toward services such as home delivery, assembly, and online shopping. This model is also on the rise in countries such as Italy, which saw a 36% increase in sales of Ikea in 2017 from 2016, with 105 million visits to the Ikea online site. For example, the development of the Ikea Locker, a 24-hour locker for the self-service collection of products ordered online, goes in this direction.

The retail world clearly is undergoing a profound transformation. On one hand, large groups of commercial distribution chains are developing online sales by exploiting the presence of physical stores and knowledge of consumers (e.g., on-site withdrawal and convenient time management). On the other hand, large groups of online sites are acquiring retail chains to offer the same types of services (e.g., see, touch, and try products and socialize in the offline world).

A conceivable future business environment mixes online and offline channels so that it is not easy to distinguish between them. In this logic, systematic monitoring of various initiatives and the user experience is necessary to improve commercial results (online and offline), customer relationships, and perceptions of brand quality.

The operating world is already talking about a phygital (figital or digical) world in which the online and offline dimensions are integrated to offer new customer journey experiences. This term expresses the shopping experience of a consumer who is increasingly connected, is suspended between the physical and digital realities, and uses multiple devices at the different stages of purchases. Consider some examples of phygital solutions such as the integration of social media into the offline customer experience, addition of VR and AR elements to see items not physically in the room, and physical creation of digital things (Astound, 2018):

– Integration of social media into the offline customer experience: A Brazilian store has linked offline and online customer experiences. Customers visiting a physical store can see digital images of how many people have liked items online. This physical connection gives consumers opportunities to obtain more information as they make purchases. This level of social and physical engagement has allowed the store to create more connections with its audience and to demonstrate how the physical and nonphysical worlds can connect.
– Addition of VR and AR elements to see items not physically in the room: A real estate company, for example, can easily create AR within a home to show how it would look with the client's furniture or new furniture. A cosmetics company can create AR experiences that show how different products can best meet consumers' needs.
– Physical creation of digital things: Nike, for example, created a phygital experience with its maker's experience. The Nike By You Studio allows customers to create a shoe from the shell of a simple Nike X white or classic shoe. The process takes 45–90 min and produces a completely unique sneaker.

These are only a few examples of the use of phygital retail from marketing through the sales funnel to the buying experience. Today's technology makes much possible, and bridging the gap between the online and offline worlds can capture and retain potential customers' attention. How can the digital be integrated into the physical marketing experience?

Today, online channels, bolstered by increasing connectivity, stand as privileged places to build and oversee relationships with existing and potential customers to create value. Considering the significant growth of the online channel, it is necessary to understand how companies can enhance and manage the product–territory link in extremely fluid environments with high connectivity and weak geographical and cultural boundaries. Comprehending the new customer journey, therefore, is also needed (Kotler et al., 2017).

7.3.1   The Customer Journey in the Omnichannel Perspective

In marketing channels, the customer path is traditionally analyzed through models that view the point of sale as the essential point of contact in the subsequent phases. The point of sale has gradually been reinterpreted as a point of purchase, a meeting point, and a point of entertainment. All these interpretations are characterized by physical contact. These models try to explain how a message is created with the aim to involve and take the consumer through a series of steps to purchase and consumption. The consumer moves through a series of cognitive (awareness and learning) and affective (feeling, interest, and desire) phases that ends with a behavioral phase or an act (the purchase).

In the new digital context, traditional models such as the AIDA model (attention, interest, desire, and action) and the Four As (aware, attitude, act, and act again) no longer seem adequate to capture the evolution of the customer journey. Digital channels have already changed significantly in the short time of their development, necessitating reinterpretation of the buying process. Initially, the web was static. It allowed navigation between pages and hypertexts, but users could not change the status or the information on sites. There was no possibility of participation except by email. In fact, websites were mainly showcases for one-way communication of their contents and offerings. Today, with the web passing through several new generations of development from web 2.0 and 3.0 to web 4.0 (Kotler et al., 2017), the Internet offers increasing interactions between sites and users of blogs, forums, wikis, chats, social networks, and sharing platforms such as YouTube. Real-time interactivity has become dominant and redesigned the relationships among the channel actors.

These developments have resulted in several new phenomena: co-production by the customer, social word of mouth, and new roles of virtual communities, among others. For example, opinions on companies, products, and brands are strongly influenced by the communities to which customers belong. Many personal decisions become social decisions through the phenomenon of social word-of-mouth, characterized by the high number of people reached and the high speed of diffusion. In the era of connectivity, loyalty, traditionally assessed by customer retention and repurchase, is also measured by willingness to recommend brands to other people (advocacy). Today, customers actively connect with each other to build ask-and-advocate relationships. Consumers establish an active dialogue among themselves that is added to and integrated with the dialogue between customers and companies. These customers generate new shared content.

Given these different interactive connection modes, the path customers go through when evaluating products and brands needs to be rethought. A possible extension comes from the proposed Five As (Kotler et al., 2017). This extension of previous models of customer journey highlights that, in these new conditions, the final goal is to move the client from awareness to advocacy through the following steps: aware, appeal, ask, act, and advocate (Kotler et al., 2017). In the era of digital connectivity, the initial attractiveness of products and brands is strongly influenced by online touchpoints, especially search engines and particularly Google, and by the communities surrounding customers that influence their final opinions.

Regarding the COO in search engines, made in Italy by Google Arts and Culture is an interesting example. As mentioned, search engines are the main touchpoint of reference. With this consideration, the Made in Italy online initiative was developed jointly by the Google Cultural Institute, Italian-Latin Government, and Italian

Chamber of Commerce. In January 2014, the Google Cultural Institute launched an online project to promote made in Italy and enhance many Italian products using virtual showroom technology (Google Arts & Culture, 2019). Exploring images, artifacts, and other content on a site edited by Unioncamere and the Ministry of Agriculture, Food, and Forestry allows discovering 168 stories and insights into the significant realities of made in Italy in the fields of artistic craftsmanship and the production of denominations of origin.

In general, loyalty is enriched by willingness to recommend products and brands to others. To understand brands, customers actively connect with each other in ask-and-advocate relationships, expressing satisfaction and dissatisfaction and continuously influencing initial attractiveness. In advocacy, three main sources of influence interact: external influence, others' influence, and personal influence (Kotler et al., 2017).

External influence comes from sources not connected to the customer, such as corporate marketing communication, brand advertising, salespeople, and customer service. External influence, therefore, is largely controllable and manageable by the company while interacting with other variables to affect individual customers. It is the first form of influence to manifest itself and thus stimulates conversation, which, in turn, generate the influence of others. The influence of others comes from those in the more or less narrow external environment close to the customer, primarily family members, friends, acquaintances, communities of belonging, and social networking contacts. At this level, the roles of word of mouth, opinion leaders, and particular customer groups (e.g., young people, women, and netizens) are fundamental. Their opinions are often the most relevant influences on purchases. It is not easy for the company to control the influence of others. The marketing community oriented to this purpose can only facilitate discussions with the support of loyal customers. Personal influence from clients results from past experiences and personal interactions with the brand, which, in turn, are influenced by word of mouth (influence of others) and advertising (external influence). While taking into account individual variability, today's customers generally rely heavily on the influence of others and the outside world. Research conducted by Nielsen in 2015 revealed that 83% of the respondents in 60 countries see friends and relatives as the most reliable sources of advertising, and 66% pay attention to the opinions of others posted online (Kotler et al., 2017).

In practice, the online route is commonly represented by the conversion funnel and its three phases: top of the funnel, middle of the funnel, and bottom of the funnel. However, this model has recently been challenged by the great changes generated by connectivity and the omnichannel approach. Consequently, the model has been expanded with new steps and more complex interpretations aimed at capturing the multidimensionality of the new customer journey. The path centers on three key variables: the purchasing channels (online and offline); the touchpoints that make up the shopping experience (search engines, comparison sites, forum and social reviews, shop windows, and the opinions of friends and acquaintances); and the activation triggers, or the events guided by the brand that lead to finalization of the purchase. Consumers dealing autonomously with these three dimensions create their own personal purchasing experiences and thus new forms of relationships with the product or brand.

7.3.2 Users' and Consumers' Searches in the Online Channel

Surfing the Internet is the first step by which the user gets closer to the product or brand. Understanding online consumers' searching process is crucial to improve the Internet presence of companies and consequently the competitive position in international markets. The Internet presents different roles for customers and companies. On one hand, it provides a huge pool of data and information from which to draw. On the other hand, the Internet acts as a place where subjects can interact and communicate even in real time with other subjects. The first nature—the Internet as a pool—is enhanced by the second nature—the Internet as a place—with the set of data and information exchanged online by subjects who comment, ask, judge, interact, and leave traces.

In the Internet pool, users ask questions to search for and retrieve data and information they need. In the past, users searched directly through the URLs identifying sites. Today, users search mainly through search engines, which are the main traffic sources for websites (Jerath, Ma, & Park, 2014). Search engines help detect, plumb, and filter huge amounts of data. They have also become response engines for users. Their main purpose is not merely to discover new information and knowledge resources but, above all, to answer questions (Nielsen & Loranger, 2006). In this context, tagging has become essential and changed the ways in which users search for and find information. Tagging consists of assigning labels or keywords to identify the contents of speech.

From a managerial perspective, companies' success depends heavily on online searches using specific keywords and search results reflecting the effectiveness of company websites (Chen, Liu, & Whinston, 2009). The types and amounts of data are growing rapidly, pushed by emerging services (e.g., the Internet-of-Things and social networks). In this era of connectivity and big data, companies have to develop skills to effectively analyze and manage the large amounts of information and in the data. While born-digital companies are prepared to handle big data, traditional companies such as Italian SMEs have to learn how to gain competitive advantages (McAfee & Brynjolfsson, 2012).

To understand users' and customers' online behavior, the distinction between conscious and unconscious search queries can be useful. Internet users' conscious queries target specific problems for which users seek solutions on search engines. These queries can be made regardless of whether users know about particular products and services. For example, a user who wants to buy a bottle of wine to give on a particular occasion (a problem) goes to Google to look for various solutions, gain information, reads customer reviews, compares brands and models, and so on. In unconscious search queries, users start from current problems of which they could become aware at a later time (more or less distant) in the face of new knowledge (which transforms the question from unawareness to awareness) acquired online without looking for it. For example, while reading an article on wine in antiquity, a user discovers that wine is still produced with those ancient techniques—knowledge the user did not have previously. The user then consciously starts seeking first general information and then the specific product. Conscious search queries are served mostly by search engines (e.g., Google) and generally start with more or less formalized problems or questions, whereas unconscious queries more frequently emerge from social networks (e.g., Facebook), where interactions among users can yield unexpected outcomes.

An interesting example for the COO comes from the results of recent research aimed at supporting the internationalization process of an Italian winery (3RDPLACE, 2018). The analysis conducted over July 2016–July 2017 highlights the high competitiveness among COOs online, where the main countries of interest and conversation are France, Spain, Australia, Italy, Chile, and the USA. Regarding Italian wine, only 7% of total mentions online globally refer to Italy (66,875 mentions of Italian wine in one million total mentions of wine). For the wine sector, therefore, it seems that, at a global level, conscious searches by online users do not especially reward made in Italy, which consequently has a rather weak presence at the start of the customer journey (3RDPLACE, 2018).

Regarding information searches, some studies have proposed a classification of the intent of online user queries (Broder, 2002; Gonzalo Penela, Codina, & Rovira, 2015; Jansen, Booth, & Spink, 2008; Rose & Levinson, 2004). User intent can be defined as "the affective, cognitive, or situational goal as expressed in an interaction with a web search engine" (Jansen et al., 2008, p. 1255). User intent concerns "how the goal is expressed because the expression determines what type of resource the user desires in order to address their overall goal" (Jansen et al., 2008, p. 1255). The query then becomes a key component of the expression of intent, which is an external representation of necessity (Pirolli, 2007). Essentially, online searches reflect different sets of underlying user objectives (Rose & Levinson, 2004). Previous studies have proposed the following main classification: informational, navigational, and transactional intent (Table 7.2).

Informational intent seeks to locate contents on a specific topic to meet searchers' information needs, which can be very precise or very vague. Users' goal is to learn something by reading and viewing web pages with their data, text, documents, and multimedia content. Navigational intent aims to reach a website, whether a specific webpage or hub site. Users may search for specific websites or simply think that particular websites might exist. Transactional intent localizes websites to perform web-mediated activities, such as purchasing, downloading, and playing games.[1]

Searching for information online does not necessarily happen in the same way for all types of products. An interesting perspective on this theme considers the

---

[1]To understand user intent, it is necessary to analyse the online keywords users employ to identify problems and their solutions. Several tools such as Google Trends, SEMrush, AdWords, and Keyword.io can be used. The starting point is always the list of words that identifies the categories of problems or needs and products (goods or services) useful for the desired purpose. To understand user intent, therefore, it is necessary to consider search engine results pages (SERP), or the pages on which search engine results are displayed. Along with user intent, observing SERPs reveals the type of content that best meets users' needs (e.g., text, images, videos, and infographics) and areas not yet covered by online offerings.

Table 7.2 Online users' search intent: A classification

Search intent	Users' goal	Examples
Informational	To learn something by reading or viewing web pages	Data, text, documents, and multimedia
Navigational	To go to a specific known website	Webpages, sites, and hub sites
Transactional	To obtain specific products or services	Purchase of products, execution of online applications, and downloads of multimedia

Sources: Adapted from Rose and Levinson (2004) and Jansen et al. (2008)

differences between experience and search goods (Nelson, 1970). Credence goods have recently been added to the previous types of goods (Nakayama, Sutcliffe, & Wan, 2010). Search goods are products (goods or services) whose specific attributes make them easy to evaluate before purchase and consumption. Examples include consumer electronics, cars, and (especially branded) consumer products that are easy to identify before purchase. Conversely, experience goods can be evaluated only after being purchased and used, as in the case of many personal services (e.g., restaurants, hairdressers, and travel). Credence goods are difficult or impossible to evaluate even after purchase and consumption. The consumer may lack the appropriate knowledge or technical training to properly assess these goods. Examples include well-being and health professional services, products, and services such as supplements and vitamins. The assignment of products to these three categories is complex and influenced by subjective evaluations. The COO attribute can transform a product in a product or brand search because its origin can aid customers' evaluations before purchase and consumption. This transformation in the product/brand search category could partly explain the Italian-sounding phenomenon.

Although the Internet serves as an important information source for experience, search, and credence goods, the types of information the consumer seeks and, therefore, the ways in which the consumer searches and makes choices differ across various product types (Huang, Lurie, & Mitra, 2009). The search mode can vary in the amount of time spent per page, number of pages searched, likelihood of free riding (i.e., buying from a seller other than the primary source of product information), and relative importance of interactive mechanisms (e.g., consumer opinions and suggestions). Previous research, for example, has shown that differences in the perceived ability to assess the product quality of search and experience goods before purchase are less pronounced in online shopping than the traditional channel (Huang et al., 2009). Examination of browsing data has shown that consumers spend similar amounts of time searching online for information on search and experience goods (Huang et al., 2009).

However, significant differences have been found in the ways in which consumers look for and buy these types of products online. In particular, experience goods require greater search depth (more time spent per product page), while search goods demand greater search width (more pages of produced views). Free riding is more common for search goods than experience goods. In addition, mechanisms used by Internet vendors to enable consumers to learn from others' experiences (e.g., consumer feedback, third-party recommendations, and multimedia presentations) increase the time spent on websites and the likelihood of buying more for experience than search goods. Empirical research has shown that the classification of search and experience goods (Nelson, 1970) provides important insights into consumer behavior in online environments.

7.4   Valorization of Fashion Made in Italy in Online Retailing

The development of online shopping has also significantly influenced the fashion clothing sector in both general factors and factors more directly connected to the specific sector (Afuah & Tucci, 2001; Vescovi, 2007). Here some results of a study are presented on Italian fashion in foreign markets (Pegan, Vianelli, & de Luca, 2013). In the fashion clothing sector, many Italian brands in recent years have added online stores to traditional single-brand stores such as Armani and Diesel that often rely on specialized companies to take advantage of the long tail (Anderson, 2006; Brynjolfsson, Hu, & Simester, 2011). Able to make a much wider range of products available online than offline, virtual shops can derive economic advantages even from niche products not convenient for traditional distribution. Focusing on the luxury segment[2] which includes the Italian products with the highest symbolic value, it should be noted that the first online stores were released in 2009 to serve the markets of North America and some European countries (UK, France, and Germany; Table 7.3).

The decision to develop online stores for the North American market is due, on one hand, to the widespread use of the Internet in this area and, on the other hand, to the greater predisposition of US consumers to use the Internet as both an information tool and a commercial channel (WeAreSocial & Hootsuite, 2018). In the omnichannel logic, the Internet, in fact, is the main source of information for the final consumer who consults it to obtain information on products, prices, and distribution even when intending to make an offline purchase. From the data collected, comparing the volume of research carried out in the USA with that on the same brand in Italy in the same period, we gain an interesting indicator (Table 7.4). As can be seen, there is a certain disparity in the fame of the different brands: for example, for every study on Ferragamo carried out in Italy, one is also carried out in the USA (100.7), but for Prada and Armani, the ratio is halved (54.4), indicating that for every two searches in Italy, one is carried out in the USA. For the other brands, this ratio is even lower.

---

[2]The information presented here was taken from a broader study on the fashion clothing sector analyzing the balance sheet data of 40 companies and groups in the sector with about 100 brands (excluding groups and companies that, although of Italian origin, have long since been acquired by foreign groups; Pegan et al., 2013).

Table 7.3 Websites and online stores of the main Italian luxury brands (year of opening of the online store)

Brand	Website	Year of opening of the online shop by country			
		USA	Europe	Japan	China
Armani	www.emporioarmani.com	2007	2008	2009	2010
	www.armaniexchange.com	2007	–	–	–
	www.armani.com	2011	2011	2011	2011
Valentino	www.valentino.com	2008	2009	2009	–
Brunello Cucinelli	www.brunellocucinelli.com	2011	2011	2011	–
Dolce & Gabbana	www.dolcegabbana.com	2011	2011	2011	2011
Tod's	www.tods.com	2012	–	–	–
Alberta Ferretti	www.albertaferretti.com	2010	2010	2010	–
Moschino	www.moschino.com	2009	2009	–	–
Salvatore Ferragamo	www.salvatoreferragamo.com	2009	2009	–	–
Prada	www.prada.com	2010	2010	2010	2010
	www.miumiu.com	2011	2011	2011	2011

Source: Translated from Pegan et al. (2013)

Table 7.4 Online brand searches in the USA and Italy

Brand	Online search in USA/in Italy (2010–2012) × 100
Salvatore Ferragamo	100.7
Armani	54.4
Prada	43.3
Tod's	31.3
Loro Piana	28.9
Valentino	24.2
Dolce & Gabbana	20.1
Brunello Cucinelli	19.7
Moschino	8.5
Media	36.8

Source: Pegan et al. (2013)

The turnover achieved by the online single-brand stores is still quite limited compared to the total turnover of e-commerce (Yoox Group, 2012). Internet sales are not only made through single-brand stores. In fact, many companies (Armani, Ferragamo, Cucinelli, Moschino, Alberta Ferretti, Dolce e Gabbana, and Valentino) now sell their products through the portals of multi-brand retailers specializing in online sales of branded clothing and accessories, such as Yoox and The Level Group. Many also ship their products overseas, guaranteeing an agile channel of access to the US market.

In conclusion, Italian fashion clothing companies seem to have moved adequately, overseeing the new online sales channel and exploiting the full potential of the Internet to communicate the brand image, promote sales, and highlight the

COO. Companies in higher segments seem to be capable not only of exploiting the network as a new sales channel but, above all, of interpreting the new communication paradigms imposed by the web. In principle, online business can also be a driver of international development by small- and medium-sized companies in the fashion sector and of enhancement of the relative COO. In most cases analyzed, however, these companies seem to use the Internet not so much as a tool to penetrate new markets but, rather, as an opportunity to consolidate their positions in markets where their brand is known, and their business is already developed in traditional channels. Consequently, in this sector, the online channel seems not to have yet manifested its potential to enhance the COO, which has been left to other channels of distribution and international communication.

7.5 Online Channel and Country of Origin: Cases in the Food and Beverage Sector

The potential of the online channel in foreign markets to enhance the COO, as in the case of made in Italy, has been addressed in several contributions (Vianelli, de Luca, & Pegan, 2012). However, even today, many companies, particularly SMEs in the agro-food sector, are not adequately structured for the online channel. Despite the great potential of online initiatives for agro-food companies, some studies (Canavari, Pignatti, Spadoni, & Sprundel, 2009) have uncovered strategies oriented toward communication purposes, such as websites used as showcase sites rather than virtual stores for online sales (Carlucci, De Gennaro, Roselli, & Seccia, 2014).

For made in Italy, the food and beverage sector is of fundamental importance but has a weak presence in the online channel. Several factors can hinder Italian exports through this channel: legal complexities, product characteristics, communication difficulties, and inability to use online commercial channels properly (Politecnico Milano & Osservatori.net, 2017). The first aspect is discussed in the following. In the age of connectivity, those without an effective online presence inevitably lose competitiveness.

7.5.1 Extra-Virgin Olive Oil, Online Channel, and Country of Origin

Olive oil production is concentrated in the Mediterranean basin, and Spain (60%) and Italy (20%) together account for 80% of the world's exports (ISMEA-Istituto Servizi Mercato Agricolo Alimentare, 2019). Recent data indicate Italy's relative position: the second largest producer country and exporter, after Spain; the leading consumer country, followed by Spain and the USA; and the top importing country, followed by the USA (ISMEA, 2018). Italy also holds an important position in quality olive oils recognized in the European Union: almost 40% are Italian brands, followed by Greece and Spain, with 29 awards each. In the national and international agri-food sectors, Italian olive agriculture is recognized for its excellence in both the quality characteristics of the production chain and the aspects of culture, territory, and tradition expressed by the oil.

However, the Italian olive oil supply chain has not yet succeeded in adequately enhancing the product for consumers even as they show growing curiosity about the product and search for more information. In this respect, the online channel can be effective as a direct channel for interaction and sales, but so far, this channel has been little used, except by younger consumer segments (ISMEA-MIPAAF, 2018). On these points, the research results are clear: there has emerged a consumer who is interested in the product and is willing to recognize the value of the origin and guarantees but needs to have more, clearer information for evaluation and is moved by a bit of verve in messages and new experiences from companies and restaurateurs (ISMEA-MIPAAF, 2018, p. 24).

Since the publication of the first studies on olive oil (McEwan, 1994; Nielsen, Bech-Larsen, & Grunert, 1998), particular attention has been paid to the geographical origin of olives, leading to two main conclusions (Del Giudice, Cavallo, Caracciolo, & Cicia, 2015; Van der Lans et al., 2001). First, the origin of olive oil is a crucial element in individual choices. Second, the full potential of the indication of its origins has not yet been exploited to differentiate and protect the product.

In more recent work, a quite strong relationship between origins and traceability also emerges, influencing the choices of consumers increasingly attentive to food safety (Gambaro, Ana, & Victor, 2013; Gázquez-Abad & Sánchez-Pérez, 2009). Product preferences are influenced by the many pieces of information consumers take into account during the purchasing process. Amid an increasingly broad range of international products, the COO and the brand become important indicators in consumers' decision-making processes, especially in the face of unfamiliarity with the product (Roth & Diamantopoulos, 2009; Vianelli & Pegan, 2014). The literature has highlighted the growing importance of the dynamics of the interactions between the brand and the COO in influencing purchasing preferences but has reached somewhat conflicting conclusions: on one hand, the COO seems to prevail (Tse & Gorn, 1993; Wall et al., 1991), and on the other, the brand does (Srinivasan et al., 2004; Verlegh & Steenkamp, 1999). In recent research with 600 respondents, perceived usefulness was increased by Italian origin and decreased by non-EU origin (de Luca et al., 2016).

Based on this empirical evidence, a possible choice to improve market power and overcome the constraints of a long supply chain is to sell products directly to the final consumers with a short-chain strategy. Doing so reduces the distance between producers and consumers and expands the market from the local to the global. In the case of olive oil, in particular, preferences vary according to the sales channel. Willingness to pay for contributions related to geographical origin (the COO) and production method (conventional or organic) varies according to the distribution form and the type of sale (department stores, specialty shops, and farmers' markets; Carlucci et al., 2014).

Regarding searching for information, the data show that the web is the main source of information for those seeking direct relationships with producers, both young people (18–34 years old, students, unemployed, graduates, and employed graduates) and adults (35–64 years old, entrepreneurs, and high-income workers; ISMEA-MIPAAF, 2018). The web, therefore, appears to be an important means of involving young people and adults, partly because it performs the function of conveying messages from opinion leaders such as cooks and nutritionists.

Although it has been pointed out that increasingly detailed information can further shift purchases toward high-quality products, there is still a transversal resistance to using the online channel for the purchase of olive oil. The consumer wants to know and understand oil and shows interest in oils of higher quality and price but falls back on lower priced products from known brands due to a lack of knowledge and oil culture. It is "as if between the analysis and the choice a potential of value was dissipated in an information vacuum that the shelf and the labels cannot fill" (ISMEA-MIPAAF, 2018, p. 59). The online channel can be used to address this information gap to show all the unexpressed potential for the enhancement of olive oil and its COO.

7.5.2 Wine, Online Channels, and Country of Origin

Even for Italian wine, online purchases are still extremely limited (Food, 2018). The data show strong percentage growth but from very low initial levels. Although late, many manufacturers are investing in equipping themselves to support the online sales channel, which is becoming increasingly strategic. Approximately 50% of Italian companies sell wine online either directly or through specialized sites, while another 17% intend to use this channel in the coming years (Food, 2018). Regarding demand, e-commerce is estimated to account for less than 2% of wine sales in Italy (online wine sales account for more than 10% in France and the UK and 20% in China). The growth rate, therefore, can only rise, and online wine purchases in Italy are forecast to reach 200 million euros by 2023. At the moment, the region with the most online presence is Tuscany, with 28% of market share, followed by Piedmont, Veneto, and Lazio (Food, 2018). The best selling denominations are brunello, amarone, valpolicella, bulger, chianti, barolo, barbaresco, barber, and franciacorta (Food, 2018).

The advantages derived from online interactions in the wine sector are manifold: two-way communication, user content creation, immediate remote sharing, extensive brand visibility, and opportunities for information searches, among others. In practice, awareness has emerged that e-commerce simplifies the search for consumers, the dissemination of knowledge about the product, and the act of purchase. In addition to the generalist platform Amazon Prime, which offers thousands of wines, several specialized sites exist. While the online channel certainly shortens the distance between supply and demand, it should also be considered that achieving a good result on the market requires an appropriate online presence. Wineries operate in complex offline and online multichannel environments. In the online sphere, it is generally believed that it is essential to have a corporate website today. An online presence is as important as a physical presence in the market. It should be noted that a website is only one component in the connection between a winery and its customers, and it is important to organize and manage channels effectively (Capitello, Agnoli, & Begalli, 2016; Wagner & Weidman, 2014).

For wine, the relevance of the COO or the region of origin has been highlighted. Especially when it is difficult to assess the specific attributes of a product, the origin serves as a sign of product quality (Olsen, Nowak, & Clarke, 2002). Research has yielded interesting external data on Italian wines abroad (3RDPLACE, 2017). Analysis of awareness scores (the degree of online awareness of a brand, product, or service), competition scores (the level of online competition within a certain brand, product, or service), and social reputation scores (online users' perceptions of a certain brand, product, or service) shows that the Italian wine sector is highly competitive, knowledge of Italian wine is medium to low, and perceptions of Italian wine are positive. In-depth analysis of factors such as the geographical distribution of online mentions (the USA is the primary source) and the socio-demo-psycho-graphic distribution of active online users allows identifying the ideal target by gender, age, and interests. The most attractive segments are 35- to 45-year-old men and millennials. Appreciation for Italian wine is often associated with a passion for travel. Content analysis of online mentions demonstrates that Italian wine is strongly associated with experience, emotion, history, and a model of life frequently emulated abroad. Regarding the price of the brands most considered, the same research shows that more than 70% of the mentions display high price consciousness, testifying to the choice orientation toward quality products (3RDPLACE, 2017).

7.6   Italian Wine in the USA: An Analysis of Google Users

Today, the international wine industry is characterized by the presence of Old World traditional wine producers such as France, Italy, and Spain and the innovative irruption of new producing countries. Employing innovative strategies in production and marketing, these new countries have gained growing global market share (Orth, Lockshin, & D'Hauteville, 2007). Understanding online search behavior is becoming a critical challenge (Gebauer & Ginsburg, 2010), especially for traditional players such as Italy, France, and Spain historically linked to wine production. Big data analytics have opened the door to numerous opportunities to develop new knowledge useful to reshape understanding of the customer landscape and to support decision-making within the wine industry. Underestimating big data can erode competitive advantages, even if consolidated, as in the case of Italian wine.

In 2017, Italy maintained its international production record, with 42.5 million hectoliters, ahead of France and Spain (ISMEA, 2018). That production, with 526 European Union awards for *Denominazione di Origine Protetta* (DOP)—Protected Designation of Origin—and Indicazione Geografica Protetta (IGP)—Indication of

Geographical Protection—wines, was made by about 46,000 wineries, revealing a fragmented sector (ISMEA, 2018). Regarding exports, Italy is the second-largest wine-exporting country in the world, both in value, after France, and in quantity, after Spain (ISMEA, 2018). Regarding import markets, Italy has a leader position in various relevant categories (ISMEA, 2018). Italy is the leading exporter by volume to the USA, Germany, the UK, Switzerland, and Canada and by value to Germany, Russia, and Switzerland. Italy is the second-leading exporter by volume to Russia and by value to the UK and the USA, the third-leading exporter by volume and value to Japan, and the fifth-leading exporter by volume and value to China (ISMEA, 2018).

Despite this international leadership and significant growth in exports (+6.4% in value from 2016 and a trend of +142% from 2000 to 2016), many companies in the sector still are not adequately structured for e-commerce (ISMEA, 2018). Although some online initiatives have great potential, some studies have revealed strategies often oriented mainly to communication rather than online shopping (Carlucci et al., 2014; Fritz et al., 2009). However, a strong percentage of growth rate emerges from this current situation of weakness. Although late, many manufacturers are investing to develop increasingly strategic sales channels. Around 50% of Italian companies sell wine online, either directly or through specialized sites, and another 17% intend to use this channel in the coming years (Food, 2018). Online weaknesses also emerge in Italian demand. However, e-commerce is growing rapidly in all sectors.

In practice, awareness that e-commerce simplifies the search for the consumer, the act of purchase, and the dissemination of knowledge of wine has increased (Food, 2018). In the age of connectivity, those without an effective online presence inevitably lose competitiveness. Focusing on the first critical aspect, improving the ability to use online channels requires understanding the new phenomenon of online research by consumers, mainly carried out through Google.

7.6.1   An Explorative Study on Online Searches for Italian Wine in the USA

In a previous explorative study (Gonzalo-Penela, de Luca, & Pegan, 2017), as mentioned in Chap. 1, we analyzed online searches, particularly those for wine in the USA, the world's largest wine market. Chapter 3 has already pointed out data of that big wine market. Here we illustrate a descriptive research to represent the configurations of online searches for wine-related information in the USA. We adopted the digital methods approach (Rogers, 2015) viewing the Internet as a source of methods rather than an object of study. We used data obtained from various SEO tools, primarily Google Trends, Google AdWords, and Sistrix. Google Trends traces trends in keyword searches from January 2004 to the present. This tool is usually used to view the long-, medium-, and short-term evolution of keywords. Google AdWords provides keyword search statistics for both general and specific topics at the national and international levels from the past 12 months. Sistrix offers website visibility reports based on organic keywords. This tool weekly queries and saves more than 15 million keywords in different Google indexes. Its reports list website rankings for these keywords and their evolution.

We considered US users' search queries on Google during 2016, highlighting and analyzing keywords' popularity.[3] We developed a three-phase research process. In the first phase, we extracted wine-related search keywords used by US users and their frequency from the Google AdWords Keyword Planner tool. Keyword extraction started from one or several seed keywords, and the main seed keyword was "wine," which returned up to 800 related terms. To gather as many more related keywords as possible, we continued using different, related seed keywords. In several subsequent iterations, we added Italian wine and its main competitors in Europe, Spanish, and French wine. Once the combinations of "wine" and "origin" were exhausted, we expanded the extraction using the seed-specific names of "grapes" and the "denominations of origin" of these three countries and finally "complementary goods" associated with wine consumption.

In the second phase, we performed qualitative content analysis to better understand users' searches. We conducted the qualitative analysis and coding process through an iterative, multistep method (multiple rounds based on query selection, classification, and characteristics treatment), guided both by data in an inductive approach and by theoretical knowledge on the subject studied (Zarantonello & Luomala, 2011). Researchers shared our coding results to reach an inter-coder agreement. In addition, we classified these keywords into three classes by intent (navigational, informational, and transactional intent).

Finally, in the third phase, we identified keywords that referred to specific COOs: Italy, along with France and Spain, the main competitors of Italian wine in the US market. We extracted the results from Google U.S. for 100 keywords for each country, analyzing the IPs of the different pages displayed on the Google result pages.

We extracted US users' wine-related search keywords and the frequency from the Google AdWords keyword planner tool from January to December 2016 to highlight and analyze keywords' popularity. Based on the wine-related keywords entered by users, we extracted 6011 wine-related search terms used by US users during 2016, with a total of 75,335,160 searches in 2016 (Table 7.5).

We then focused on terms with high search frequencies and, in particular, the top terms for Italian, French, and Spanish wines. As seen in Table 7.5, champagne is in the top position, followed by Italian prosecco and moscato, and then cava, the first Spanish wine.

To better understand the meaning of the numbers in Table 7.5, we analyzed the composition of the search keywords frequencies (Table 7.6), distinguishing between

---

[3]According to the definition of SEO, keywords are words and phrases searchers enter into search engines, also called search queries (https://moz.com/learn/seo/what-are-keywords, 2018; retrieved May 25, 2018).

Table 7.5 Top 10 keywords of wine-related search terms extracted (U.S., 2016)

Ranking	Keyword	Searches
1	Champagne	2,255,000
2	Wine	1,988,000
3	Wine and spirits	1,966,000
4	Prosecco	1,311,500
5	Moscato	1,081,000
6	Bodega	987,000
7	Wine rack	928,000
8	Pinot noir	868,500
9	Cava	751,500
10	Vineyard	701,800
. . .		
6011		75,335,160

Source: de Luca, Pegan, and Gonzalo Penela (2019)

Table 7.6 Extract of the findings from the top terms for Italian, French, and Spanish wines (U.S., 2016)

Top Italian, French, and Spanish wines keywords	Number of search keywords	Search keywords frequency	Head keywords frequency	Long-tail keywords frequency	Keywords average
Champagne and related keywords	61	3,158,180	2,255,000 (71.4%)	903,180 (28.6%)	15,053
Prosecco and related keywords	173	1,968,576	1,311,500 (66.6)	657,076 (33.4%)	3820
Moscato and related keywords	18	1,866,602	1,081,000 (48%)	785,400 (42.0%)	46,200
Cava and related keywords	43	857,860	751,500 (87.7%)	106,360 (12.3%)	2473

Source: de Luca et al. (2019)

head keyword frequency (one keyword) and long-tail keywords frequency (two or more keywords).[4] According to the literature on the long tail (Anderson, 2006), the concept of keywords demand is highly relevant. It indicates the low number of queries that direct large amounts of traffic, along with the volume of less-searched and phrases that can bring the majority of search referrals (Brynjolfsson et al., 2011). For instance, when comparing prosecco and moscato, the first has more search keywords (173) but a relatively shorter long tail (33.4%), with a low average of frequency for each long-tail keyword (3820). Moscato has a higher long tail (42%),

---

[4]We decided to use these numbers (1 for heads and 2 or more for long-tail keywords) because the first keyword captures the majority of users' searches.

Table 7.7 Example of output for keywords analysis (U.S., 2016)

Ranking	Keyword	Total 2016
7	Moscato	1,081,000
25	Moscato wine	447,600
46	Moscato d'Asti	284,100
631	Moscato wine price	13,580
649	Moscato red wine	13,210
1062	Vino moscato	5570
1454	Elio Perrone moscato	2740
1674	Italian moscato wine	1980
2155	Moscato Italian wine	1000
2306	Moscato wine Italy	840
2354	Moscato wine price Walmart	790
2920	Wine moscato price	440
3073	Italian wine moscato	380
3445	Moscato red wine price	270
3873	Moscato di Scanzo	190
4016	Moscato Italy white wine	170
5369	Moscato giallo wine	100

Source: de Luca et al. (2019)

with only 18 keywords and a higher average of frequency for each long-tail keyword (46,200). This trend could reflect the growing moscato trend in the USA.[5] Table 7.7 gives an example of moscato wine output.

To deepen understanding of these results in the second phase of this research, we performed qualitative content analysis to identify codes for search keywords for each wine considered (prosecco, moscato, champagne, and cava). The content analysis of 925 search keywords involved ex-ante and ex-post coding. Table 7.8 presents the interpretive coding scheme (see the Appendix to the chapter). After a multistep coding process, the authors agreed on eight codes: one code related to the wine variants of the specific four categories considered; two related to the concept of the COO and the more specific place of origin of the wine analyzed (e.g., prosecco Treviso); one code related to brand; and three codes related to buying intention (place of purchase, price and delivery service, and gift and related service).

From the content analysis, we can draw some findings. Regarding champagne, the top searched for wine variety in the US market, users search primarily for brand and gifts, while price does not seem to be relevant. In the case of prosecco, we note

---

[5]As pointed out by Drinks Association (2017), E. and J. Gallo Winery, one of the biggest US wine companies, coined the term "moscato madness" to describe the rapid grow of this wine in the US market. In 2015, more than 20 million people in the USA bought moscato over a 3-month period. This fruity grape probably is a gateway into wine for first-time drinkers and is most popular with millennials. A recent *Wine Searcher* article noted that the site was "rather shocked to see that the year-to-date figure of 273,261 was far in advance of that for prosecco, which has only reached 128,615 keyword searches in the same period," making moscato the most-searched sparkling wine in the world.

Table 7.8 Coding and categorization of Google keywords: Examples from Italian, French, and Spanish top wines in the US market (2016)

Codes	Italian top wines				French top wines		Spanish top wines	
	Keywords	Search frequency	Keywords	Search frequency	Keywords	Search frequency	Keywords	Search frequency
Wine variety (head keyword)	Prosecco	1,311,500	Moscato	1,081,000	Champagne	2,255,000	Cava	751,500
Wine variants	Prosecco white wine White wine prosecco Sparkling white wine prosecco Red prosecco Prosecco red wine	2500	Moscato red wine Moscato giallo wine	13,480	–	–	Cava sparkling wine Brut cava Cava rose Cava brut champagne	35,930
Country of origin	Italian prosecco Italian prosecco brands Best Italian prosecco Prosecco Italy	5130	Italian moscato wine Moscato Italian wine Italian wine moscato Moscato wine Moscato Italy Moscato Italy white wine	4370	French champagne	23,200	Spanish cava Spanish cava wine Spanish cava brands Cava Spanish sparkling wine	8170
Place of origin	Prosecco Treviso Prosecco valdobbiadene Colli asolani prosecco Prosecco valdobbiadene migliore	3180	Moscato d'asti Moscato d'asti wine Moscato di scanzo	296,730	–	–	–	–

	Prosecco		Moscato		Champagne		Cava	
Brand	Valdo prosecco Zonin prosecco Dicello prosecco Mionetto prosecco Prosecco Valdo Prosecco brands	16,103	Elio Perrone Moscato	2740	Cristal champagne Mumm champagne Taittinger champagne	200,865	—	—
Place of purchase	Where to buy prosecco Where can I buy prosecco Buy prosecco Buy prosecco online Prosecco buy Where can I buy prosecco wine	3490	Moscato wine price Walmart		Buy champagne online Buy champagne	7960	Buy cava	130
Price and delivery service	Prosecco price Prosecco wine price Price of prosecco Price of prosecco sparkling wine Bottle of prosecco price Wine prosecco price Best price prosecco Best prosecco prices Prosecco wine price range	37,870	Moscato wine price Moscato wine price Walmart Wine moscato price Moscato red wine price	15,080	Champagne prosecco price Champagne wine price	360	Cava wine price Cava champagne price	1600
Gifts and related services	Prosecco gift basket Prosecco gifts delivered Prosecco delivery gift	1390	—		Champagne gifts Champagne gift baskets Champagne gift delivery Champagne gift ideas Send champagne gift	48,140	—	—

Source: de Luca et al. (2019)

that US users most often search for brand, price, and delivery service keywords, while searches for a specific origin are not as relevant. For moscato, users search frequently for contents about specific places of origin, followed by price and delivery service. The most frequently searched keywords for cava wine are related to wine variants and the COO.

In line with the literature (Jansen et al., 2008; Rose & Levinson, 2004), the coding scheme also supports the classification of user intent as navigational, informational, and transactional. Determination of users' search intent is based on the wording and the structure of keyword phrases used when performing searches. In addition to the core keyword, transactional searches contain a modifier that indicates and supports purchase intent. For example, a keyword modifier such as "cheap," "price," "deliver," "buy," "sale," "deal," and "discount" next to a core keyword strengthens the transactional intent. Navigational and transactional searches are categorized by specific search keywords or search modifiers for each class. Navigational searches include a core keyword; a term such as "web," "website," and "official website;" and letters associated with a top-level domain whose last segment is the domain name (e.g., "com," "net," "it," "es," and "fr"). Navigational searches can also consist of the domain name without a top-level domain suffix. In the case of the wine sector, it was possible to recognize domain names in search queries using a database of the names of sectorial websites. During the SERPs analysis phase, we developed a specific database of domain names, first, isolating the websites extracted from the Google results pages and, second, eliminating the top-level domain.

We specifically aimed to highlight transactional keywords due to their relevant implications for decision makers. This type of keywords allows identifying search queries closer to the time of purchase. Following this classification, the codes for place of purchase, price and delivery service, and gift and related services in Table 7.8 reflect the transactional intent for the wines considered. These codes include specific search modifiers such as "price," "buy," "gift," "deliver," "order," and "purchase." Our analysis found that prosecco has 32 transactional keywords and a frequency of 42,750, moscato has five transactional keywords and a frequency of 15,870, and champagne has nine transactional keywords and a frequency of 56,460.

To better understand the scenario of Old World wine in the US online market and the competitive position of Italian wine compared with French and Spanish wines, we conducted the third phase of this study. We identified 2206 keywords including European DO terms with a frequency of 11,634,770. Among these, Italian DO terms (1232), followed by French (495), and Spanish (479) DO terms, stand out. We extracted 1111 keywords directly mentioning Italian (473) wine and compared the total to those for the top traditional wine countries, Spain (323) and France (315). This analysis highlighted the visibility of European wines and vineyards in the US wine market search niche. For example, we could analyze how European DO sites rank in Google U.S. based on any category of terms and which US site is the best to publish or sell a specific blend type. For keywords referring to a specific country such as Italy, we studied Google U.S.' results for 100 keywords per country and analyzed the internet protocol (IP) addresses of the different pages. The resulting distribution of national sites (Table 7.9) based on IP addresses shows that the

Table 7.9 Pages hosted in different countries for the search of Italian, French, and Spanish wines in the US market

Page host country	French wines	Italian wines	Spanish wines
USA	69.86%	72.95%	69.43%
UK	9.24%	8.24%	12.86%
Netherlands	6.62%	7.86%	6.90%
Switzerland	–	–	2.29%
France	3.33%	–	–
Italian	–	2.81%	–
Spanish	–	–	2.19%
Europe	2.00%	1.95%	–
Other countries	8.95%	6.19%	6.33%

Source: Adapted from de Luca et al. (2019)

regional search results are composed mostly of US and UK sites, while the visibility of European sites barely reaches 3%. In the data, we can observe that Italian wine sites, along with other European wine sites, have rather low visibility: 2.8% for Italian wine searches, ranked second behind French wine (3.3%) and before Spanish wine searches (2.1%).

Table 7.9 shows the countries hosting the webpages in Google U.S.'s SERPs.[6] These figures are based on website analysis of the countries where the IP addresses are hosted. As seen, even though the searches were aimed at finding information on Italian, French, and Spanish wines, the selection of pages displayed in Google U.S.'s SERPs are mostly from the USA (approximately 70%), while the pages hosted on European countries account for less than 3% of the selection made by the Google algorithm. Thus, the possibility of ranking in the USA is limited not only by the problems described but also by the existence of established websites that are very difficult to outrank.

7.6.2   What Can Google Say About the Relevance of the Country of Origin for Wine?

Regarding the specific research on Italian wine in the US market, we can propose some conclusions. Among Italian wines, the top positions of prosecco and moscato in the wine-related search keywords extracted in 2016 seem to reflect awareness of these wines in the US market. Our analysis allowed us to point out the diversity of the new customer journey in the online context for each wine variant considered and

---

[6]Google's ranking algorithm gives prominence to pages based on the languages in which web browsers are configured and the hosting locations. Thus, for any search made from the USA, Google selects pages that match the browser's language, usually English, and pages hosted on servers in that country are considered to be more relevant.

the different roles of traditional levels of differentiation in the wine sector, such as the COO. By coding and categorizing the keywords, we found, for example, that in the case of prosecco, keywords related to brand are more frequently searched than the general COO, and "price" is an important search term. For moscato, the specific place of origin seems to be more relevant. For champagne, the top wine searched in the US market, users tended to be more interested in specific brands. For cava, the keywords most frequently searched were related to wine variants and the COO. These results could suggest that price and service are important queries for Italian wine; in particular, for prosecco and moscato, brand and origin, respectively, seem to be important. The findings for champagne are rather different. In this case, the keywords seem to relate mainly to brand and gifting. Price is not relevant because Champagne is considered to be a premium or luxury product, and it does not seem to be important to refine the search with other additional terms. For cava, users seem to search mostly for informational details on wine variants and COO brands. In the present case, we found informational intent (keywords in the categories of wine variants, country of origin, place of origin, and brand) and transactional intent (keywords in the categories of place of purchase, price and delivery service, and gifts and related service). We did not identify any keywords related to navigational intent. This finding means that web users and consumers do not often search for a specific wine site but mostly search to obtain information for purchasing purposes.

The third phase of this research highlighted the weak position of Italian wine in the US market and the low visibility of Italian wine online sites, as well as other French and Spanish wine online sites. Investment in customer knowledge by utilizing user-generated data and organic keywords is relevant for wineries that need insights into consumer behavior. One of the leading factors for success in the online market is on-page keyword optimization. If the keywords that users are searching for do not appear on the firm website, it is highly unlikely to rank for those keywords. To drive traffic using organic searches, therefore, wineries need to optimize their web content for organic keywords. They need to find the keywords users actually use when looking for Italian wine and then optimize their website pages for these organic keywords. The results of this analysis of keywords and long-tail wine-related terms can be used to improve the optimization of digital marketing campaigns. These results indicate that wineries can improve their content marketing and inbound marketing strategies by using contents that correspond to transactional niches with higher commercial potential.

7.7   Conclusion

This chapter has reviewed the online channel, which is assuming a growing, pervasive role in the system of entry modes and marketing channels and is evolving into a complex omnichannel dimension. The online channel manifests its relationships at the business-to-business and business-to-consumer levels, directly or indirectly linking producers and consumers from the COO to the market of destination.

The online channel, therefore, has effects at both the level of entry modes and the level of marketing channels. After a detailed description of the development of the online channel and the emerging omnichannel perspective, this chapter addresses studies on the relationship between the online channel and the COOs that do not seem to have a consolidated theoretical framework yet. In order to contribute to this field of study, this chapter presents empirical evidence related to cases of particular products–markets collected through the analysis of secondary data and the results of recent empirical research in the fashion and agri-food sectors.

The advantages derived from online interactions are many and mainly connected to two-way communication possibilities, user content creation, immediate remote sharing, extensive brand visibility, and opportunities in information searches. This study also shows that sectors are different from each other For example, in the case of fashion, it is above all the brand that conveys value, but in the case of agri-food products, the brand can take second place to the COO. In the latter case, the available data show that e-commerce simplifies the search for consumers, the knowledge and dissemination of the product, and the act of purchase. While the online channel certainly shortens the distance between supply and demand, it should also be considered that achieving this objective requires an appropriate online presence. In this era of connectivity and the omnichannel context, an online presence is as important as a physical presence in the market. In this context, the relationship between the online channel and the COO is twofold. On one hand, the COO serves as a sign of product quality, especially when it is difficult to assess the specific attributes of the product. On the other hand, the online channel, if used effectively, can become an important vehicle of the valorization of the COO for the target market and, therefore, if recognized in terms of premium price, for the appropriation of value by producers and other online players.

References

3RDPLACE. (2017, December 21). *L'external data intelligence per le scelte di business. Un esempio concreto.* Retrieved January 30, 2018, from http://3rdplace.com/news/lexternal-data-intelligence-per-le-scelte-di-business-un-esempio-concreto/

3RDPLACE. (2018, January 15). *External data intelligence analysis. Italian wine—2017.* Retrieved January 30, 2018, from http://3rdplace.com/news/3rdplace-vinventions-analizzano-mercato-del-vino-italiano-allestero/

Afuah, A., & Tucci, C. (2001). *Internet business models and strategies: Text and cases.* New York: McGraw-Hill.

Ahmed, S., & Kumar, A. (2015). Opportunities and challenges of omni channel retailing in the emerging market. *Journal of Retail Management and Research, 1*(1), 1–16.

Anderson, C. (2006). *The long tail: Why the future of business is selling less of more.* New York, NY: Hyperion.

Astound Group. (2018). *Phygital marketing & customer experience.* Retrieved December 4, 2018, from Astound Group https://www.astoundgroup.com/astound-insider/phygital-marketing-customer-experience

Bassi, M. (2018, June 25). *Alibaba: Online è come offline*. Retrieved March 21, 2019, from Mark Up https://www.mark-up.it/alibaba-online-e-come-offline/

Beck, N., & Rygl, D. (2015). Categorization of multiple channel retailing in multi-, cross-, and omni-channel retailing for retailers and retailing. *Journal of Retailing and Consumer Services, 27*, 170–178.

Bellini, M. (2017). *La SmartAgrifood per Cisco: campi connessi, analytics, startup e Open Innovation sino all'Industria 4.0*. Retrieved June 18, 2019, from Internet4things https://www.internet4things.it/smart-agrifood/la-smartagrifood-per-cisco-campi-connessi-analytics-startup-e-open-innovation-sino-allindustria-4-0/

Bertoletti, C. (2017, November 21). *Auchan Retail, Alibaba e Ruentex: Un'alleanza strategica in Cina*. Retrieved from https://www.mark-up.it/auchan-retail-alibaba-e-ruentex-unalleanza-strategica-in-cina/

Bettucci, M., D'Amato, I., Perego, A., & Pozzoli, E. (2015). *Omnichannel customer management. Come integrare i processi fisici e digitali*. Milan, Italy: SDA Bocconi.

Broder, A. (2002). A taxonomy of web search. *SIGIR Forum, 36*(2), 3–10.

Brynjolfsson, E., Hu, Y. J., & Rahman, M. S. (2013). Competing in the age of omnichannel retailing. *MIT Sloan Management Review, 54*(4), 23–29.

Brynjolfsson, E., Hu, Y., & Simester, D. (2011). Goodbye Pareto principle, hello long tail: The effect of search costs on the concentration of product sales. *Management Science, 57*(8), 1373–1386.

Canavari, M., Pignatti, E., Spadoni, R., & van Sprundel, G. (2009). Nuove dinamiche nel commercio dei prodotti agroalimentari: resistenze all'adozione dell'e-commerce nelle relazioni B2B. *Economia Agro-Alimentare, 3*, 103–118.

Capitello, R., Agnoli, L., & Begalli, D. (2016). Online communication approaches and social networks in traditional wine regions: A case study from Italy. *EuroMed Journal of Business, 9*(2), 129–148.

Carlucci, D., De Gennaro, B., Roselli, L., & Seccia, A. (2014). E-commerce retail of extra virgin olive oil: An hedonic analysis of Italian SMEs supply. *British Food Journal, 116*(10), 1600–1617.

Chen, J., Liu, D., & Whinston, A. (2009). Auctioning keywords in online search. *Journal of Marketing, 73*(4), 125–141.

Cito, G., & Paolo, A. (2014). *Italia Caput Mundi*. Milano: Rizzoli Etas.

de Luca, P., Pegan, G., & Gonzalo Penela, C. (2019). Insights from a Google keywords analysis. What can the internet tell us about Italian wine in the US market? *Micro & Macro Marketing, 1*, 93–116.

de Luca, P., Pegan, G., Troiano, S., Gallenti, G., Marangon, F., & Cosmina, M. (2016). Brand e country of origin: Una ricerca sulle preferenze del consumatore di olio extra-vergine d'oliva. In *XIIIth SIM conference—Marketing & retail nei mercati che cambiano* (pp. 1–6). Cassino, Italy.

Del Giudice, T., Cavallo, C., Caracciolo, F., & Cicia, G. (2015). What attributes of extra virgin olive oil are really important for consumers: A meta-analysis of consumers' stated preferences. *Agricultural and Food Economics, 3*(20), 1–15.

Digital Commerce Institute. (2018, July 10). Retrieved from https://digitalcommerce.com/D

Digitas Study & Wincor-Nixdorf. (2012). Retrieved October 7, 2018, from http://www.exaqtworld.com/en/solutions/store-to-web.php

Drinks Association. (2017). *"Moscato madness" drives export boom to US*. Retrieved June 20, 2019, from Drinks Association http://www.drinkscentral.com.au/4751?Article=moscato-mandness-drives-australian-export-boom-to-united-states

Food. (2018, April). *Dossier vino*.

Fritz, M., Canageri, M., Cantore, N., Deiters, J., & Pignatti, E. (2009). Commercio elettronico e fiducia: analisi preliminare del potenziale in filiere agro-alimentari internazionali. *Economia agro-alimentare, 2*, 63–83.

Gambaro, A., Ana, C. F., & Victor, P. (2013). Influence of subjective knowledge, objective knowledge and health consciousness on olive oil consumption - A case study. *Food and Nutrition Sciences, 4*, 445–453.

Gao, F., & Su, X. (2017). Online and offline information for omnichannel retailing. *Manufacturing & Service Operations Management, 19*(1), 84–98.

Gázquez-Abad, J. C., & Sánchez-Pérez, M. (2009). Factors influencing olive oil brand choice in Spain: An empirical analysis using scanner data. *Agribusiness, 25*(1), 36–55.

Gebauer, J., & Ginsburg, M. (2010). The US wine industry and the internet: An analysis of success factors for online business models. *Electronic Markets, 13*(1), 59–66.

Gonzalo Penela, C., Codina, L., & Rovira, C. (2015). Recuperacion de informacion centrada en el usuario y SEO: Categorizacion y determinacion de las intenciones de bùsqueda en la Web. *Index Comunicacion, 5*(3), 19–27.

Gonzalo-Penela, C., de Luca, P., & Pegan, G. (2017). Insights from Google search user-generated. In *Convegno SIM—il marketing di successo: Imprese, enti, persone* (pp. 1–6). Rome, Italy: Società Italiana Marketing.

Google Arts & Culture. (2019). *Made in Italy*. Retrieved July 2, 2019, from https://artsandculture.google.com/project/made-in-italy

Green, D. (2017). *Amazon oltre l'e-commerce: contro l'apocalisse del retail scommette sul negozio fisico. Ma lo fa alla sua maniera*. Retrieved July 20, 2019, from Business Insider Italia https://it.businessinsider.com/amazon-oltre-le-commerce-contro-lapocalisse-del-retail-scommette-sul-negozio-fisico-ma-lo-fa-alla-sua-maniera/

Griswold, A. (2016). *Amazon is planning a line of tiny grocery stores*. Retrieved June 20, 2019, from Quartz https://qz.com/806389/amazon-amzn-is-planning-a-line-of-tiny-grocery-stores-fol lowing-walmart-wmt/

Host Milano. (2016, May 7). *Coerenza e servizio le richieste del consumatore 2.0*. Retrieved April 20, 2018, from http://host.fieramilano.it/coerenza-e-servizio-le-richieste-del-consumatore-20

Huang, P., Lurie, N., & Mitra, S. (2009). Searching for experience on the web: An empirical examination of consumer behavior for search and experience goods. *Journal of Marketing, 73*, 55–69.

ISMEA. (2018). *Vinitaly: Il punto ISMEA sul settore del vino Italiano*. Retrieved August 4, 2019, from ISMEA http://www.ismea.it/flex/cm/pages/ServeBLOB.php/L/IT/IDPagina/10268

ISMEA. (2019). *Scheda di settore—olio di oliva. Maggio 2019*. Retrieved August, 12, 2019, from ISMEA http://www.ismeamercati.it/flex/cm/pages/ServeBLOB.php/L/IT/IDPagina/3523#MenuV

ISMEA-MIPAAF. (2018). *Gusto in-EVOluzione*. Retrieved July 20, 2019, from ISMEA-MIPAAF http://www.ismea.it/flex/cm/pages/ServeBLOB.php/L/IT/IDPagina/10271

Jansen, B. J., Booth, D. L., & Spink, A. (2008). Determining the informational, navigational, and transactional intent of web queries. *Information Processing and Management, 44*, 1251–1266.

Jerath, K., Ma, L., & Park, Y. H. (2014). Consumer click behavior at a search engine: The role of keyword popularity. *Journal of Marketing Research, 51*(4), 480–486.

Klaus, P. (2013). Exploring online channel management strategies and the use of social media as a market research tool. *International Journal of Market Research, 55*(6), 829–850.

Kotler, P., Kartajaya, H., & Setiawan, I. (2017). *Marketing 4.0*. Milan, Italy: Hoepli.

Lazaris, C., & Vrechopoulos, A. (2014, 18–20 June). From multichannel to "omnichannel" retailing: Review of the literature and calls for research. In *2nd International Conference on Contemporary Marketing Issues (ICCMI)* (pp. 1–6). Athens, Greece.

Levy, M., Weitz, B., & Grewal, D. (2013). *Retailing management* (9th ed.). New York: McGraw-Hill/Irwin.

McAfee, A., & Brynjolfsson, E. (2012). Big data: The management revolution. *Harvard Business Review, 90*(10), 60–66.

McEwan, J. A. (1994). Consumer attitudes and olive oil acceptance: The potential consumer. *Gracas y Aceites, 45*(1–2), 9–15.

Nakayama, M., Sutcliffe, N., & Wan, Y. (2010). Has the web transformed experience goods into search goods? *Electronic Markets*, 251–262.

Nelson, P. (1970). Information and consumer behavior. *Journal of Political Economy, 78*(2), 311–329.

Nielsen, N. A., Bech-Larsen, T., & Grunert, K. G. (1998). Consumer purchase motives and product perceptions: A laddering study on vegetable oil in three countries. *Food Quality and Preference, 9*(6), 455–466.

Nielsen, J., & Loranger, H. (2006). *Web usability 2.0. L'usabilità che conta*. Milan, Italy: Apogeo.

Olsen, J., Nowak, L., & Clarke, T. (2002). Country of origin effects and complimentary marketing channels is Mexican wine more enjoyable when served with Mexican FOOD. *International Journal of Wine Marketing, 14*(1), 23–33.

Orth, U. R., Lockshin, L., & D'Hauteville, F. (2007). The global wine business as a research field. *International Journal of Wine Business Research, 19*(1), 5–13.

Parker, R., & Hand, L. (2009). *Satisfying the omnichannel consumers whenever and wherever they shop*. IDC Retail Insights report.

Pegan, G., Vianelli, D., & de Luca, P. (2013). Il ruolo della distribuzione nella valorizzazione dei marchi made in Italy ad alto valore simbolico in USA: Casi, esperienze e criticità. In G. Aiello (Ed.), *Davanti agli occhi del cliente. Branding e retailing del Made in Italy nel mondo*. Rome, Italy: Aracne Editrice.

Pirolli, P. (2007). *Information foraging theory: Adaptive interaction with information*. Oxford, UK: Oxford University Press.

Politecnico Milano & Osservatori.net. (2017). *Osservatori digital innovation. Le infografiche 2017: I numeri chiavi dell'innovazione digitale*. Milan, Italy: Politecnico Milano.

Rigby, D. (2011). The future of shopping. *Harvard Business Review, 89*, 65–76.

Rogers, R. (2015). Digital methods for web research. In R. A. Scott & S. M. Kosslyn (Eds.), *Emerging trends in the social and behavioral sciences*. New York: Wiley.

Rose, D. E., & Levinson, D. (2004). Understanding user goals in web search. In *WWW 2014* (pp. 13–19). New York, NY.

Roth, K. P., & Diamantopoulos, A. (2009). Advancing the country image construct. *Journal of Business Research, 62*, 726–740.

Srinivasan, N., Jain, S. C., & Sikand, K. (2004). An experimental study of two dimensions of 825 country-of-origin (manufacturing country and branding country) using intrinsic and extrinsic cues. *International Business Review, 13*(1), 65–82.

Tse, D., & Gorn, G. (1993). An experiment on the salience of country of origin in the era of global brands. *Journal of International Marketing, 1*(1), 57–76.

UPS. (2016). *Pulse of the omni-channel retailer*. I. R. Insights. Retrieved May 27, 2018, from https://www.key4biz.it/wp-content/uploads/2016/09/IT-UPS_research_white_paper_A4_IT_29-07.pdf

Van der Lans, I. A., van Ittersum, K., De Cicco, A., & Loseby, M. (2001). The role of the region of origin and EU certificates of origin in consumer evaluation of food products. *European Review of Agricultural Economics, 28*(4), 451–477.

Verlegh, P. W. J., & Steenkamp, J. B. E. M. (1999). A review and meta-analysis of country of origin research. *Journal of Economic Psychology, 20*(5), 521–546.

Vescovi, T. (2007). *Il marketing e la rete*. Milano: Il Sole 24 ore.

Vianelli, D., de Luca, P., & Pegan, G. (2012). *Modalità d'entrata e scelte distributive del made in Italy in Cina*. Milan, Italy: Franco Angeli.

Vianelli, D., & Pegan, G. (2014, January–June). Made in Italy brands in the US and China: Does country of origin matter? *Journal of Euromarketing, 23*(1&2), 57–73.

Wagner, S. L., & Weidman, L. M. (2014). *Reputation management on the internet: Content and impact of Oregon wineries' websites and Facebook pages'*. Paper presented at the 8th AWBR international conference, Geisenheim, Germany.

Wall, M., Liefeld, J., & Heslop, L. (1991). Impact of country of origin cues on consumer judgments in multi-cue situations: A covariance analysis. *Journal of the Academy of Marketing Science, 19*(1), 105–113.

WeAreSocial & Hootsuite. (2018, January 30). *Digital in 2018*. Retrieved January 31, 2018, from https://wearesocial.com/it/blog/2018/01/global-digital-report-2018

Yoox Group. *Annual report 2012*. Retrieved November 20, 2013., from http://cdn2.yoox.biz/yooxgroup/pdf/annual

Zarantonello, L., & Luomala, H. (2011). Dear Mr chocolate: Constructing a typology of contextualized chocolate consumption experiences through qualitative diary research. *Qualitative Market Research: An International Journal, 14*(1), 55–82.

Chapter 8
Conclusion to the Country of Origin Effect on Decision-Making in Practice

Abstract This chapter provides a brief overview of the objectives of the book and discusses the main findings. In particular, the chapter takes up each theoretical research question that inspired the research process and offers the reader an attempt to answer based on the main results obtained. Giving space to the voice of companies and their stories has once again made it possible to see how difficult it is to translate principles easily shared on a theoretical level into strategies and actions implemented on a daily basis.

8.1 Introduction

The purpose of this book is to contribute to the still very lively debate on the topic of the COO, focusing on the perspectives of companies entering foreign markets. In particular, this study has investigated the main challenges companies operating in sectors with high product typicality face to be able to create value for foreign clients (the value creation process) and to make sure that their final target clients are able to recognize the value of the COO (the value appropriation process). In fact, with the different entry modes and the international marketing channels needed to penetrate foreign markets, the risk of hindering actual perceptions of the initial COO value created by manufacturers is high.

This book is aimed at providing useful theoretical and managerial contributions by giving space to the voices of manufacturers, importers, and retailers to understand their perceptions of the COO effect—voices so far neglected compared to the emphasis put on the consumer perspective in the academic literature. Without claiming to be exhaustive, the methodological process of this study involving a constant dialogue between theory and practice has allowed us to grasp various companies' visions of the relevance of the COO effect in their international marketing strategies, particularly the criticalities and opportunities offered by different ways of entering foreign markets and the subsequent marketing channels. This rich, varied framework of practical business experience is intended to suggest to the reader answers to the initial research questions that guided and inspired all the

G. Pegan et al., *International Marketing Strategy*, International Series in Advanced Management Studies, https://doi.org/10.1007/978-3-030-33588-5_8

work. A brief discussion of the main results of the various research questions follows.

8.2 Main Findings About the Role of Country of Origin on Decision-Making in Practice

Regarding the meaning and strategic relevance of the COO in companies' perspectives, the study provides an articulated overview. Certainly, in accordance with the theoretical background, for companies characterized by high product typicality, the COO represents a strategic driver in which to invest to create value in the foreign market. The experience gathered by the various companies involved shows how the COO effect has favored their processes of internationalization. In international marketing strategies, the concept of product typicality facilitates access to foreign markets. As suggested by the categorization theory applied to the study of the COO effect, it is seen that in conditions of strong national typicality (i.e., when a product is considered to be typical of a country), the COO determines a more favorable assessment by the consumer, increasing the propensity to buy the product. The COO's potential intrinsic value, in the case of Italian products, stems from strong, positive associations present in the minds of consumers and, therefore, can rely on this positive stereotype of the country, supporting the company in creating a distinctive value proposition in foreign markets.

According to the companies, the COO certainly can simplify the purchasing decision-making process by offering synthetic cues to product quality. In the specific case of the declination of COO in made in Italy, it is very clear that the emotional component often plays a role in influencing foreign customers' choices. In the international imaginary, Italian products evoke symbolic values linked to the *bel paese*, lifestyle, elegance, refinement, and the so-called *bello e ben fatto*. The positive halo that surrounds made in Italy supports the consumer in making selections from among the myriad of products available, acting as a heuristic (sometimes an affective heuristic) to a priori judge product quality and make faster decisions with less cognitive effort.

However, two interesting aspects regarding the first research question emerge: the simplification that analysis of the COO concept assumes from mangers' point of view and the interconnection between the COO and the brand in strategic-operational management. Regarding the first aspect, according to the managers interviewed, the sub-components of the COO that can influence consumer behavior are the country of production, the country of design, and the country of the brand. The companies involved in the study never mentioned the distinctions proposed by academic studies, such as those relating to the country of the parts and the country of assembly. This result seems to support the idea that the COO of the brand is becoming more important in the production dimension. In other words, the analysis of the COO from a business perspective significantly simplifies the structuring of strategic theories, focusing more on consumers and their associations. From a theoretical perspective, this study seems to support some scholars' conclusion that an excessive research focus on the COO from the consumer perspective risks losing the meaning of an assessment of the COO effect from the managerial perspective. Regarding the second aspect, the voices of the companies interviewed highlight the strong link between the COO and the brand and the difficulty from the managerial perspective to separate the size of the COO and the product brand in the process of creating value for the market and appropriating that value by the company abroad. In fact, even in situations of high product typicality with ideal conditions to exploit the COO effect in creating distinctive positioning, companies stress the need to invest in the brand to maintain long-term competitive advantages. The COO effect must be combined not only with qualitative excellence and a strong product culture but also with investments in the creation of a brand with a name capable of evoking and communicating the values and promise of the company.

Focusing on the second research question, the voices of the various companies and the cases analyzed highlight that the challenges faced to correctly exploit the potential intrinsic value of the COO are always demanding, regardless of the different strategic entry modes, the marketing channels used, and the context of the product–foreign market considered. The presence of the potentially high intrinsic value of the COO (often an affective–symbolic value) is not sufficient to create value. This value becomes effective only if it is appropriately spread and communicated to the final market through and along the channel. Relationships with the partners in the marketing channel must be built and nurtured through a constant biunivocal dialogue on when it is possible for the parties involved to effectively exchange value. What the sources of value for the company's intermediate and final interlocutors are and how the COO can help determine this value along the marketing channel must first be understood.

For example, the experience of the exporting companies studied highlights that the strong link with the territory of origin, typical of sectors such as wine, is a driver for international marketing strategies. However, this intrinsic value of the COO in the product offering of the exporting winery risk to remain a mere potential if it is not properly exploited along marketing channels. This risk is also especially evident in traditional export markets, such as the USA, where there is a knowledge gap between the distribution partners, who often are highly expert, and the end consumers, who generally are not very competent. In a market context with new exporting countries offering competitive prices and willing to adapt the product, the end customer is generally not very attentive to the real country of manufacture unless guided in the choice of wine by the importer and retailer. The importer who oversees the foreign market in both off- and on-trade markets can fill this knowledge gap by playing a primary role in ensuring that this COO value is correctly perceived by the end market and appropriated by the producer. In this case, the importance of rereading the COO in the light of local specificities and investing in the brand emerges. The difficulty in making the extreme complexity of some DO perceived abroad, the basis of the differentiation of Italian wine, and the proliferation of Italian-sounding products (e.g., prosek) also encourage wineries to shift resources to investments in marketing and brands through intense partnerships with importers. In-coming actions in which importers can learn about companies' products and territories and the supervision of foreign relations by manufacturers have emerged as essential.

Important challenges also arise for companies that decide to use entry modes based on agreements such as franchising, licensing, and strategic alliances. As mentioned, in the case of contractual agreements, the risk is shared between the partners who can contribute equally to the promotion of products in foreign markets. In addition, the modalities of entry through contractual forms can contribute to cultural mediation between the COO and the country of destination. This approach, therefore, should favor the company's ability to promote the COO throughout the marketing channel, creating value for the final market and then appropriating that value. The link between the COO and contractual agreements can be twofold: on one hand, contractual agreements are an important tool for the valorization of the COO in the foreign market; on the other hand, the strong image of the COO can favor the possibility of concluding agreements in the target markets. The close relationship between the COO and the brand is certainly more evident here than in the export context and requires that the company monitor this relationship to understand its evolution in the particular outlet market. The cases analyzed confirm that the presence of an initially strong product typicality must be enriched by the values of the brand and, above all, adapted to the specific context, particularly in markets very geographically and culturally distant from the domestic one.

The importance of the relationship between the COO effect and the brand effect is especially important in the context of direct investments of greenfield types. The companies interviewed support the idea that in international marketing strategies, the brand is becoming more important than the country of production. In other words, in direct greenfield investments, there is a need to implement strategies to create a culture that enhances the origin of the brand, strengthening the positive associations with that brand in the mind of the consumer. In this regard, some companies point out that investing in the brand first requires differentiating themselves from other brands not made in Italy, even if presented as they are. They also insist on the strategic importance of investing in a brand name that, in addition to its denotative function, is capable of clearly communicating the image of the product's typicality, benefits, and values to the end market. This need emerges when the company has to invest directly in foreign markets with traditional outlets, as the case of Italian products in the USA, and in distant markets such as China. Although companies operate in different markets and product contexts, the reasons for this similarity can be attributed primarily to the acceleration of economic development in recent years. Increasing globalization has led to the rapid dissemination of information on new products and brands even before their actual presence in foreign markets. Consequently, familiarity with products and brands also exists in early stages of the product life cycle, as is the case with some products in China.

The relationship between the country and the brand image should take into account different cultural contexts, particularly in emerging markets. For example, in China, the purchase of a well-known brand contributes to the acquisition of social respect through the display of social status and the communication of personality and uniqueness characteristics. In addition, the increasing internationalization of companies has influenced competitive dynamics. Companies with the same country of brand origin often compete in foreign markets. In some cases, it is seen that the image of the country can enrich the image of the brand without being particularly distinctive. The companies studied, while benefiting from positive COO effects, also believe that the creation of a strong brand reduces any negative side effects, such as food scandals, political problems, and the weakening of the image of their country. Managers see a brand not only as a means to confuse the product origin when the COO effect is negative but also a tool to create a brand culture of origin based on positive perceptions of the country. If, from the consumer's perspective, the brand origin exists only in long-term memory and constitutes a strong brand association, any negative changes in perceptions of the country of brand and the country of production are likely to have lesser impacts on the brand image. In this perspective, the study seems to confirm what has emerged in the literature on the need to invest in consumer awareness to create a culture that enhances the brand origin, strengthening the positive associations with the brand. This need becomes strategic for companies to differentiate their products and services from foreign brands, which is sometimes underestimated in consumer studies.

It has emerged that the online channel is assuming a growing, pervasive role in the system of entry modes and marketing channels and is evolving into a complex omnichannel dimension. The online channel has effects at the levels of both entry modes and marketing channels. Studies on the relationship between the online channel and the COO have not yet developed a consolidated theoretical framework. The analysis of some cases shows that the benefits of online interactions are many and mainly related to two-way communication possibilities, content creation for users, immediate remote sharing, wide brand visibility, and opportunities to search for information. The study also shows that the sectors are not all the same with respect to the relationship between COO and brand. For example, in the case of fashion, the brand primarily transmits value, but in the case of agri-food products, the brand often occupies a secondary place behind the COO. In the latter case, the available data have shown that e-commerce simplifies consumer research, product knowledge and dissemination, and the act of purchase. The online channel certainly reduces the gap between supply and demand, but achievement of this advantage requires an adequate online presence. To obtain an effective online position, the company must invest in digital activities (SEO and SEM). In the age of connectivity and the omnichannel context, the company must analyze the different touchpoints in which the product, brand, and COO can interact with the customer both online and offline. In the online context, the COO effect certainly can perform the role of simplifying the process of searching for customer information. To achieve this effect, companies should review their international marketing strategies, analyzing, for example, Google keyword searches to understand the type of information sought and at what stage of their target clients' journey a particular search takes place. Once these keywords are identified, the company has to invest in communication with content marketing actions on its website that attract the various market targets to be reached. In this context, the distinction between the communication channel and the distribution channel fades, requiring that companies overcome the real challenge omnichannel marketing imposes: to offer a consistent customer experience across various touchpoints. The COO effect, even if positive and strong in the omnichannel perspective, is even less obvious because the same distinction between modes of entry and marketing channels becomes more fluid here.

Regarding the third research question, the role of the importer, as mentioned, has emerged as fundamental to creating value for the market and appropriating that value by the manufacturing company. The characteristics of the importer, particularly the level of commitment, coverage of the foreign market, and high expertise in product and regulations, are fundamental in the evaluation and choice of the partner on which to rely. These characteristics thus influence the partnership relationship that is created, facilitating and hindering the processes of creating value for the market and appropriating that value through the positive COO effect by the company. The value of the COO largely depends on the knowledge and skills of importers, who are generally considered to be very well prepared and therefore able to interpret products, territories, and countries. In many cases, a synergistic relationship is created between knowledge and commitment. The will to give centrality to the product in the assortment leads the importer to acquire more and more skills that enable enhancing the product of a particular territory with its target audience. In turn, the increased product knowledge makes the importer more involved and, therefore, more inclined to invest in products made in Italy. This positive approach, however, tends to be lacking when the importer is sales oriented, which negatively affects the degree of importer's commitment toward winery's offering and, more generally, the quality of the distribution relationship. The rather superficial knowledge of the common consumer often tends to reduce the recognized value of Italian products. In fact, according to the respondents, the main obstacles to the appropriation of value by wineries are the DO's complexity, inexperienced consumers, and rising prices.

In the decision-making processes of importers, the declination of the COO in made in Italy is considered to be fundamental because it represents an element of distinction and quality that allows them to grow. Importers perceive as crucial their role in transmitting the characteristics of the product and the philosophy of the manufacturing company to the final consumer, especially when the distribution chain is long and has many intermediate actors. Importers believe that the strong national typicality of the product offers significant growth opportunities for both wineries and importers, and consider this typicality as to be a strategic resource for differentiating and acquiring new market segments. Importers consider the producer's commitment to investing time to learn about the peculiarities of the outlet market and support the distribution partnership to be fundamental. It is not enough to know how to make a quality product. The producer must also know how to make the market, and building that market requires his/her direct, personal onsite presence to be able to adapt together with the importer his/her value proposition to specific local needs.

Particularly interesting is the in-depth study of the role of the COO effect in the context of retailers' assortment strategies, a subject so far little studied in the academic literature on the COO. The success of companies in foreign markets depends not only on the ways in which they enter and manage the international distribution channel but also on their ability to influence the choices of the retailers that include in their assortment products of domestic and foreign companies. The role of distributors is fundamental because they constitute the link with the final consumer and can decide whether to include products in their portfolios. Manufacturing companies, therefore, must study the behavior of these intermediaries, understand their needs, and create synergies based on mutual benefits. In other words, this analysis suggests important guidance for manufacturers on the marketing investments necessary to create value for their COO among retailers. The specific focus on US retailers provides interesting insights into the COO effect on their assortment choices. The results on the retailers' buying behavior are very articulated and take into consideration the different dimensions of the COO. First, it emerges that the COO in general can affect the choices of retailers, with no differences between high- and low-involvement products. Nevertheless, if we make a distinction between the country image and the country of brand, the findings indicate that, in most cases, the country macro image does not influence retailers' intention to buy. In contrast, the country of brand image has strong positive impacts on retailers' intention to buy and is mediated by consumer attention to the COO when considering premium products. Second, product typicality influences the intention to try foreign products with a strong COO for both high- and low-involvement goods, but the effect is higher for high-involvement products. Third, the results point out that the relationship between the country of brand image and retailers' intention to buy is mediated by the store image. However, similarly to consumer attention to the COO, the store image is a mediator when considering premium products. Finally, manufacturers have to deal with the phenomenon of foreign-sounding brands, which is very strong for both value and premium products.

8.3   A Brief Overview of Challenges Faced by Producers in Exploiting the Country of Origin

In sum, this book emphasizes that, in international marketing strategies, companies should develop a capacity to redefine the COO effect, using language appropriate to the different channels and cultural diversities present in specific business contexts. Indeed, the relationships between the COO and its sub-components (the country of manufacture, the country of brand, and the brand origin) are very dynamic and constantly evolving. Consequently, companies must invest time and resources to monitor foreign market trends without ever taking anything for granted. Only in this way can they be able to transform the high intrinsic value of the COO into value actually perceived by the foreign market.

Today, more than ever, a sort of triumph of territorial specificities and differences emerges in the global context, as the removal of geographic barriers and the interdependence of markets seem to reduce cultural, social, and economic differences. Consumer globalization and homologation demands coexist with consumer seeking authentic local traditions with the aim to defend the cultural heritage of their lands of origin. This coexistence can be seen in the West but is increasing even more in Asian markets. People are always looking for new ways to define themselves through their choices to consume products and brands that help communicate their identity to others. The ability to adapt, therefore, is more essential than ever to create value for the market for the company and society as a whole. From this perspective, the results confirm what management scholars have theorized about the need for companies today to equip themselves with personnel with multicultural skills, capable of rereading and correctly interpreting the different contexts in which the COO effect must be valorized. As the representative of a food company (company F) analyzes: "The made in Italy is only a basis. Then you have to adapt your business to the local context."

Company's relationships with distribution partners must be built and nourished through a constant biunivocal dialogue that makes possible the effective exchange of value by the parties involved. What the sources of value are for companies' intermediate and final interlocutors and how the COO can help determine this value along the marketing channel must first be understood. Reliability, trust, authenticity, flexibility are some of the fundamental characteristics on which the relationship between the company and the partners of the marketing channel should be based in order to create value for the market.

The main obstacles to company growth in foreign markets, even traditional markets, include confusion, poor product knowledge, and poor market perceptions of the real peculiarities of authentic products, leading to unwillingness to pay the price differential. This knowledge gap must be filled to exploit the positive associations in the minds of the foreign consumers that, if not effectively solicited and strengthened, reduce the intrinsic value of the COO to mere untapped potential for business growth. Making strong investments in communication activities to educate foreign consumers and partnerships with distributors, usually more sensitive and attentive to quality and authenticity, is the main challenge for companies seeking to increase their presence in foreign markets, including traditional ones.

Furthermore, appropriately dealing with retailers is essential because they can be influenced by the COO in different ways, especially if they sell premium products with high product typicality. Hence, when entering foreign markets, manufacturers, especially those selling high-involvement products, should be aware that they have to empower the link between the brand and its origin. They should also develop correct positioning of their products to limit competition with foreign-sounding products.

Selling a product in the US market is quite different from selling it in the Chinese or the Indian market. This finding sounds like a trivial, outdated claim. Yet, giving space to the voice of companies and their stories has once again made it possible to see how difficult it is to translate principles easily shared on a theoretical level into strategies and actions implemented on a daily basis.

CPSIA information can be obtained
at www.ICGtesting.com
Printed in the USA
LVHW020333111121
702938LV00001B/19

9 783030 335908